Life Addict

The tide that

Life Addict

The tide that takes us

To

Brother Steve.

Thought I'd bring in your 50th year with a few fond memorys.

Stay Gold

[illegible]

xxx

x.

Some names, places, times and events have been altered or changed for various reasons.

Published 2020 by Temple DPS.

British Library Cataloguing in Publication Data
A catalogue record for this book is available from the British Library.

ISBN: 978-0-9562432-8-7

Design and print management: G & J Hughes

It was the middle of 2002. I had just won the regional heavy weight stamina strength championships. Over the past 12 years I had won a series of bodybuilding shows and was aiming at becoming a British bodybuilding champion in the under 85kg section.

I had taken the mantle of being Bury's No.1 after Rob Worthington had retired from bodybuilding but it created a lot of competitive rivalry. Everyone wanted that mantle.

I'd tussled with various training partners but they weren't beating me, my ego, nor my pride, were ever going to allow that to happen. This caused a lot of bitterness towards me and I was seen as arrogant and self-righteous but I'd won what I had on merit. These fools used belittlement and devious ways of leaving me out of things or talking underhandedly behind my back. Training partners put me in dangerous positions whilst spotting me on heavy sets. No one ever beat me in the gym though and couldn't stay up with me for very long. The only thing I was beaten by was the undercurrent of negativity that kept coming my way.

Like a breeze in the wind or the push of a tide, I knew I had to go if I wanted to fulfil my dream. If I fought against the undercurrent it would take away the focus of my goal. So at this point I left the gym.

The Quiet Angel

While heading to the gym across town a car pulled up at the side of me. I saw a blank expression hiding in the shadows of the vehicle, a square jaw and some large shoulders. Then, came a smile I recognised all too well.

It was a friend of mine named Andrew Whittle. I had given him a little help around the gym. We had the banter and had struck up a nice bond. He didn't owe me anything, though, and at the time we weren't close friends as such. But with little more than a brief explanation he was willing to change gyms and help me out at mine.

My will to win had made me self-absorbed. I may have moved gyms but I had to win the big titles to shut the haters up for good. In going against them I had become more like them. I was never jealous or wanted to take anyone down but, still, it was all about me, me, me.

Andy was turning up but was always under scrutiny.

"Pick the fucking bar up." I'd yell.

"What fucking time do you call this?" He had come in five minutes late.

"Fuckin' spot me properly, for fuck sake." I'd thrown the weights to the floor. It was non stop. Andy stayed quiet. He turned up to every session. He took the embarrassment of being humiliated by my actions yet never called me to anyone; I went on to win the British title.

A year later I was training up to do a stamina strength contest, which was to be held at my old gym. I'd heard threatening rumours after I had won the British title and further belittlement was sounding around my ears.

At our gym and training up to the contest, the bars were bending, the squat, the dead lift, bench press and the bent over row. There was never any less than 200kg to 300kg on the bars and it felt like there wasn't enough oxygen in the room for us to train. We were passing out, pale faced or puking. Andy wasn't competing but he kept with me anyway. On the day of the contest I wanted to enter the gym alone in order to end the pathetic threats I'd heard but as I arrived

Andy was waiting by the door and came in behind me. No one did anything and the talk stopped.

A few years on

By this time my wife had left me and I was out on the streets, living out of my car. I'd gone to see Andy. He'd instantly seen the condensation against the car window and my clothes that had become my bedding. The dirty protein shakers and empty tuna cans at the base of the passenger seat.

"Pal, come and stop with us for a while. Josh and Nick can share rooms," he said with a concerned look upon his face.

"No mate. I'm not fit to be around anyone at the moment," I dishearteningly replied. I was facing a few unsettling days in court due to violence or driving offenses at the time.

"There's a room here whenever you want it pal. Remember that." I felt embarrassed by Andy's kindness.

We had gone inside his house. He was sat looking after his children and I had found out at this time that he had once been a powerhouse martial artist and had turned down fighting for the British team to look after and provide for his family. He could have kicked me through the wall back at the gym if he had wanted to, but he didn't. He could have called me all the names under the sun if he had wanted to, but he didn't.

He was the arms beneath the weights that helped me to win the shows. He was the punch bag to my aggression that prevented me having a go at anyone else and he had turned up to the contest just to make sure I was safe.

I realised at this point what a real man was and that I was nowhere near.

I asked Andy, "Why did you stay with me when I was such an arse hole?"

His reply: "You never look down on me like some do and you always come and see me when you've time." His instant thought was to appeal to what he had liked about me.

"I'm not talking about now Andy; I'm talking about then."

"I knew you had a dream and I just wanted to help you out." It was a totally selfless act.

Although I was way off course at the time, I'd sensed the pitifulness of my self-righteous attributes and how lonely and angry I'd allowed my world to become.

I saw in Andy the person I was once on the way to becoming but mostly I saw the person that I wanted to be.

Just like God had sent Andy (the quiet Angel) I had to find a way of somehow making the dark times interesting and the good times great, and as long as I was breathing I had to be living. I had to find a way on to God's great tide of life once more.

Introduction

I started thinking about how the mind works; how it changes with the various experiences we come across throughout our lives. Was the highest high a drug? Was it love? Was drink, stress or drugs the biggest killer? Why the outrage? The violence? The torment?

When considering the highest highs, I would say that for me they were when I was either alone, but with a good mindset putting me in a positive place, or alternately when I was surrounded by people of a good sort: people who have lived, people who have been tested yet still choose to do right by themselves as well as by others; people who make a difference.

In my opinion, the highest high starts the same as the lowest low. It's not about drugs, stress, drink: no, it comes before all that. It's about the influences that either build or destroy our minds. It may lead to addictions or stress, it may lead to greatness and joy, but it all starts the same: human behaviour, the influence that triggers all. But unlike most addictions, this is one you can't always walk away from.

I'm going to take you on a forty plus year trip that is my life: a string of stories that have formed my path and along the way trying to analyse the varied aspects, influences, distractions and motivations that have made me the person I am today. In my life, I've taken an interest and participated in several sports and hobbies varying from dancing, skating and martial arts, right through to writing. I've also been a reputable doorman for the best part of twenty-five years; an occupation where a lot of my life's lessons have been learned.

In everything I've ever aimed for, it's always been about how to make the heart sing; passions that nourish and fuel the soul, giving back to give forward, always with God in my heart. When all this comes together (in my opinion), this is when you are living, but when you can't ever let this feeling go, that's when you've become a life addict.

Starting out in Life

When thinking back to my earliest memory I can quite clearly remember my first day at nursery school; 3 years of age. I'd be sitting with my legs dangling over the school's sand pit, swinging my legs from side to side when I was accompanied shortly after by two other boys; one smaller and darker than me, the other a little taller and a little paler. Before long we were all swinging our legs, no one speaking but all of us relaxed in each other's company. After a short while the taller kid said, "Anyway I'm Sean."

Then the short kid said, "I'm Scott."

Then me, "I'm John."

The small kid's full name was Scott Lea. The taller kid's name, Sean Joyce, and from infants through to secondary school we were pretty much inseparable.

The school I went to was based between a council estate commonly known as Dickey Bird, the other side, the nicer side, being Walmersley. I lived up Fairfield, which ran from the back of Dickey Bird. Our house and street were pretty nice but most the kids I hung with were from the estates. I spent a lot of my youth hanging around on the council estates (especially as I got a bit older).

Sean, Scott and I were always practicing Karate in our play times at school and often ended up fighting in the school yard. In class we drew pictures; pictures of sharks, and soldiers at war, pretend this, pretend that. We had a lot of fun with our drawings. Sean was the most philosophical, Scott just laughed at anything and I was the dreamiest. We fed off one another's interests. To this day, I can only smile when thinking of the fun we had whilst playing together at school.

At school I was well liked and never had any problems with anyone. Although I'm not certain this would have been the case had I attended another school. When it came to school work, you could say I was a little behind the door, I wasn't, I was a lot behind the door. By six, I still couldn't spell my name properly. I was writing with my right hand (I'm left handed), upside down and right to left; a really awkward style, as you can imagine. I was in some special classes and once a week I'd have to stay behind for an extra lesson.

I wouldn't say I was dumb; I just wasn't programmed like the other kids in the class. I was into what I was into and luckily, throughout the best part of my school life, the stuff I followed, that tide that took me, was of a wide interest at the time. Most kids did their homework and perhaps liked their TV shows and interests as a side line. I was into playing with Star Wars toys, playing out and riding my bike so that's what I did. My Dad used to say, "How come you never have any homework like your sister does?"

I'd just shrug, "I don't know."

I didn't focus much on school work. Even at a young age my reality came from within me, from my dreams so why would I need the three R's? My mindset was: To have fun, to play and to dream. In this day and age, I'd be diagnosed with double dyslexia, they'd be doing tests on me in a lab!

There was never attention brought to my obvious lack of school intelligence. In fact, at one point I was that far behind that the teacher let me leave class to draw a mural of the brass band for the school concert as I was known for being a good drawer at the time.

Part One
Sensing The Tide

Chapter 1

When Mum steps up

It was the start of a new term and, as always, I was looking forward to spending time with my school pals, enjoying another fun year. When we arrived in class, Sean, Scott and I were messing about as usual, when out of nowhere came this loud croaky voice, "Right, can everyone be seated please." As we turned and took our seats, we were soon to realise that the croaky voice (resembling a witch) would have the face to back it up, beamed straight out of the Wizard of Oz. Her name was Miss Right; no doubt she will still be a miss. Anyway, within weeks of her being at our school she had started designating lots of work. Then came our first lot of homework and as usual I hadn't done it.

She was going through the homework later that week when I heard my name mentioned. "John, your homework isn't here, where is it?"

"Err, err, I forgot to do it," I muttered.

"Can you come to the front, John?" she croaked. As I went towards her desk she put her hand up, as if to say stop, then she said "This is for everyone." I was in front of the blackboard stood in front of the whole class when she proclaimed, "This is for anyone who thinks it is ok not to do their homework." At this point she pulled a large thick plastic metre rule from the side of the blackboard then told me to hold out my hands. I wasn't quite sure on what to expect, but I honestly didn't expect this.

She started thrashing my hands from the longest distance, her face almost mutilated with anger not unlike the emperor from the movie Return of the Jedi. As I looked around the class I could see a room full of dumbfounded kids all looking like they were about to cry themselves. Their saddened, shocked, scared faces I remember all too well. Then I saw the saddest face of them all: mine. In the cupboard at the back of the class I could see my reflection peering back at me, a darker image obviously, but clear nonetheless. My cheeks, bloated and red, my eyes afraid and not quite sure of the punishment I was getting. Teary, yet still trying to hold back the tears in a bid to save a little personal pride. The beating seemed to take forever before I was finally told to go back to my seat. I was six years old.

The weeks that followed, believe it or not, were worse. Even when I had attempted to do my homework because of its poor quality, I was getting punished even more. I was called out in front of the class on numerous occasions to get a beating. She even leathered me once, in a fit of rage. She had made me read in front of the class and I had choked. She dragged me into a cupboard by my hair then locked me in the dark on a few occasions. I was greeted with an everyday occurrence of her abruptly shouting and belittling me in any way possible. My friends Sean and Scott would comfort me at the end of most lessons. My eyes were regularly filled with tears and upset, even though at this point I still hadn't completely broken down.

At home, as usual, I never said anything with my mindset that adults know best and that it must be me doing something wrong for this to be happening and because I mainly played outdoors; no one really noticed any change in my demeanour. The thing my Mum and Dad did notice was that I was doing my homework. I would get "Bloody hell, what's up with you?" from my Mum.

The following week, upon learning my spellings for Friday's spelling test, I'd put all my efforts into getting them all right. I couldn't properly read the words but I could recognise them if I was to look at them all enough. It was the first week in which I had asked my Mum and Dad to help me out, which they did. Come Friday, I knew I had nailed it.

It was the day of the test; I went straight to work. When

the test was finished I felt an instant rush of confidence, my first well done. We swapped our papers with the person next to us, marking each other's tests before handing them back. I looked down at the test to see, ten on ten. Boom! I was smiling inside and out. A wave of relief hit me and I was looking forward to shouting out my result. The teacher started to ask names, with everyone shouting out their marks. Then it got to my turn. "Ten miss," I said, beaming cheerfully. Looking around the room, the other class members all looked happy for me.

Miss Right paused for a second motionless, but clearly unhappy about the outcome. "Who has shown John their work? Come on, own up." She quickly went to the blackboard, picked up the board duster and threw it straight at my head. "Get out, get out of the class room now!" My happy world had come crumbling down once more. I didn't have much logic towards things to start with, so you could imagine how I was feeling at this time.

The following week I was reading the final part of red book three at the side of Miss Right's desk. When finished I was hoping to go up to the blue books. Most of the class were around three colours and eight or nine books ahead of where I was, so I was quite excited to have bridged the gap a little. I got to the end of the book and in my kid sweet voice I ask if I was getting my blue book. Miss Right froze again, no movement. "John, you are not ready to move on yet. I'm going to put you back to red book one." With this, and for the first time, I instantly broke down. Tears were bouncing off my cheeks, an inconsolable little boy, broken and humiliated. She told me to stop crying. She was full of her usual anger as she turned to her favourite instrument. The cane didn't hurt anymore; how I felt inside was much worse.

The following day whilst walking to school I had a lot on my mind, no understanding of my problem, but an understanding that it had to stop. When getting as far as the little stream that was hidden away behind some trees just before the approach to the school gates, I suddenly just stopped. I quickly looked around to see if anyone was about then swiftly shot down to the side of the stream, making sure I was out of sight. From this day onwards, the side of the stream was my school.

I'd watch the rats trying to come up from the sewage and when the odd one did get out, I'd run as fast as I could down the banking. I'd play with sticks, breaking them evenly then placing them in the stream, like they were racing each other. I shifted my mind to a nicer place. Later in the day, I'd slip out after hearing the final school bell, usually tagging along with a couple of pals before heading home. My mind was at ease, not my happiest, but not sad either. I wasn't sure of the outcome, or when I'd have to go back to school. I dealt with the now, and for now I had made everything ok.

Around ten days had passed when Mum called me into the front room, "John, have you been going to school? We've had a phone call asking why you've not been in."

"No, I've been going in," I sheepishly replied.

Mum and Dad didn't push the issue, just kind of looked at each other. "I wonder what they are talking about then."

"I don't know, can I go and play out now?" I said, quickly dodging the subject.

A few more days went by. I was getting ready for school when Mum and Dad were quietly talking but in that way when you know it's about something serious. I already felt a little unnerved. When they'd finished I heard my Mum say, "John, come in here a second, we need to have a word with you." Head dipped and reluctant, I walked into the living room. They asked me why I hadn't been going to school then told me not to lie. I said I didn't know. Mum and Dad weren't angry as such but wanted some kind of answer from me. "Well you're going to have to go in John, you can't be missing school." I quickly shook my head, both scared of going back to school and scared that I might be about to get in trouble with my Mum and Dad.

They questioned me a couple more times. The pressure hit, then within seconds I started lashing out frantically, an angry, desperate cry, "I'm not going to school, I'm not going." My Dad pulled me to one side and as he did I grabbed on to him, holding on to his leg, crying uncontrollably.

Both parents sat me down. I looked at their faces; you can tell with a parent when they are angry, when they think you are trying it on. You can also tell when they know there's a definite problem. I could see, as they looked at each other, all types of questions were going through their minds but I also knew they weren't mad at me and wanted to hear what I had to say. Both a little distressed, obviously upset about my outburst.

Dad: "John, we need to know what's wrong. Just tell us what's wrong. You're not going to get into any trouble."

My eyes and face were in tears, blubbering, but more at ease, I wanted to talk, but couldn't get anything out. "Miss Right, she keeps... Miss Right, she keeps..." I started still crying, constantly sniffing, whilst attempting to wipe my teary face; I couldn't finish my sentence.

Mum and Dad attempted to guess at what was wrong but I was too busy choking back the tears so couldn't get the words out. Even at this young age I had a lot of pride about letting anyone know if I had problems, perhaps a little too locked up for a kid so young. They carried on with the guess work then Dad said, "Has she been bullying you? Has Miss Right been bullying you John?" I nodded then wiped my eyes. A sense of relief came over me both knowing my parents knew what was happening and that I wouldn't be going back to school until things were sorted.

I'm not sure exactly what went on with my Mum and Miss Right but I can guess it wouldn't have been too pleasant for Miss Right. Back in class she seemed totally transformed; manners, patience, her whole demeanour. Oh yeah, I also got my blue book, she never bothered me again!

I suppose after this I should have shown signs of aggression or behaviour disorders perhaps, but no, nothing. As soon as the ordeal was over I was back as happy as I had ever been; back in my own little world.

Throughout most of my life I've always had that thing where people feel safe in my company. I've been influential to some and a help to anyone who has needed me. Being honest, until writing this book I've never realised why I'm so quick to protect or why I don't have any time for bullies (unless they need help to change their ways, if perhaps they have had their own issues or been misled). With every set back, there's always a lesson learned. If I'm going to make this relative to later life, I'd say that any person can send another a certain way. Everyone has been put upon at some point. Everyone can lose their way but there is always room for understanding before judgment. There are bullies that have no remorse. But let's be positive here. The main lesson I learned from all this was that one person can change everything; one person can make all the difference and in this case that one person was my Mum.

Rocky

A collection of motion pictures had made its way onto the big screen around this time, the name of the movies: Rocky, starring Sylvester Stallone. In 1982, I'd watched Rocky 3, at the cinema, then later, hundreds of times at my aunty Cinnie's house. She always let me pick Saturday's movie, even if it was the same one every week, with Rocky 4, pretty much the same deal. As I got a little older I started watching the older Rocky movies, especially Rocky 2. In Rocky 2, the character, Rocky is getting laughed at (whilst shooting a commercial) because he can't read. I couldn't understand why I'd get so upset whilst watching this scene, but I think I know why now.

The Rocky movies themselves have served like a bible for us kids who struggled to read, but who aspired for greater things. The bible doesn't always come in the form of a book. God will always send you a message that is suited to you. The Rocky movies, to me, was that bible, that message, almost a picture of my life to come, in so many different ways.

A new era: The 80s

Flicking through the time lapse; going into the early 1980s. I had a load of good friends, the main ones still Sean and Scott but growing friendships with lads named Des Hutchinson, Alan Hall, Dennis Egan (Spam), Pete McGuirk, John McEntyre, Brendon O'Shaughnessy and a kid named Steve Smullen.

At weekends I would spend a lot of time at Sean's house; it was the BMX era. Sean had a piranha, and I had a kumara (from the 1982 movie ET, ridden by Henry Thomas - Elliott). I loved the American look, the movies, their way of life and so had US flags on all my bikes. We would smash up and down the sand hills, sort of like they do in the Spielberg movies. Then we'd build ramps and jump into a body of water in the Walmersley area, known as the lido (an old outdoor public swimming pool). Evenings would bring midnight feasts at Sean's with his brothers, Mike and Martin educating us on certain subjects, with the ones I found most fascinating being bodybuilding and sharks.

On week nights Scott, Alan, Des, Spam and I were at the youth club most nights. Me and Scott were always practicing the Bop, a 1950s dance. We also learned to dance like Michael Jackson, Elvis and Shaking Stevens, who was Scott's favourite. I had a few girls I was chasing, one called Louise, the other Julie; both sweet girls. On Tuesdays and Thursdays my Dad took me wrestling, and afterwards we would visit McDonald's, new to Bury at the time. After that, I'd go back to my friend's house, Ian Sawden (who came wrestling with me) and watch the series Night Rider starring David Hasselhoff; we loved it. I was a competitive wrestler at seven years old, trained by a guy named Ken Stevenson. I also raced bikes on Sunday mornings for a guy called Mr Mann. Although I liked wrestling, biking and chasing girls, I knew there was more. There was that little bit of something still missing, a power play, something to really get into. I was yearning for a passion.

Chapter 2

Breakin'

The first big tide

I was watching TV sometime in 1982, when a group of dancers came on. They were throwing themselves around on the floor, spinning on their heads and backs. The music was so upbeat, smashing my soul. Their track suits were shiny and their trainers carried an infamous swoosh. Americanised, stylised, the full package; right away I knew this was it. I started practicing that very day; in fact; from this point on, it was all I wanted to do.

My friend, Louise Burke and I both had a spark for the dancing so had started practicing in her garage. I wasn't very good for quite a while but I loved it all the same.

One day me and Louise had a walk up to the top hill as we called it. It was a big grass hill with a road at the bottom where everyone used to hang out. On this day we'd seen two lads dancing on a piece of lino on the road at the bottom of the hill, looking like the pros we had seen on TV. We went over to talk. The lad's names were Graham Gabriel and John Young, both good lads, style and flair in their dance. This was the game changer.

I danced everday with the two, I loved it. It was the summer holidays and every day, without fail, I was on that hill. We danced on concrete with a thin piece of lino thrown over. With great music and sunny, long days I never wanted it to end. Fourteen months on and by the middle of 1983 I was very good. I could do every move and like a gymnast at the box, my strong point was spinning round on my hands then going into the move, the flares. I was hitting windmills with no hands, bouncing from one move to the next. Momentum was the key. I had learnt that the smoother and speedier you came out of one move, the more active and precise you went into the next. It all started with a move known as `the crazy legs'. For me style was also essential; it had to look good.

I'd hidden away from most of my friends whilst practicing so hadn't really shown anyone what I'd been doing. Anyway, it had got to the time for the school disco that was taking place at the nearby St Bede's church hall. I had recently purchased my summer clothes, ready for my holiday; this was the first time I had worn them. Getting ready I was buzzing. My grey Nike shirt and tracksuit pants and some fresh Nike Jammer trainers; smelling the leather, holding them up like a trophy, already feeling a radiating sense of elevation.

As I walked into the church hall disco I saw my pal Alan Hall.

"Fuckin hell," he said (we had all just learned how to say the 'F' word). "Are your underpants Nike as well?" We both laughed. Bear in mind that not many kids were wearing branded names at this time. We were around an hour in to the night when over the speaker came the track A.E.I.O.U by Freeze, with a circle of dancers already formed. Alan and I pushed to the front to watch (this was the first breakin', not on TV, that had been witnessed on our side of town).

"Fuckin hell, John, they're good, are you better than that?"

"Yes," I confidently replied. "Fucking miles better." The next thing I knew I was on the dance floor tearing it up and even in mid-flight I could hear roars of approval from the side lines. When I arose, everyone was clapping and smiling. I realised I had just become the king of the world with the breakdance craze about to get massive. Shortly after this I was told about Bury town centre; that on Saturdays it was like breakdance central, that it was everywhere and that I would love it.

Me and Louise had been practicing our dance routine for some time now, it had been rehearsed to a fine art. We were already talking about our descent onto the Bury dance scene. Louise was a massive fashion victim, so was talking about our clothes and how we should look whilst dancing together. So we both took a trip to JD Sports to sort some matching outfits. We had picked out matching Nike cagoules and white silky Adidas trousers, already having matching Nike trainers. The sky blue swoosh from our trainers matched the sky blue lines on our pants and the sky blue upper part of our jackets; then us, both with sky blue eyes and pretty faces. I was feeling the explosion before it had even happened. These were awesome times; every step of the way was exciting.

We had reached Saturday and I was stood at Louise's door ready to go. On the bus into Bury not much was said; a bit of nervous excitement I think. When hitting the town centre it was exactly how people had said. Just on the corner near the record shop, Vibes, there was a dance off and a circle of people already formed. We couldn't believe it, but this was nothing. After a while other kids were starting to make their way through a dark side alley, hearing voices of, "Let's go to Boots" and "It's rocking at Boots."(This was an undercover space outside the store, Boots pharmacy.) When following all the other kids through the alley we soon arrived at the side of Boots. Wow. It was like a stage scene; a massive circle of people with everyone dancing. There were steps leading up to a hair dresser with every one dancing on every level. California had just arrived in Bury.

Louise and I slowly started making our way to the front of the biggest crowd, where everyone was watching the main dancers. When getting to the front I was ready to go but with the older dancers jumping in and Louise a little nervous, it was going take some time. Our time eventually came; with an empty space, we now had a few seconds to make our mark. I put my hand at the back of Louise and gently pushed us both forward to take up the space; a quick glimpse, a nod and then off we went. Two eight-year-old kids, matching outfits and dancing in sequence; Yes you've guessed it, we brought the house down!

Literally seconds after making our exit we were shaking hands, getting pats on our backs and making new friends (the most noted of them being a kid named Paul Burdaki). The kid was as cool as you like. His boots were covered with graffiti; he wore a slender, shiny Kappa tracksuit, with wet look curly hair (the look back then) and had the biggest boom box I'd ever seen (again graffitied and banging out some seriously good sounds). Paul instantly took us under his wing and by the end of that afternoon we had danced at all the Bury hot spots, as well as met most the names and faces about town at the time; Elliott Norton, Tez Monaghan, Jason Floyd, Louis Douglas, Ste Rammy, Matt Walsh, Joe Jarrett, Woz Dick, and Ste Duckworth to mention but a few.

From this day on I'd be practicing practically anywhere I could; the hill, Louise's garage, Alan's spare room, in front of Des Hutchie's house, the school yard, school halls, school corridors. I was all over it. It all brought Saturday: the best day of the week. Dance battles, living for every up beat moment.

In 1984, a couple of motion pictures had been made; one about the California Venice beach scene, which was named Breakin', featuring Ice T. The other movie, set in the Bronx of New York (my favourite of the two) was named Beat Street and starred Rae Dawn Chong, featuring Grand Master Flash. I was taken along to watch the movie with my dance mentors, now friends, John, Graham and Ste Rammy. When watching the movie, you could sense the adrenaline in the air. The dancing on the screen was a step up from anything we had ever witnessed. The dance battle between the Rock Steady Crew and the New York City Breakers set to the track Breaker's Revenge was the best dance battle I'd ever seen. I wanted so badly to be part of it.

While the soundtrack to the movie played out at the end credits John, Rammy, Graham and I all ran to the front of the theatre onto the small stage in front of the screen. We all then kicked off with some crazy legs and swipes. Next we started belting into a four-man whirl of no handed windmills, virtually in sync. When we arose we got a standing ovation from everyone in the audience. It was absolutely magic.

In this year I became part of the crew, Street Level Juniors, the younger end of the older professional crew by the same name, I also won the Bury and area junior solo breakdance championships, and had become renowned throughout town for my dancing. I was invited to dance at many places; some professional events, people were proud to know me and have me come down to dance for their friends, my cousin Lee Armstrong (aka Timer) one of the many. The girls I used to chase were now chasing me, and into my final year at primary school, I was the king, still thick as fuck, but who cared. I was now a shepherd with a following.

Summer holidays, 1985. I was around 10\11 years of age. Breakin' was rife. Bury was a little, big town, it was small but served to have lots of talent and lots of things going on. By summer this year, a notorious night club named Atmosphere had opened its doors for a break dance Saturday afternoon. So every Saturday we had a full blown disco, lights and hip hop DJ; it couldn't get any better. Because this was the first and only place of its kind, it would bring in breakers from up and down the country. I was now dancing as part of street level, the pro crew, as well as having my own dance crew made up of me, Alan Hall, and a kid named Paddy O'Conner. I would dance with Alan and the crew on the side lines, and at various events, but would always make myself ready for the main battles, for when they came. Burdacci was the main coordinator, sending you in against the other top dancers, trick for trick. We danced against the UK no1s, Broken Glass, a kid named Danny Price leading the pack, also dancing against a pre- take that, Jason Orange. As a pro, I would get to dance with Street Level's main crew, John and Graham, Ste Rami, Daz Harrison, Ray Satchell and our king popper, Ste Duckworth. We won a string of contests, and one of our crews even made it to the overall dance nationals.

Anyone who didn't know me when I walked in would want to know me before I left. As I've said before, these were magical, magical times, a sense of passion, adrenaline, fame and belonging, a beautiful memory of a time so care free and without any fault whatsoever. Awesome!

Chapter 3

Breaker's revenge

September 1985: The start of the new school year

It was off the back of the greatest summer ever known, a four year build of excitement leading to this point. I had started at a new high school, St Gabriel's RC in Bury. I was just expecting a carry on from the previous year, after all I was the king of the world, right? A lot of people knew who I was and had seen me dance at some point but for some reason it didn't seem to matter. The school was huge, so as much as I was known by some, others didn't seem too bothered about breakin' or breakers.

The thing that I had missed was this: As I'd been enjoying summer at what seemed like the height of the dance craze; while I was dancing in the halls, the disco and in competition, I hadn't noticed that no new breakin' movies had been released, nor any new music made its way into the chart. I hadn't even noticed that a lot of my pals had given up the ghost and weren't practicing anymore. I hadn't noticed that in the short time from summer until now, breakin' was on its way out. When practicing in the corridor, no one was watching. People were pulling their faces and muttering "What's he doing? Has no one told him breakin' is out?" It couldn't be, I thought, ignoring the initial signs.

Classes at our school were mixed so both clever and thick kids were put together. My pal Scott had left to go to another school. Sean and I were placed in separate classes so we didn't see each other, only in passing. Most of my classes were with new people that I didn't know. With most kids from my old school in a different form layout, I was stranded. I wasn't mixing well, nor was I doing well in any of my lessons. Neither teachers nor the students I got put with knew anything about me. They were either 'not rights' or people who read books, none of them my kind of people.

Even my school uniform didn't look right; I'd picked the wrong pants. They looked alright when I was buying them but when I'd come to put them on a few weeks later they were way too tight. I had pointed shoes, which were cool last year but now and like breakin', were out of fashion. Think of Johnny Depp as Willy Wonka to get the right picture.

Within a month or two of being at my new school I seemed endlessly involved in fights. I even got suspended for three days for banging a kid in the middle of the classroom; I didn't like being called a scrubber. My clothes weren't just out of fashion; because of the fights I was having in the yard they were also covered in shit and torn. I noticed all the kids who had looked up to me not long back were either shying away, looking in the opposite direction, or actually joining in going against me. My family had recently moved up to Dicky Bird council estate so this really didn't help my case. There was a lot of snobbery at my new school. If you weren't part of Brandlesholme or Greenmount, or the football clique, you didn't fit in. I was quickly hating my new school.

It wasn't like even when you won the fight you'd be left alone. There was still a lot of torment. I had battered everyone who had bothered me but it didn't seem to make a difference. I missed a lot of school in my first year. If I had been an arsehole when a breaker then fair enough but I wasn't. I was confident and believe it or not, there are so many people who will want to rock or knock that out of you; more than what you think. Why? You'd have to ask them.

I did meet one friend in this year though. His name was Simon Jaworskie. Simon was one of the cleverest kids in the year. He was part of the Brandlesholme football crowd and was well known and liked throughout the school. I think I was standing on my own when he first came over to talk. He was a nice kid and even in my least approachable state, he managed to pick up on my interests. Although very much chalk and cheese, he managed to tap into the better side of my persona. It's funny when you've got lots of friends you never really pay much attention, but in an area where you haven't any, it can make the world of difference. A good person never forgets who was there for them when they needed someone.

At night things were much different. In 1985 I was part of the Willow Street Massive. Our turf was the Bob Shop and Smullens off-licence. There was me, Des Hutchinson, Chris Hutchinson, Chris Lawrence (Logs), Alan Hall, Jason Garside, Dennis Egan (Spam) and a kid named Steve Smullen (Eddie). There were a few others who came and went but this was the main crew. Des was our mentor. He was the best junior footballer in Bury, and was the cock of the year above. He was our education when it came to girls, as well as various other daft shit he got us into. A scary thought when thinking back.

We usually had a posse of girls who hung around with us as well. Again there were different names and different faces but plenty of 'em. I was the outcast at school but at home it was different. We were all big Rocky and Arnold fans. In fact, we knew a lot and were fans of lots of things mainly to do with sports, girls and movies. We talked a lot about stuff we were going to do when we got older. We challenged each other to do varied tasks, mostly dangerous stuff; hanging from bridges, climbing drain pipes, running over cars, playing chicken on the motorway, hot wiring cranes at the building sites...

I remember once, Alan and Logs had dared me to eat this chocolate bar they had. I agreed but then they told me it was a laxative and that they were saving it for Smullen. They said it would make me shit if I was to eat it. I don't know why, but I didn't believe them. Well it's not that I didn't believe them; I just didn't think a chocolate bar could make you shit. So there I was eating the chocolate thinking, "Yeah, whatever," both Logs and Alan shaking their heads knowing what's coming.

I went home to have my tea: nothing. I sat and watched a little TV: still nothing. I decided it was time to get ready and go back out. I'd made it as far as the church, which was a couple of hundred yards from where I lived, when I felt my guts suddenly give way. Then came the noises, then the smell. As quick as I'm writing it, it had happened. It was already shit water in my underpants. I think "Fuck." I get behind the Church, pants down, butt against the wall. It was coming out of me like shit coloured custard. I'm making that "ooor ooor" kind of sound whilst waiting for it to finish. I got some leaves and quickly cleaned my butt, thinking that's that.

I was then walking down the main road, when same again; splat, splat, explosion. I had to shit at the side of someone's wall in plain view of oncoming traffic. Pride was out the window on this one. After this, things started to ease up a little as I made my way down to Logs' house but I was seriously stinking by now. I got about ten feet from where he lived, when it starts again. I made a dash. All the crew were outside the house waiting.

"Logs, let me use your toilet. I need a shit, badly."

Logs guarded the doorway, "I warned you! You can't go in, you fucking stink."

Logs was being a real arse and wouldn't give an inch so I told him that I'd shit on his lawn if he didn't let me use his toilet. He laughed saying, "Go on then." So I did.

Everyone was like "Ooooh, you dirty bastard!"

Logs was going mad. "You should have let me use your toilet then, you fuckin' dick."

My night was cut short. I ended up stopping at my auntie Cinnie's. She was feeding me soup the following day as I had looked like a washed out panda. Auntie Cinnie shook her head, "Bloody hell John, when are you going to learn?"

Then her son, Phil added, "You won't be turkin any birds looking like that."

Back to the story:
We would usually rob Smullens store most weeks. Our favourites were alcohol, chocolate and videos. None of it was really enough for George (the owner) to notice, but enough for us to get trashed. We would always give Steve (George's son) the videos back through the week. We mainly watched the Arnold and Sly Stallone movies amongst the other action and horrors we wouldn't otherwise be able to get our hands on. We weren't really big on drugs and none of us smoked. We did experiment with poppers, aerosols and magic mushrooms though, always laughing our heads off shortly after. We got in some fights (but only when needed) and as a team we always won, mainly thanks to Des who could hit as hard as any man. On the punching machines at the fair, I can't remember anyone ever beating him; he was twelve at the time. We hung out with various girls. We had a lot of young testosterone and were very eager to learn about the opposite sex. We didn't get to hang on to our virginities for very long. We crashed parties, got chased off peoples' property by owners and police, put bangers through letter boxes, played knock a door run and so the list goes on.

Thinking back, even though those things were wrong, we were so absent minded that it almost made it alright. If I was breakdancing on the bowling green, it wasn't to tear up the green, it was just to dance. Although we got chased with baseball bats for that once! We ripped up the fence at the tennis club just to go in and play tennis. Even when we broke into the newly built warehouses, it was only so we could stand on the base of the doors and use the chains at the side to pull each other up to see how high we could get before having to jump off. We got chased off six police vans for that one. I remember me and Des having to run through someone's house because we were cornered. Once we got through the house, both laughing, we had to fly through a ton of bushes and different gardens until we finally made it back to his house. We were rolling about in stitches, green faced and cut to bits. Great times!

We had full blown Rambo knives, sharp as you like. Not because we wanted to hurt anyone; it was just for the fact that we wanted to be Rambo. There was very little, if any, malice in what we did; we were just kids being kids, 80s style. This may seem like bad behaviour but we were never cruel, unlike like some of the supposedly 'better kids' that were at our school.

Back to school

As Christmas neared I was, as usual, practicing my breakin'. I was now immensely good; back flips into front flips, one handed handstand bounces, moves flowing smoother than a river. Even though I knew a lot of people had shrugged me off, I reckoned with how good I had got I would still be able to blow people away with my dancing. I just wanted to show what I had learned; it was kind of all I had at the time. When at the disco I appeared smart with good clothes, so initially a few people seemed to take a touch more time letting on or being ok. Simon had been trying to introduce me to a couple of his friends with not much luck, but a few had warmed to me a little. And even though I wasn't in any of Sean's classes, we were seeing a touch more of each other so things, in general, were starting to go ok.

It had got to a part of the night when one of the classic breakdance records had started to belt out from the DJ stand. I looked around and fortunately a dance circle had formed and magically, everyone wanted to watch. A lad named Alex Morris, a dance fan who had liked me, was straight over, "Come on, John, you'll rip these to bits." So off we went. I went straight in, adrenaline rushing, a sense of cocky confidence as I whipped into my first dance run, the crowd loving it. I got up from my first run receiving cheers and pats on the back. There were some surprised faces though. Obviously a lot of these kids didn't know me and had written me off as some kind of dosser. I reckon a few knew they had got me wrong. Anyway, back at it and my finale of the windmill, which was now, 'bounce off the surface rapid'. I flung myself in and off I went.

It only took a couple of seconds before I felt myself getting shifted to the side of the dance floor. I was getting kicked in the head by a group of older lads, flipped over onto my back. Within a second, a dark shadow came from behind and careered straight into the lads. It blasted them out of the circle, powerful and brutal, towards my aggressors. I wasn't sure of what was happening. A few seconds later I felt myself being lifted back to my feet; a big lad, abrupt looking, but a guy you could tell was fair. After getting me up and seeing I was ok, he started to speak. "You've got a real talent there pal, don't give up." It was so sincere it dug right into my soul. I went straight back in and finished my run with an awesome array of my finest moves.

The guy who stepped in was named Julian Parkinson. I think he may have been cock of the walk at the time. No one bothered me again after that. Again there was the same message of that one person being able to make all the difference. My last dance in front of an audience: a great experience rather than a bad one.

The following year: 1986

I'd carried on with my dancing until there was literally nothing more I could have learned. I even invented some of my own moves, but unfortunately breakin' had died. The school disco was my last dance. What I got from this, and also through Julian's actions was that I carried on an extra year. I finished what I started. I honestly couldn't have got any better or tried any harder. I gave it enough time to know that it wouldn't return. No regrets, looking to find the next big wave.

Breakin' did return but it wasn't until sometime in the early millennium, and I did dance again. In 2004 I danced with the LA breakers in Florida, USA. My dream of dancing over in the states was met. In 2009, age thirty-five, I was able to dance with some of the original Rock Steady Crew at the Lowry in Manchester; a dream I'd kept since 1984.

People seem so hell bent on dispelling God but with patience and belief there are very few of my prayers and dreams that haven't been answered, regardless of how big or small. I've witnessed, but have had to work for, a lot of the happy endings in my life; all well worth it though. God will never challenge you on anything you can't win or learn from.

Chapter 4

Bad habits, losing friends, losing popularity.

Same bad habits, making friends, gaining popularity.

During the tough time at school, mid 1985-1986, I had done a lot of boxing. I had five fights and five wins (not the billed fights, just a club against club type of thing). I was an awkward fighter, fighting from both stances. I thought that when I joined, I'd be set up with a class of heart felt Rocky types. However, because I was awkward to fight, some of the kids used to complain because they couldn't get to me or fathom out my quirky odd style. I got pretty decent and liked the training but found most the kids I was fighting with were the kind of kids who needed a way out in life, boxing being that. I was looking for a way in, to have that upbeat feeling and although boxing was my favourite sport to watch on TV, I knew this wasn't the tide that was going take me. I stuck with boxing for around 14 months but it wasn't the spark I wanted.

The Brat Pack

A crew of young Hollywood actors had just come onto the scene. They were known as The Brat Pack. I was with Smullen and Logs at the time. Smullen was babysitting for this hot Italian looking girl named Paula, messing about sniffing her underwear and putting her bra on his head. Me and Logs were laughing whilst getting drawn in to a movie we'd been watching on TV. The movie was named Risky Business. It was about a kid who got caught up with a hooker then got chased down by this weird dude named Gweedo, the killer pimp. The guy was throwing wild parties; his charisma was second to none. I couldn't take my eyes away from the screen. I'd just been introduced to Tom Cruise. There was also another actor, he was starring in a big block buster at the time, About Last Night, but I'd seen him in a few earlier movies named Oxford Blues, Class, and St Elmo's fire. The guy's energy was bouncing from the screen. His movies involved school and college parties combined with wild, outlandish fun. The actor's name was Rob Lowe. He was the king of The Brat Packers at the time, and again like Tom Cruise, he was massively cool. I saw myself like both these characters; not trying to be someone I wasn't, more of an extension of what I already was. But I didn't want to just act out this life style, I wanted to live it.

In my second year at school trouble would ease up a little. The fighting I had done in my first year left a lot of people a little more reluctant to want to cause me any more problems. Because of my dancing and how good I was at most sports, I now seemed less of an outcast (at least to some). I did get suspended for fighting though and although my pal Simon invited me up to his house on numerous occasions, apart from one kid named Ewan Stevenson, none of his other friends seemed to want to take me on.

It got to Simon's 13th birthday and he had invited me to his party. It started at Simon's house (a jelly and ice-cream type of party) then we jumped on a bus and headed into Rochdale to watch a double bill at the cinema; Karate Kid part 2, starring Ralph Machio, followed by Three Fugitives, starring Nick Nolti. Whilst we were on our way into Rochdale, looking out from the bus, I pointed out my house as you could just see it from behind the buildings. I had recently moved back up Fairfield from Dickey Bird. My house was a neat looking white cottage. When the other kids saw, I could see the cogs in their minds start to turn right away and, sad as it seems, their acceptance of me seemed to change from this point on. Bear in mind, as much as the 80s were upbeat, people flowed with their emotions, passions and feeling. The 80s was also the 'yuppie' decade; a lot of these kids had parents in high power jobs which caused an 'us and them' type of attitude. The stuff they'd seen on TV obviously rubbed off on them too.

Anyway, back to the story. Things were on the up:

A few months in and coming close to my 13th birthday; the start of my teens. With college movies in mind and my tunnel vision insistence that it has to happen; it just has to happen! I've always had tunnel vision. So at 12 that vision just sort of said, "Tom Cruise and Rob Lowe are cool. They have wild parties. I want to have wild parties and be cool like Rob Lowe and Tom Cruise." Was it selfish? No, because at that age you shouldn't even know what being selfish means; you are about to become a teenager.

The invites went out. I basically just asked everyone that I knew whilst passing. Simon's pals were a little reluctant but once one said yes, they all did. We had girls from the block, older girls from school, even older girls from other schools. We had the years below to the years above. This was the first party of its kind and as I said, I'm a shepherd; I do what others only think about. Tunnel vision and no thought for consequence. I would lead the sheep to water and we'd all get fucked up together.

The party went down a treat. The house, garden, beds, everyone was either, making out, talking shit, dancing or fighting. I remember being in the front garden when a kid named Ryan Monaghan had jumped from a bedroom window. He then fell off the porch and on to the grass. Everyone was like, "Whoa."

Ryan gets up, about 11 years old at the time. "There's a girl up there, she won't go with me", "Have a beer Ryan. Take it easy," I say. I put my arm over his shoulder.

"Cheers, John,"returned a quiet, drunken mumble. Everyone laughed and patted Ryan on his back. Everyone got off with everyone that night. Necking: the in thing at the time. The rich mixed with the poor, the top sets with the bottom; it truly was mint.

The following week, if I'm trying to explain it, was like the Michael J Fox movie Teen Wolf. When he's walking down the halls after the basketball game; High fives, everyone stirring, not a conversation went on that hadn't mentioned the party. Only in my second year, I was once again king of the school. The same outlandish behaviour that had killed me was the same behaviour that got me back on top. The fact is, it was never intentional. I did what my heart told me to do and when left to my own thoughts, the worst type of behaviour became a positive aspect in more ways than one. The school had come together. Simon, Gilray and Rob were talking to Des, and Neil Hanley (another clever kid) was getting on with Spam, and everyone seemed to just get along. I made it cool to be a little crazy. As they say, God moves in mysterious ways. If things are done with good intention and everyone gets something good from it, how can it possibly be a sin? I threw a host of parties. The first five throughout 2nd and 3rd year were the wildest. The parties became legendary.

Throughout 1987 I was the party boy. I was also into skating (I'll talk about this more in the next chapter). This was the Beastie Boy era (a rock, rap band of the time) so my not right behaviour was accepted; even more to the point it had become an influence. On the council estates this stuff was just the norm but when hanging around on the posh estates it was like who's this crazy kid? I wanna be like that. And before long, everyone was. We were all jumping off cars, stealing VW signs off the fronts of vehicles (Beastie Boys were wearing VW signs on a chain around their necks). We wore, Jean Jackets and Levis, whilst swilling bottles of Bud.

Now all these once 'well-to-do-with' yuppie kids were all going for it; mad as fuck. I'd created a party epidemic with most these kids opening their doors to hold a huge party at some point in their school or early college lives.

I'd get suspended again in early third year, three years on the trot, but not for fighting this time...

My mum used to do ouija boards at some point in the mid-seventies, possibly early eighties; an end of the night, pissed up party piece around Christmas time. Anyhow, I was telling the stories and how my house was haunted. Kids were shitting themselves but were still very curious, especially the girls, to know a little more; we were in music class at the time. A couple of weeks down the line I was being mithered to do a ouija board whilst in class. We were left alone in the sound proof room for an hour. No one ever came in and none of us could even play a tambourine or had any remote interest in what we were meant to be doing. I don't even know what we were meant to be doing, so I agreed. We had a guard at the door, keeping an eye out. I'd cut up pieces of paper and prepared them into letters and numbers, yes and no. We used a tumbler from the cafeteria for the centre piece and basically that was it. We were talking to spirits in our music lessons. Right away, people started to talk. So I'm showing the kids in the room next door and next door to that The kids I was showing were then telling their friends, so even the years above were now making ouija boards whilst in music class. And so it began.

Anyway around three or four months went by, everyone was buzzing about meeting spirits and getting caught up with it all. It was all a lot of fun but not for long! A girl from the year above had gone flying out of her lesson and straight in to see the head master. She had told him what was going on. She'd had a bad experience with one of the ghosts so was obviously upset. So like anything, questions are asked; one then another, then the question of, "Well who started all of this?" So that was that, another three-day suspension; but this time getting suspended was cool.

The last big party

It was the holidays before the start of fourth year. I was 14 at the time, known for my parties and wild ways. I was the all American kid but I lived in England. I had never gravitated to anything English; I'm not sure why. But like anything, you don't have to travel to be like your idols, you just do what I did and create your own scene, easy.

It was the dawn of what would be my last major party. At the time, I had a string of friends from all walks of life. I hung here, there and everywhere. Very free spirited, caught up in a self-made wonderful world. Amongst others, I hung out with a group of older girls: Joanna, Lisa, Sharon and a girl named Sarah. The 'it' girls from up Jericho.

I had a thing for Sarah and as it turned out she had a thing for me also, even though she was a few years older. We'd listen to records whilst in Joanna's room and even though I'd had experience with other girls, when it came to Sarah, it felt like it wasn't forced. She'd put her head against my shoulder with 'The first picture of you, the first picture of summer' playing in the background. I was just sitting there smelling her hair, entranced by her sweet smell and by the melody, butterflies in my stomach. Nothing needed to happen. She was mature but she liked me, even though I was always pretty quiet in her company.

We'd been talking one day whilst we were in Joanna's house. It was just me and her, and I couldn't help but look right into her eyes. She had soft brown eyes and an infectious smile and before I knew where we were, she had moved towards me with her hand at the side of my face and gently started to kiss me. My frickin' legs were shaking, it was brilliant! So was I growing up? Was I starting to appreciate the finer things in life? We will see.

Party time

This party was the wildest. I was trying to be a touch more mature as I knew Sarah was on her way so didn't want to be acting like a total dick, as per usual. Even early on you couldn't see through the house. There was barely any standing room and the garden was rammed top to bottom with crazy kids ready to go wild. Initially, when Sarah arrived, I wasn't drinking much but as the party started to unfold I began to have a sense of fear. I was a little nervous and stuck for words so I had a few more drinks to boost the confidence a touch. As the party drew on we were sat on one of the sofas and had started making out. Nervous and anxious, I drunkenly thought that if I didn't try it on, I might be seen as frigid (especially with her being older and more mature,) bear in mind, Des had been my mentor. So I started getting a little flighty with my hands. Sarah quickly grabbed my hands and puts them back to her shoulder. She tells me it's the time of the month, then we carried on. I didn't have a clue what the time of the month was, not a clue. So without even asking what she meant, I try it on again. BANG! She slapped me so hard I fell to the floor. Sarah was up on her feet then out the door. Joanna, who was sat nearby, followed after her. I made my way outside, Sarah stood clear.

"What's up with her? Do you think she will still want to go out with me?" I asked Joanna.

"Erm, no John. I don't think so, not tonight anyway." I didn't really have a clue as to what just happened.

A couple of minutes after they had left I went back and told my pal Paul Scanlon (Scannie) about what had gone on. He passed me a bottle of beer and we spoke whilst standing at the front gate. Another beer, then another took our pissed conversation outside the gate and into the middle of the street. Whilst we talked a car pulled past and stopped in front of my house. A guy got out looking pissed off. He saw me and Scannie. "Hey, where's Peter?" he ranted.

Not knowing what he was talking about I say, "Who?" with a slight smile on my face. The guy then spotted Pete, his son, vomiting and sliding down the wall. He then asked if it was my party, so I nodded whilst trying not to laugh. "Where are your parents? Isn't there any parental control here at all?" he blazed.

I looked at him in disgust."You what? I didn't invite him; I don't even know who he is!" I think I remembered him coming in with a kid named Matt McTague, but not 100%.

The guy then puts his shapeless son in the back of his car, still going on about parental control to the point that it had got boring. Me and Scannie just kind of looked at each other then looked back at the guy. "Fuck you, you fucking dick. Get fucked," we both went at it. We swilled a little more beer before looking at each other again and laughing. We then threw our half-filled beer bottles at the car as it screeched off up the street, a quick high five and another drink.

Fucked up and down about being dumped, I made my way into the front garden. I started on at Des, saying I had tried it on with Sarah off the back of what he'd said. I was angry so started a fight with him but to little avail. After Des had battered me in the nicest way possible, just enough to have left me paralysed but not enough to have knocked me out, he sat me down and explained things to me, my older brother influence. The last thing he said to me was, "John, you're my best friend. It doesn't matter what state you're in; I'll always be your friend." I hugged Des. I was a pissed up emotional mess, great times.

As I walked back up the garden a little later on. I think I saw Joycie battering someone on the front lawn. Then I see the window is smashed, Tudor fucking glass. Spam had blood all over his hands and as I walked back into the house, the cupboards were open, my Mum's cigarettes gone. Puke and shit was everywhere. There were burn marks, radiator hanging off the wall and plates smashed. People were passed out or vomiting and crying. It was total fuckin' oblivion. Party over.

The next day I got worded up by my parents. My Dad started off calm but finally hit the roof, fair-play. The parties quietened down for a short time after that and when I did start throwing them again I had given up drinking so kind of kept my eye on things a touch more. Still pretty good though, happy days.

A few weeks had passed and I was broken hearted over Sarah whilst I trained in the shed my Dad had recently built for me. I was playing tracks such as Van Halen's, Why can't this be love? Berlin, even fuckin' T'Pau. I had depth, feeling, and it hurt. It took me a good two weeks to get over the breakup of the relationship that never was. Ok, maybe not that much depth then. Anyway, after a brief interlude of sparked emotion, I decided that chasing girls was no more; not for now anyway. So it was back to shallow, selfish and full of shit and what better way to take me away from all this thought and feeling stuff but to get involved with a new passion: the straight up hard core remedy for not giving a fuck for anything.

Chapter 5

Possessed to skate

A touch of science before we get started:

The brain: the muscle, the organ releases serotonin which is a feel good hormone. It makes you feel upbeat, heartfelt and gets the adrenaline going. When we watch stuff on TV it is absorbed into our memory, giving us the urge to want to get involved. Like when I was breakin', I can recall my feelings, what the kids were like, how good the times were and so it makes us want more. The muscle memory has indicators directing us to varied paths that guide our most positive thoughts and so life addictive people (people who love living life to its fullest) will chase the same path. They already know how to mentally assimilate those same feelings. Like a heroin addict who has had the taste, he's been to that place and he needs to go back otherwise he goes nuts; well that's the same with life addicts also.

I'd been skate boarding for a while but only as a bit of fun. After watching the movie, Back to the Future, starring Michael J Fox, skating had ventured back into the public eye. It had never really been big in Britain up until this point. I'd be standing in the bus depot when I first saw a crew of skaters. They were flicking out hockey stops, their boards looking neat with wide fish tails. They had different coloured wheels. The kids were cool; cool clothing, cool in their manner. I'd seen all this before.

After seeing this, there was a feeling, that same feeling of something good about to happen. When I say God acts in mysterious ways, this was it. After seeing those kids on their boards I really wanted it. Well, I prayed and shortly after, it all just started to happen; positivity breeding positivity. My pals Stu and Alex shared a Varaflex board and had started hanging with a kid named Martin Livesey, another skater that I already knew through breakin'. So when I said I wanted to skate they took me to that place. The place this time being the city of Manchester.

There was Stuart and Alex, Martin, Cleany, Javie' a kid called Porky and another lad named Pete Dutton. We had gone to a place called American Sports and wow! The boards in there were awesome. I knew I had to have one. This was it. Then we went on to another shop named 50\60, a punk type skate shop on the Affleck's Palace, Northern Quarter side of Manchester'. The place was cool and right away there was that welcoming sense of belonging; a place I wanted to be.

I don't really remember how every detail went following the initial transition onto the skate scene, but it moved pretty fast. My full team of pals were all now into skating. Everyone loved it. Stuart and Alex had built a quarter pipe at the side of their house and me and Spam had built a massive jump ramp near us. I skated everywhere. There was a motion picture out at the time named Thrashin', staring Josh Brolin and Robert Russler. We played it to death. Then there were the skating videos.

After a short while the shop known as 50\60 became Split Skates. There was a path for us to ride our boards through the shop. We sat in the skate part of the shop every Saturday morning. The owners, Anne and Granvil, had skating videos on the TV whilst we bought new bits to put on our boards. We regularly spoke to a kid named Dillon, who worked behind the counter. Our favourite video was named Animal Chin starring the Bones Brigade, Steve Cabballero and Tony Hawke. There were also Streets of Fire featuring Christian Hosoi and Molecules in Motion starring, Mark (Gator)

Ragowski. These were the main guys at the time. I skated a Steve Cab, then later a Gator and a Hosoi; all my favourite skaters. We argued over who was best. We knew every name from routing through both Thrasher and R.A.D magazine. We knew the tricks and had seen the parks, their set ups but it was now time to create our own. Like I've said before, you don't need to go to the U.S. to be like your idols, you just need the right people and the right frame of mind.

We were regulars at the Manchester law courts where they had large concrete banks (concrete angled slabs with a slight lip that would follow on in file) and became pretty incredible bank skaters; I think because, initially, we had little access to anything else. It was the same with the fly off ramps. Where I lived, we only had the one ramp. We had to get it on a down-hill slope to get to a decent speed so we could smash out high aerials. The kids on the street all wanted to skate. Mums and Dads came to their front doors to watch. We taught all the young kids how to do kick turns on the ramp and laughed our arses off watching them try. Before long I wasn't just the king of the school scene and the party scene. I was now a well renowned part of the skate scene and like breakin', it was just about to get massive.

In Manchester, they had just erected a mini half pipe in the upstairs of Split Skates. Now Saturday morning was ramp skating then on to the banks in the afternoon and Sunday, pretty much the same deal. We had a crew of around 40 or 50 lads, all from Bury, catching the early 90 express bus into Manchester. It was rife. Me and a lad named Stuart were the main skaters to come out of Bury at the time. The banks were our patch. We'd get set up whilst everyone was practicing, then when we were ready it was just a case of 'get out of the fuckin' way!' and off we went. But the kids loved us for some reason. We also had groups of girls who came down to watch us but I didn't really entertain them, I just wanted to skate. Stuart ended up going out with one of the girls I had turned down. My mind was solely focused on skating. I loved it and it was just about to get even better.

I'm not sure how or why but, before I knew it, skating was arriving big in Bury. We built an indoor half pipe at Goshen Sports and had a full street set up in the main hall at the leisure centre. I mean, wall ramps, pop offs, ramp to ramp transfer and landing pad. We had quarter pipes and mini hand rails. We had it as good as any indoor pro contest. It was awesome. I got sponsored around this time by Split Skates. I worked all day Sunday, (then later Saturday and Sunday) at the Goshen ramp and Saturday night at the leisure centre where I was a skate warden at both. I was skating all day, all night, all week. We were soon getting named and pictured in R.A.D magazine. We were asked to skate and give the pros a taste of the Manchester street scene; we killed them on the banks. We also got to skate with some of the bigger names including Jesse Martinez and Natas Corpus. Ultimately, we got to skate the Goshen half pipe with Steve Caballero, Lance Mountain, Mike McGill and Tony Hawke, all our heroes.

I was one of the first Northwest skaters to land a hand rail slide. It was at the law courts in Manchester. Literally, I smashed myself to bits. I think the only reason I carried on was that there was a big crowd of people all watching. Whilst attempting the trick I cracked my back, head, arms, legs and ball sack on the concrete step and rail to a string of, "Whoa," "Ouch," and "Oh shit." I went a little Happy Gilmore: "f'in this, f'in that," throwing and smashing my board against the wall. But, honestly, when I finally ollied on, got my balance, slid down the rail and on to my wheels, shit me, it was all well worth it. What a massive rush that was.

On the Bury half pipe I was flying. I always got there an hour or so before opening time, the caretaker opened up then left me to it. I'd have a coffee or three whilst warming up on the ramp, initially steady lip tricks and grinds. I'd always start my morning listening to a bit of The Smiths, The Cure or New Order; nice and steady. After around an hour I'd get to it. I'd change the music to thrash metal; Suicidal Tendencies, Red Hot Chilli Peppers, and bands of that sort. I've got to say the music really did it for me. I was ripping out some serious aerials, foot plants and inverts. By the time people started filling up the place I was in the zone, three hours' practice already under my belt. It became so popular that the ramp was open at night throughout the week. I was there nearly every night. I lived for it.

One night we were all at the ramp and I said to my pals Peter Dutton, Porky and John Kenny, "Pick any move and I'll do it." I was hitting inverts, backside airs, front side judo airs off the extension, front side rock n rolls...

Then Pete shouted, "Mc twist and shout." This was a 540 degree inverted aerial but I thought, fuck it, here we go. I threw myself in. I made the full twist, and back, on my wheels, but then slid on my knees. It was a good effort though and what an uproar.

When my pals from the estate came down (most of them were just messing about, not mad interested) I'd get my pal Alan Hall to dangle his legs over the front of the ramp, then I'd do an aerial over them. Alan always made me laugh. He'd always be calling anyone he didn't know: "John will tear you up, you are shit. Tear 'em up John." He was the harshest kid I ever met. I was embarrassed but couldn't help laughing. Great times.

12 months on: School high life and haunted house fun

Outside the skating arena all was well. We had lots of parties, everyone was at it. I'd stay sober, kind of the more mature of the bunch. As well as acting like Tom Cruise and Rob Lowe, I'd now taken on thinking I was Patrick Swayze also. I was regularly training with weights and had earned myself a nice little six pack. I quite regularly showed it off with my party piece of putting a coin in my abs; my abs gripped the coin and the girls loved it. I had succumbed to the ladies once more, but didn't have to do much chasing this time. I was the bollocks.

Haunted house

My house had become as renowned for its haunting as it was for its partying now. Literally everyone had witnessed something. There were green outer rims and facial changes in the mirrors and lights going on and off. It even felt like a pole was going through the side of my shed once. My pals Paul Holt and Craig Colker shit it and ran off home.

There was a condensation face, that wouldn't rub off (it looked like Jesus with the crown of thorns). It may have been a sign, but it just shit me up. Kids were talking about being pinned down, unable to move. Most of my family have witnessed this also.

There was a night when Sean, my sister Karen and her mate Janine were stopping over at my house. We were hearing bangs all through the house and lights were going on and off. Then we saw a green orb, clear as day, make its way through the dining room. It was Proper freaky.

My little sister Deb was often seen to have black pupils. She was always pointing to stuff and coming out with weird shit. She was around two years old at the time. I remember coming home late one night; I'd been to a party. Debra came flying out of her bedroom in her little pink baby grow then, tight as you like, grabbed the back of my leg. Her pupils were black. "Get away from me," she warned but not in a kid's voice. I shit myself, locked myself in the bathroom and slept in the bath all night. My pal John Kenny, an Oxford Uni grad, said to me recently, "I'm a man of science, but honestly there's just shit about your house that can't be explained." I mean literally hundreds of kids were witness to something. Even big Des and his brother Chris, after seeing a massive shadow then something grabbing them, took an early trip home on that night.

My Dad thought we were all full of shit until one day something ragged his head backwards. He first thought it was Deb, then he realised no one was there. The hairs on his arms stood right up, it was all so mad but funny at the same time.

Capturing the scene of the 80s school life wave

I was the school athlete, even though I wasn't a lover of football. I was captain of the running teams for all distances. I was a strong part of the rugby team and had won the all school fitness challenge. I had a string of girls doting over me; I'd wink at them and they would go red and weak at the knees. In lesson though, I'd sit with some of my original school friends: Alice OBrien, Alison Berry, Candy Hakin and Grace Gibbons. Unlike the other girls who hung on all my bullshit, these just laughed at my obvious stupidity. I reckon they still fancied me though. It was all good.

I had a regular on\off relationship with a girl named Emma. We tended to fall out a bit when we were going out together but were always good friends and loved the drama\romances that kept re-emerging between us throughout our time at school. I remember first asking her out after I'd been mesmerised watching her tap dance. I'd gone into the prom room where we had our break. I'd got a ring pull from the top of a can to use like a ring. I then proposed to her on one knee, asking if she'd go out with me. The whole place was clapping and laughing. This was the kind of daft confidence that would win all the girls over, I mean everything was just fun. On our being cool days, we may get away with being seen like our idols Tom Cruise, Patrick Swayze or Rob Lowe but on most days we were more like the goonies, or them pervy kids from that movie, Porkys.

Classroom fun

I remember, there was this one teacher that we all fancied named Mrs Wiggins. She was quite sweet looking but it was more the fact that she had huge boobs! The main reason we liked her so much. In class we soon fathomed that if we had a problem with what we were doing then Mrs Wiggins would come over to the desk and lean forward whilst explaining things. This left us able to look down her blouse. I'd call her over and as she arrived I'd get a dig from my pals Rachael and Shenade, the word "Perv" whispered in my ear. I'd quickly look down the teacher's top as she glimpsed over my page then lift my head quickly when she was done. "Thanks, Miss," I'd say with a big smile on my face. St John was the best: He'd call the teacher over but when she'd arrived at his desk his face would go a beetroot colour as he smiled ear to ear knowing everyone knew what he was up to. He'd always smile around the room looking embarrassed as we all looked on laughing and flicking small pieces of paper at him.

Mr Howarth was another teacher we had fun with, but in a different type of way. Mr Howarth was a science teacher. He was quite strict, kind of old school, but that wasn't the problem. The problem was that both his eyes pointed outward (kind of like crazy eyes from the Adam Sandler movie Mr Deeds). We'd be messing about when Mr Howarth would shout "You, boy" from across the classroom. "Who me?" "Me sir?" No one having any idea who he was looking at, which only added to his frustration. However, on this occasion it was me that was in bother. I wasn't the only one who got in trouble though because my pals had started laughing also, we all had to stand outside the class. When the teacher finally came to deal with us, he kept asking what was wrong with me because I couldn't stop giggling. "You, boy," he starts at it again. Des did an impression of Mr Howarth, where he shouted "You, boy" then pointed in the opposite direction. This image playing over in my head only made me worse.

"Right," he said. "What's your name? I'm reporting you to the head master." I figured if he didn't know my name then I could give any name. "Rob Lowe, sir," I offered. I wasn't really lying; I really did think I was either, Rob Lowe, Patrick Swayze or Tom Cruise at this point in my school life. My pals had then started laughing for saying I was Rob Lowe. The teacher just shouted and bawled, really losing his shit this time. Then another teacher started to walk down the corridor, Mrs. Buggy. She started asking what was going on, seeing

Mr Howarth very much distressed and me laughing.

"John, what are you up to?" she asked. Mr. Howarth chirped in, "John? I thought you were called Robert? What's wrong with you, boy?" The other kids were all now sliding down the walls in stitches. Mrs Buggy stepped in, massively unimpressed. "I'll take care of this Mr. Howarth, this way John." Mrs Buggy said very little as she marched me up to the head master's office. She then stupidly walked off leaving me on my own. I gave it a few seconds then sneaked off, all Spider Man like under the science lab windows then safely hid in the toilets until the bell went and it was time to go home.

As far as school went, I was clever enough to copy someone's homework before I went to class, so I didn't get in trouble, but that was about it. I liked Religious Studies, having always enjoyed the stories from the Bible. The only lesson I excelled at though, was drama. My drama teacher, Mr Keating, told me I was the best actor in school and said he didn't want me failing my exams due to poor English, reading and writing. He said I had the option to stay behind once a week to do the course work, so I agreed. I ended up getting an A and when I learned my lines for the school play, he helped a lot with my mispronunciations and the words that I struggled with. When we were in class he had me look like a pro, taking the embarrassment factor out of the equation for me. He was a great teacher, even though he would regularly say, "See, you don't have to be clever to be a good actor" after I'd put in a good performance.

I starred in a stage version of Macbeth, I was Genghis in the school play, Dracula Spectacular (also starring a pre-Emmerdale Lisa Riley). Later on I was part of a travelling show to do with the rain forest, starring Julia Kearni, a little after she had finished starring in the TV series Brookside. The play brought media attention and we all appeared on Granada Reports. Then I got selected for a small role on the Johny Ball Show. I appeared on Look Northwest as one of the skaters to do with the re-birth of skating. I was in the 'hunk of the month' edition of Mizz Magazine, followed by doing some modelling for a catalogue. And I got my one and only cover photo on a lesser known skating magazine, as well as having been pictured and named in the bigger magazines also.

The world truly was my oyster. Unfortunately, with this kind of attention there's an ego that arises. You don't sense it at first; it's just cocky confidence to start with. It's only when things start to get taken away that it affects you; only then you realise just how far there is to fall. Things stayed pretty good up until the back end of fifth year; then a slight demise, a string of opportunities missed. Then BANG: another big wave hits, but this time I'm under it.

Chapter 6

The mood changes

Near the end of my final year at high school, several opportunities were knocking at my door. However, at school things were starting to change a little around the halls. Parties, trends and so on with a slow, yet sure, new wave starting to arise: Raves and indie music. I'd been an indie music fan myself: The Smiths, New Order, The Cure. But this had just been part of everything else I'd been into such as rock, thrash metal and hip hop. I think it may have been me who originally got my pals into this type of music. They were listening to stuff like Wet Wet Wet and Curiosity Killed the Cat when I initially started to broaden their horizons. But now the indie scene had started becoming a way of life. It was the next big wave, but not for me.

From wearing T-shirts cut into vests and knee length board shorts, my pals had started wearing long sleeved nylon tops with scruffy jeans, branded with the names of their new favourite bands: The Charlatans, Happy Mondays and The Stone Roses. They had long floppy haircuts, were pale looking and actually held their shoulders inwards to look thinner, like their idols. A whole demeanour change had started to occur throughout the school. It was only a minor demise, but I'd sensed the change. Just like I could sense something good about to happen, I could also sense when things were about to change for the worse. Back then I was blaming the trend but looking back, I think it was more about me.

I had always prayed from being very young. I had always prayed for a lot of things to be a certain way, to achieve certain things. I know that when I was a kid, a lot of other kids also used to pray for things, but speaking to those same people in this day and age, most of them don't anymore and I think I know a good reason as to why! One of my main prayers was, when I was round 16 years old, to get started on building a bodybuilding career. But for God to get me started at this intended age, all other ventures and avenues would have to cease. The obstacles in my path would have to be removed to create an opening.

God knows how badly you want things. He knows that if it doesn't happen, you will never be the you that you want to be; nor will God be able to guide you on what you are meant to be and what he knows will be right for you.

A lot of people cease to pray because the dream they choose, the feeling they want, the life they want comes with a sacrifice. The road to follow is there but not always the easiest road to keep on, unlike the seemingly easy path in their dreams. Because things don't happen overnight, people have a tendency to give up on their dreams, themselves, and on God. Life's path is a lot harder to spot when you are young; I initially couldn't see it.

Within a twelve-month period, I was fully ready (and obstacle free) to start my bodybuilding career. Unfortunately, God's great gift would initially look more like a curse than a blessing.

I'm not really sure where to begin with this one. School was still lots of fun.

In our posse there were lots of girls. The most noted was one of the lad's girlfriends. She was quite a lot of fun most the time, but she was gradually taking our pal away from the skate scene and made it known that she was the boss in their relationship. So as a bit of a laugh I started poking fun. His girlfriend didn't like it so we ended up having a big argument. My pal had organised a party; normally I was first to know but for some reason it had been kept from me. When it got down to it, my pal's girl had said she didn't want me there. The girl changed her mind shortly afterwards, but the fact was, was that my so-called pal had chosen a girl, he hadn't known long, over a guy who was supposed to be one of his best friends. The tide was turning.

The clique had become more of a clique, but was unknowingly separating into smaller groups. I was still part of it, but it didn't stop me mixing, and being right with everyone else. The sarcasm wasn't funny anymore either; it seemed more underhanded. If an issue had been discussed away from the group, those involved would talk in code, knowing what each other meant but not wanting the person they were taking the piss out of to know. It seemed a little wrong to me. I wasn't the one being segregated, but I'd been there in the past so I knew what was starting to happen.

These people being left out were my friends; choices had to be made. One of the lads was taking the piss out of Sean, thinking he was being clever. Luckily Sean wasn't behind the door so just ended up banging the kid in the school yard. My pal Simon had also become a little more segregated. I'd heard a few of the lads calling him, underhandedly, behind his back like I had with Sean. I should have really said something then. The next issue though, I couldn't walk away from.

Simon had purchased some tickets to go and watch a band. Being thoughtful, he had bought a couple of tickets for his friends, part of the clique. I was walking down the hall with the two lads at the side of me. They were laughing, saying how Simon had bought some tickets for them to go to this concert and they had told him that they couldn't go. These lads had then gone to the gig and put the stubs from the show on Simons desk with a message saying, "Great gig Simon, sorry you missed it." I was fuming.

So with the tide now turning, my mind had an overwhelming sense of right and wrong. This moral virtue of making the decision to either stay with the cool kids who initially didn't want to know me or step up and help out the kid who had given me his unconditional friendship at a time when no one else would. I was a little more aggressive knowing things were changing, perhaps it had reminded me of how I felt after falling from grace after the breakin' era had ended. It could have been a heightened sensitivity or a bad memory perhaps but I'd been through it; still, that didn't mean that my friends would have to.

I decided I was going to teach these kids a lesson and ended up giving one a crack at the youth club. I then got into it with the other kid shortly after.

Now I had meaning. I could sense the difference between bullshit, fickle friends and what's real and do right by it. The only problem was, I liked being on a high, I enjoyed being popular. Like I said, I'm a life addict, I need that passion, that attention; without it I go berserk (like a drug addict). By the end of term, I was missing more school, opting to go to the skate park instead but nothing too noticeable. I had battered another pal over some shit to do with a girl (he had been bad mouthing me). Then I got partially expelled for hitting another kid (for reasons I won't go into, but he did deserve it).

The tide of change was also starting to happen within the skate scene. The fact that I was on my own told me something was wrong. I got to Split Skates and it was closed. Then I went to the original skate shop, American Sports. I went into the shop, talking to a kid called Bec.

"So they told you then?" he starts.

"Told me what?"

He then went on to explain that a few of my crew had been down a couple of weeks earlier and he had asked them to see if I'd be interested in going pro and doing the British Isles pro skate tour. I saw my arse for a second thinking "sly bastards." But I'd not missed it, "Fuck it", I thought. "Let's do it." Bec got me set up with some free wheels, a £200 board. It was an Eric Dresson, Santa Cruz which wasn't a board I would have chosen but Santa Cruz was a leading brand so I didn't complain. He mentioned that Converse Cons were sponsoring the event then gave me six boxes of free shoes and stickers to take with me. I got some Jimmy Z clothing thrown in as well. The tour was set to start in the holidays; no problems there.

I had been selected to do another modelling shoot but had to turn it down to go on the skate tour. It wasn't a problem though. The tour was a blast. I got to skate with some of the main US pros up and down the country. We set off on a Friday and came back on a Sunday evening, most weeks. When back in Bury though, skating was the lonely man's sport. At the ramp, I literally had it to myself most days. As sad as it seems, I enjoyed it. A little like breakin', I would hit my best level, right at the end and on my own. I carried on skating until the skate parks all closed. The skate shops all closed and the weather became drastic. God's way of telling me it was time to move on. Again: no regrets.

The next door to close was the acting. After three and half years of doing performing arts, I got what seemed like a chance in a life time deal. I had auditioned and had been selected to tour with a large international company, travelling Europe, shooting advertisements and starring on TV. Me and my Dad went along to find out more. When at the event there were hundreds of young hopefuls all wanting to jump on the fame train, but for me it didn't feel right. The guys doing the promo tour were all a little odd. I sensed a seedy demeanour. I wasn't stoked; there wasn't that upbeat feel of something good about to happen. You only have to look at the stories of the youthful 80s Hollywood to know what might have happened.

When leaving the venue my Dad just sort of went quiet. "If you want to carry on going there, you'll have to go yourself." My Dad wouldn't tell me what I could and couldn't do and although I was a little pissed at him at the time, I kind of knew where he was coming from. God, a little like my Dad, doesn't take your free will, but he will give you a warning. He acts like a beacon to keep us safe and in this case, it worked. I didn't go on the tour and after the holidays I never returned to acting.

Most people can admit when they have had a bad feeling about something or someone, but haven't gone with their gut feeling. This is God's way of telling you to stay clear. Remember, God doesn't take away free will, which means, unfortunately, every one still has the right to be an arsehole if and when they want to be. People are quick to moan when shit happens, stuff like, “There is no God” and “Where is He when you need Him?” But you can guarantee most of them will have had some sort of message saying to stay away, something isn’t right, but have ignored it. I know this as I was about to do the same.

Chapter 7

The drugs just didn't compare

So God had put an end to skating and He'd done it in the sweetest possible way so I hadn't had to make a decision. The acting was a dark void; the missed modelling went to a better choice then never re-opened. I didn't like rave. I didn't like drugs. I realised that some of my pals weren't really my pals, and that this rave scene just wasn't for me at all. God had done me proud. I had prayed to get started at the gym at 16. I was 16 with my path clear as day as to what was coming next, gym life practically calling my name. So what did I do? I went to raves. I got full of drugs. I stayed with the old crew. For the first time in my life I was a sheep; a fucked up disobedient sheep.

Six months down the line

I'd been to college and got expelled. Firstly for hitting a guy through a volley ball net. I then got a final warning for having a fight at the college disco. Oh yeah, I hadn't done a scrap of work either. I saw Sean just before I was about to get expelled. I asked him what he was up to. He too was leaving (I'm not sure of the reason why). Sean asked me what I was waiting for, insisting they were going to throw me out anyway. He said I may as well just go. So I did. Me and Sean went into Bury and got drunk in a bar named The Knowsley that afternoon. So the first friend I had met from school was the same friend I'd be having a beer with when leaving. It wasn't exactly cap and gown stuff, but it worked for me.

Luckily, we'd nailed the celebrations at the school prom the previous year. The only people I kept in touch with down the line were Simon and Sean, my first ever friends from both schools.

Back to the club scene

From a guy who was the king of clean, I'd been to party after party without any temptation; high on life. Well I wasn't high on life any more. In little to no time I wasn't just having a touch of the bad stuff, I was getting trashed. Three or four ecstasy pills a night. Three to four speed balls, which was a cocktail of deadly drugs, a couple of acid tablets and around ten pints to wash it all down. I was fucked. Because there wasn't any type of depth to this type of life style, the only thing that made anyone laugh were the stories about things I had done whilst being fucked up, so I got more fucked up off the back of it. I'd get pissed about people telling stories about shit that hadn't happened, so when wasted I had a tendency to bang the kid talking bullshit, even though I'd talk a ton of bullshit myself. Yes, you've guessed it, I was a dick. I did have some funny stories though.

The acid trip

Acid had always acted differently every time I had taken it. I remember watching the World Cup with a few pals in 1990. I was watching my favourite footballer, Paul Gascoigne, when I saw something pass by the outside window. I actually believed it was Predator; something moving but no one there. I was going mad. Stuart had to close the curtains so we could finish watching the match.

I got to a point where I was well into drugs, taking them during the week and looking for parties to turn up to even when uninvited. House parties were the most fun. I liked hanging on the rougher estates because they seemed more real to me; my kind of people. I remember being at this one party, stood in the corner of the room after dropping a couple of acid tabs. The house was decorated in an old look Spanish style. There were ukuleles and old pictures on the wall and those Spanish looking dolls on the fire-place. I was just standing there glaring, taking it all in, when one of the Spanish dolls looked to be dancing. My eyes widened. I then started grabbing hold of people saying, “Hey look at the dancing dolls” whilst chewing the insides of my cheeks.

I soon realised that I was seeing things and had become paranoid, like I was about to explode. I quickly left the house but when I got to the main road it didn’t look right. It was widening and narrowing. The cars looked like they were going too fast. They were too loud. They were too near. I stood for a few minutes but couldn’t cross the road. I couldn’t gauge anything. I ran back into the house luckily spotting a kid I knew; his name was Ernie. Although Ernie was part of the rough and ready outfit, he was liked by the cool kids also.

I stumble over towards him. “Hey Ernie, I can’t get across the road. Can you help me cross the road? "Licking my lips then grabbing at his sleeve.

“Urm, ‘ey kid, you look fucked.” He turned to his mates, “I’m going to have to look after this dong.”

We walked out and, like a kid with his mum, I grabbed for his hand as he walked me over the road. His friends then came out to see what was going on. Ernie just shrugged, as if to say, “what can I do?” so all his pals opted to leave the party with him. He then walked me all the way to the interchange as I chewed his ear off.

Years on, me and Ernie ended up working together and whenever out on Christmas do’s and what not, he was always my right hand man; always getting me out of trouble and getting me home safe. I always find it funny, that when meeting someone, the initial influence is often the same influence throughout. Poor Ernie, if he had only walked away that night.

Other than daft stories I can’t remember having a single good time whilst on the drugs; they were a very low distant second to the natural highs I’d witnessed whilst skating or breakin'. The club nights went worse; I realised I had become the booby prize to get stuck with. My aggression levels were through the roof. I'd had a bit of a dig at my pals for being a touch sly with Si, but I was being an arse with everyone and for no real reason.

As the sarcasm at school had dissipated, everyone was all 'love and peace'. I should have been happy really but it all just seemed too false. I couldn't acclimatise. The lads weren't being false. They are still the same today; same music, same attitudes. Looking back, it seems more like they were faking it trying to be like me when at school. You didn't have to be good at anything, you just had to be nice; stare at a big light and throw your hands up. What the Fuck. I had to be working at something, I wanted to be the best, I wanted to be the centre of attention, and less than twelve months earlier I was.

I turned quite violent. I remember starting what became a very messy fight up in the toilets of a big club in Liverpool. The police were brought in and the club closed down early that night. I remember everyone talking about the idiots who had started the fight, they didn't know; I was that idiot. If I talked about fighting I only mentioned the ones I'd won, I kept quiet about the ones that I didn't, wanting to be seen as the big man. I was bored with the whole scene, literally fighting to get attention. I wanted so badly to go back to how it was at school.

At this time, there was no one being arsy, I wasn't dropped like I was when dancing. I was scared of losing my friends but couldn't put anything positive forward. I'd hit the top of the big wave, but had now been taken down by an unseen undercurrent I hadn't seen coming. Smashed by the next big wave, I wouldn't be able to, nor want to, get back on to.

Sean was trying to do right by me; he warned me that I was getting too caught up with the drugs and the drink.

"You can't even go to the cinema without having five beers, there's something wrong John." Sean always played it straight. I was taking drugs even when I was on my own.

I'd go skating on whizz. I'd feel indestructible whilst riding down the centre of the main road. Cars were blipping me with the sounds of "Get off the road you cock head" and pleasantries of that sort. I'd even be high when I was going to the pictures, but I never told Sean. My pal and ex-girlfriend, Emma, tried being there for me but I didn't take her on, sometimes being arsy with her. When she eventually moved on, I insulted her and her new boyfriend when seeing them out. I saw the upset in her eyes. It was totally unnecessary but a way I could get attention. It was a sad time. The only thing I had right was that I still hated drugs; I never enjoyed them, it just helped to take away the feeling of being a no one. Ego and popularity are worse than any drugs, once people start to look the other way, you're fucked.

Final night out: The last straw

The last night out I went on I don't really remember. I remember seeing a pal, one of the cleverest kids in school, the guy who had it made. He was fucked. He didn't have the answers to everything, just like I didn't.

It was on this night that a kid named Alley hit his first ecstasy pill. He had never taken drugs before. He died on the same night. Everyone talked; they were going to change their ways, but they didn't. Alley had made them see the light: they hit the drugs that weekend.

I can't remember having much empathy for Alley because I was too fuckin' selfish, but I honoured his death by doing the one thing he would have wanted; not making the same mistake he had. I walked that night and never returned.

The kids were all good kids when thinking back. I think this was just an awkward age, a strange time in life for everyone. Even the earlier stuff that went on: laughs became sarcasm and sometimes that could turn a little nasty. As teenagers, being a bit dickish goes with the territory unfortunately.

Chapter 8

God opens his doors

So I walked away from the club scene, the drug scene, my past and my memories of it all. I was looking for the next big wave. It was more of a puddle than a wave to start with. A few weeks of being away from the club scene, the new tide would gently appear, small at first, then slowly upwards and onwards. This time it was God who would open his doors.

The good things I had done in the neighbourhood whilst growing up would be the things that were going to come back and help me out. Throughout my time at school I had always taken time out for the kids on the estate. I had organised bonfires. I got everyone on board, even my mum and her pal Anita would do their bit when it came to guarding the bombie. In the summers I had everyone using my ramp and the kids loved to just watch. We went sledging down the big hill, camping in Ashey Valley and other stuff where I had looked after all the kids, keeping them safe. I was like the local hero.

I started at the gym as intended, but whilst I walked home I'd see the local kids all playing football at the spare ground, at the back of the church. Not having much to do after training, I started joining in. As the days started to get darker and as summer started to fade, the kids were now at my door because their parents didn't want them playing out too late. They said it was ok though if I was there. When I came home my dad used to say, "Your crew are outside." There was around 20 or 30 kids waiting for me most nights.

I'd walk the kids home after playing football, then it was usually me, a young kid named Paul Harrison and a kid named Sean Schoffield left at the end. These two I had looked after like little brothers from when they were very young. They lived near so we always hung out at the end of the night talking about horror movies or football. It was always fun listening to the two of them. After playing football one night I realised how dark it had got. The mums and dads were cool about me walking all the kids home; in fact that was the only reason they had been allowed out. But the weather was turning a little bitter so I knew the football wouldn't be happening for long.

I don't know where it came from, perhaps God, but I had the idea to ask the local priest if he could open up the hall so we could play football inside. So one night I called down. The priest was a friendly chap and although he couldn't agree to opening up the club for football because of damages, he said that I could use it to start a youth club and to leave it with him. Two weeks later we were open. There were around 30 to 40 kids to start with, everyone mainly just messing about or playing pool. The age range was as close as two years younger than me (I'd just turned 17) down to kids aged 10 and 11. The older kids were chasing the younger kids about giving them dead arms and brass knuckles, roughing them up but only fun stuff. The club looked to have little scope but the fact that more and more people were turning up; it had created interest.

During a meeting, I made the point of offering to separate the age groups and adding more games and interest. The secretary of the club liked my ideas and agreed to Sunday nights for over 13s and Monday nights for the younger end. We had volunteers from everywhere and the plans and ideas ran smoothly. God enjoyed the fact I was doing something for others but also something that kept me busy, safe and out of trouble. The Sunday night was more my night with kids nearer my age and a few nice looking girls; it was getting pretty good.

Aside from all this, I had to get a job. I had a string of part time jobs including working for Burger King which I left when they made me walk around Bury dressed as a bag of chips.

I also worked at the video shop, which was the best job ever. I even did a bit of babysitting, worked on the market and had a paper round but needed something full time. I ended up getting an apprenticeship in engineering, but had to work as a car mechanic to start with. I was proper shit at it but we had a few laughs. The only real problem I had now was coming down from the drugs.

I figured that because I never liked drugs in the first place and that natural highs were way better, it was just a case of being able to walk away and that was that. I wasn't aware of the side effects. After 16 month's of battering varied drugs, it wasn't going to be that easy. Within a month or so, I found myself struggling to think straight. It was like having a permanently bad headache. I remember thinking to myself, "This can't be how my head is always going to feel." In bed I was sweating ridiculously, followed by cold shivers through my body, having to wrap myself up in blankets. My vision always seemed dark, almost like I was seeing through someone else's eyes. I never felt like I was fully in the room. I misunderstood conversations because I couldn't focus on anything for any length of time. If I'd had a few extra brain cells to spare it may have been a little better but it was a dark void, a little scary sometimes. The good thing was, I wasn't going back on the drugs. I had got used to this way of life.

I was talking to young Sean and I don't know if it was there and then or just the first time I had actually noticed but everything had become clear again. I was so appreciative of the gift of total vision and a fresh mind. It was awesome.

I'd like to say that I never touched drugs again but that would be a lie. However, it was only ever when I was going through bad times, usually injury related, Christmas outings and the odd Good Friday. It was only now and then, perhaps once or twice a year, but by my late twenties I never bothered at all. The good thing that came out of taking drugs and drinking heavily is that I know why people do it: Everyone wants a break from their own mind sometimes. Our minds can get a little plagued; life gets to us. For most people, alcohol or drugs gives people that freedom that they need. It didn't for me though, I was an absolute fuckin' idiot.

These days when my head's up my arse I tend to just go for a run in the hills or hit the punch bag and clear my head out naturally.

1993

By this time I was a fully qualified fusilier (army regiment). I had won Mr Bury, Mr Yorkshire and was competing as a small national level bodybuilder.

So like before, I'd had a bad time then found a place that does it for me. I've ridden the wave of success and was back on top. I had the girls chasing me and the world was my oyster again. All this was off the back of helping a few kids out.

Bury was my California again only we weren't comparing moves anymore; we were comparing abs. We hung out in town in our gym gear; tight T shirts, Golds Gym vests and 'ten men' walks in baggy pants. It was stupidity and vanity at its best.

My rival this time around was a kid named John Latham. We were at opposing gyms. He was the young 19 'year' old up and comer at his gym and I was the young up and comer at ours.

John Lathem: "Hey John, looking well. Arms are looking good but I'll tell you what the ladies are going mad for these legs, they love the tan John." I weighed him up. He did have a better tan but I had better hair. He had the better shoulders but my chest was bigger. He looked like one of my favourite bodybuilders, Lee Labrarda but I wasn't going to tell him. We had a lot of fun. Even in the night clubs, we'd be comparing girls we had met on the night.

"Not bad John but you should have seen the one I had last week, out of sight," I couldn't help but laugh. We may have been in the 90s, but our banter was from the 80s and possibly still is. Me and John had some great laughs, it was the most fun rivalry to ever come about and still good friends today.

All the teenage kids at this time had some sort of Americanised image going on. For example, my cousin Warren Hey had this blond, James Dean thing happening (although most people thought he was aiming to look like one of the Bros twins). It got him the birds though. And when I ran into my old pal Alan Hall, he now looked like something out of a US boy band. Then there was Ryan Monaghan, the kid who jumped out of the window at the party. He now looked like a Davidoff Cool Water commercial. They all hung with a kid named Soul Fuckin' Soul? The name alone told you this kid was going to be cool. This dude had long blond locks and looked like he'd just finished shooting the movie Point Break. Bury was Hollywood.

I was back on the A-list, the final year of my teens. Clubs and pubs were free and there was no waiting in queue. I remember it regularly being me and my pals, Chris, Lee and sometimes John. We'd be sat with groups of girls we barely knew. I remember once a girl shouting to her pal from across the room. "Are you coming?" I was stood between the two and shouted back, "no it's just the way I'm stood". The girls started to laugh and the next thing we were all having a drink together. We honestly couldn't fail.

We may never have been very famous but we were definitely 'Bury famous'.

Chapter 9

Little Sean

I had built the youth club around the idea of all the young kids wanting somewhere safe to play especially in winter time but I mostly spent time with Sean. He was about 10 years old, going on 30; wise beyond his years and with a heart of gold to boot. I remember being at the back of St Bedes and I'd been kicking the living crap out of my sports bag, ranting about how I'd just finished last at my first bodybuilding contest. Sean appeared holding his football and looking a little confused, so I tell him what's gone on. He looked at me a little precariously then simply said, "John, you know you're going to be the best someday. Don't let it bother you." He decided not to play football that night and opted to walk me up to my house. He bigged me up the whole way, knowing that feeding my ego was the best way to cheer me up. He was 10. I was 17.

Sean would regularly come with me to where I baby sat. He also came with me when I was working at the video shop. He'd sit with me all day watching movies like Predator, Aliens or some Freddy Kruger. Sometimes I'd have both him and my little sister, Debra, with me watching movies they shouldn't be. I was never alone. I'd also look after Sean for Malc, his Dad. Malc had recently started seeing a lady named Alice who he had met at work. I knew he'd had a tough marriage previously, so thought I'd help him out a little. Sean was usually passed out on the carpet when his Dad came to pick him up. It was only when I saw him tucked up under his blanket that I'd realise he was still only a little kid.

When I took him to play football, he went at it like a mini Paul Gasgoine. He was small but strong as an ox, an outstanding player. He was already part of Manchester

United's School of Excellence and had a clear view on becoming a professional footballer. There was no doubt to his amazing ability. The kid was on his way. All heart, all fire, all desire. Malc was always very proud. Our conversations were usually always about Sean.

It was sometime in November 1992. I saw a lad named Noel Worsley running up the street. He looked panicked whilst trying to speak, "Sean's just been run over!"

As we got to the scene I think the ambulance had just left. I remember feeling very anxious and in that brief moment I remembered back to when I'd been run over, around the same age. I remember it being quite bad, having to have my fingers and the back of my head stitched up, but I also remember recovering quite quickly. This thought allowed me to feel much more optimistic.

Luckily Sean had made it. He had a lot of swelling around his brain but he was talking and the doctors had said he could still make a full recovery. I'd moved a little away by this time but I still came up to see Sean throughout the week. Malc and I were always optimistic of Sean's full recovery and our moods picked up whilst we spoke.

After a while Sean was talking clearly. His old personality had started to shine through. We had him up and walking a little too. A few more months went by and we were into early summer 93. Sean was making his first appearance back at the youth club. It was really nice to see that the kids who he had originally hung out with had carried on seeing him whilst he was ill. All his old friends had turned up to help him out: Noel, Kate Doody, Paul, Danny Mullen, Andy Cuffright, the full crew. And so he made his first steps into the bigger world. Everyone at the club doted on him and his willingness to want to help himself, magic.

Unfortunately, after a couple of months the improvements in Sean's health seem to grind to a stop. He knew it too. You could see his frustration, knowing he wasn't healing. He became more violent and often swore a lot. I think it was in a bid for attention or maybe just to be able to laugh a little. Malc and I never mentioned anything but we both knew things weren't going to improve enough for young Sean to be up and running again. Seeing a kid who had so much heart; watching him, knowing he was never getting better, sensing how badly he wanted to break out. It broke me in two some days. There were even a few days where I went up to see him but I never went in. I struggled at times but I'm glad to say I stuck with it, knowing it was the right thing and that he was my friend. I may have been an egotistical prick on the surface but I can never be accused of not being there when it counted.

A break in play, time to let loose

I had organised what would be my very last teen party. It was on New Year's Day 1994. 1993 had been a great year but with my worries for Sean, seeing him more and more. I felt I needed to blow-out.

This party was actually organised by my Mum but I'd invited so many of my own friends, I kind of made it my own. I'd given up drinking but around Christmas time every year I liked to let loose. In the past I'd always behaved pretty good at my mum's parties but this time I felt I needed to be away from all my thoughts and feelings, even if only for one night.

A few of us kicked it off with a few beers, followed by a few shots. I started feeling it but in a good kind of way. Everyone was enjoying the party. So it's gotten later into the night and I was talking to a girl who I'd known a little. I also knew she'd had a thing for me in the past, so a little showing off in front of the lads as well. After a while of talking I asked the girl if she wanted to come with me to the kitchen and grab a drink. She thought it through for a second but then told me she was seeing someone. Instantly angered at her rejection I loudly replied "who?" in which she sheepishly replied "what?" seeing me about to lose my shit. I hadn't even fancied the girl. I'm that full of myself the girl had insulted me just in saying no. I was Mr Bury for Pete sake. She should have been fuckin' honoured. The milk had instantly turned sour.

I headed outside as Mark Holt shouted after me, "John, where are you going?"

I had been out with a girl who lived up the street a few years back and I regularly still flirted with her so I presumed (like I did with most girls) that she still fancied me. Stupidly, and in a state of rage was somehow planning on asking her out again.

I got to her door then knocked but no one answered. That only made me worse and within seconds I was kicking and punching at the door. The girl's dad came to the upstairs window then asked what I wanted. He was being quite polite to say I'd just put a big hole in his front door! By this time Holty and Tommo had managed to get a grip of me, dragging me away from the house.

When we were back near my house I picked a fight with Tommo, punching him into the side of someone's car. Then I punched Holty into someone's garden. I don't remember anything after that.

I woke up the next morning and Mark came into my room after stopping over the night before. Within minutes he started telling me about how I had hit him and Tommo and that I even had a fight with a neighbour. I hadn't remembered that or having a go at my dad about the fights we used to have when I was younger. He told me about smashing Jane's door in, whilst somehow trying to ask her out. Then he told me the worst news of all; that I broke down crying at the end of it all. Shit, I could handle destroying the neighbourhood and upsetting everyone but publicly crying:"Noooooooo!"

This was the start of 1994 and it wasn't going to get any better

I don't know what it is, but when it rains it pours.

Human nature thinks only of itself. Your own mind fails to see the light; it's like shit just falls from the sky, uncensored. The only thing you can do is hope things get better.

STAY GOLD.
Nature's first green is gold,
Her hardest hue to hold,
Her early leaf, a flower,
If only so an hour.
Then leaf subsides to leaf,
So Eden sank to grief,
So dawn goes down today,
Nothing gold can stay.

This Robert Frost poem was featured in the 1983 movie, The Outsiders. The main character played by a then 15, year-old C. Thomas Howell. He's a dreamy kid living in an area that is surrounded by violence, poverty and negativity. His friends are all losing their shit, bit by bit. As they are looking to the ground, he is looking to the sky, to the sunset. His friends all love his beautiful mind and heart. He's trying to understand the poem but as a positive. His caption in the movie is 'Stay Gold'; as in keep hold of the magic, nature's first green, hold on to it. This has been my saying since high school. It was a stunning performance and gave me much meaning. I say it often so I keep looking towards the sky when times seem hard.

Back to the story

I spent '93 being mean and lean but now I wanted a season off to fill out and put some extra muscle on. Unfortunately, that means looking chunky and chunky means less attention. We had also started going out in Rochdale where I wasn't really known, so even lesser attention. So even though only vanity it was the first step to feeling shittier about myself; ego being the worst drug of all. My moral compass told me I was going to be a bodybuilder and so this had to happen. I didn't let ego stand in the way of my passion. I had also learnt that some people only chase you when you're winning, when you're looking well. One minute I was the bollocks, then the next I was like yesterday's spaghetti. A lesson I was learning all too well.

By the middle of '94 my ego was nowhere to be seen. I had become used to the lesser attention and the real world needed me more: I had a friend who was battling to stay alive. Sean's health had seriously diminished. He looked different now that the swelling on his brain had worsened. He was always disruptive, biting his own arms and lashing out uncontrollably. His eyes had veered to the side with him frothing at the mouth; it was the worst thing I'd ever had to see.

I had stopped at my Mum's after going up to see Sean the night before. I was working as a mail man, Malc had got me the job a year or so earlier. I'd brought all my things with me so that I could leave my Mum's ready for work the next morning. As I was getting ready, I could hear Malc trying to wake Sean, "Come on Sean, time to get up. Come on Sean." There was a niggling feeling but I brushed it off and didn't think too much about it. I told myself, "He's alright."I presumed all was well before setting off to work. After about an hour of being in the office, I realised Malc wasn't in. "Stop being stupid John, everything's fine," I kept telling myself.

Ten minutes later, my pal Gaz Scully, Sean's cousin, approached me. "John I'm sorry to tell you this but Sean died last night in his sleep. Malc's just phoned in." Gaz was allowed to go, but because I wasn't an actual relative, I wasn't able to. I felt destroyed that day and couldn't wait to get away from the office.

At the funeral there was a great turn out. At first I felt ok but as the funeral came to an end my thoughts and feelings had started to get the better of me. I kept seeing Sean, he was playing football. He was telling me about his dreams, sat with me at the video shop. He was everywhere. So when I saw the coffin I instantly burst into tears. It wouldn't stop. I couldn't get his memory out of my head. What a waste. There was so much more he needed to do. When the funeral was over I was inconsolable, I couldn't deal with anything more to do with Sean's death. A work mate, by the name of Steve Jenks, took me home because I couldn't face the burial. I went and sat behind St. Bede's for the rest of the day; a cloud thick in thought and memories of my little pal. R.I.P. Sean Schofield my heavenly brother.

I didn't know it but I'd lose a lot of people all within a couple of years of one another.

I lost Allie to drugs, my uncle Teddy to lung damage, Auntie Doreen to gangrene, Uncle Pat drank himself to death, my pal Steve Smullen took a heroin overdose and, later on, Nick Harrison. A kid who I'd looked up to since I was very young, the first cool kid influence on the block. He committed suicide aged 34. I never attended any of the funerals. I like to remember people in my own way. I'll make the time for people whilst they are here. I don't deal with death particularly well, sometimes I don't deal with it at all. After Sean's funeral I don't think I went to another until well into the millennium. Apart from training hard, I don't remember much good coming out of 1994, and even into '95.

Following Sean's death, our own crew of friends started to break up. New relationships formed, people did their own things. They ventured to pubs and clubs, the youth club wasn't such a big deal any more. Then there was the wave to move me on.

Backing the younger end of the club, there was now a large committee of doctors, solicitors and overly protective parents, in other words, a lot of wankers. No one was happy that I'd got everyone back outside playing football even though this was where the club had all stemmed from. Now health and safety wouldn't allow it. Parents were worried that their precious babies wanted to play two seconds away from the club, uninsured. What the Fuck. So I got voted out at my own youth club. The lady secretary had loved my ideas when it was bringing in attention and good funding but now it was all set up, I was no longer needed. Her words, "The children look up to you and see you as more of a friend, but we can't keep you on with you not following any of the health and safety regulations."

"Get fucked." It was time to move on.

I didn't see it but an undercurrent of incidents was coming. Another life to walk away from and another tide making its way towards me. It was more of an undercurrent that would eventually become a tide, but perhaps the most inspiring tide of all.

End of part One

The Chrysalis

Whilst I was trying to break through as a bodybuilder, avoiding injury was always a big issue. I'd steer clear of fights, anything high in aerobics that may affect my growth. I'd even walk slower in order not to burn muscle whilst at work. Apart from the odd blowouts here and there (pressure releases) I had done everything I could have to stay 100% focused whilst working my way up. Five years of straight dedication. Even though my reading was poor, over the past 3\4 years I had put all my efforts into reading about nutrition and acting on what I had read in terms of diet for muscle growth. And even though I had struggled to read, I never had a problem taking anything in and, more importantly, remembering it. I was training with some big names in the weight room. In '95 I won the North West Championships, then later, the drug free novice UK.

Despite everything looking pretty good on paper (being where I wanted to be, having respect from some of the upcoming pros, no drink or drugs, nor any real problem to speak about) I just wasn't happy. Sure I'd had problems leading up to this but that wasn't it. So what was it? As I said, I'm a life addict, I need that buzz; God's best zest. You can be doing all the things you want, but without that zest it's just never going to work. I was chasing a wave I couldn't see. I didn't know where to look for it. The swim was hard and draining and I still saw nothing. But it was on its way, it had to be.

My introduction to working the doors: The new wave

Sometime in 1994 I was 19-20 years old. Being a big lad, and being well known around the gym, I'd been getting several offers to do door work. I'd say, "No, I'm a bodybuilder, I don't want to get injured. No, I don't want to get involved with all that." I was hanging with door lads and standing on the door waiting for them to finish their shifts. I knew doormen on the clubs and pubs and had trained with most of them at some point. I was surrounded by doormen but still it just wasn't for me. God was guiding me on this path but I couldn't see it. The waves were pushing me in the direction, to ride that bigger wave.

Out of the blue I ran into my old pal Sean Joyce. Sean had made it quite big as a club DJ. I'd heard his name mentioned a few times over the radio. We got talking. He was running a few events, a couple a month, at a night club not too far from where I lived. I told him the same as I'd told everyone else but he was persistent, "John, just check the tickets, keep the trouble out. It's a good crowd, won't be any bother." I felt I as if I was letting him down if I didn't. He was my pal, we'd had each other's backs since knowing how to walk.

"Ok," I said. "I'll do it."

Sean was like the key master to my life. He was the one who had opened the door to bodybuilding, now he was opening up the door to the security industry, spooky. So I worked Sean's door on a couple of occasions. All went well, but then I got into a little trouble.

Three guys started messing with Sean's decks; his brother, Sam had pointed it out. When I approached the situation I really didn't have a clue what to do so just grabbed for one of the guys. The other two then quickly pushed me back. My fist clenched, all of us stared at each other waiting for someone to make the first move. I had no idea how to address the situation. A guy walked in, "Hey you three, fuck off back in there." The three saw the guy then walked straight out. I looked across to see the doorman from the rougher part of the club.

"Cheers, pal," I let on. He wasn't a big guy but he had a way with people. I didn't really understand it at the time though. He was called Sean Patrick. After a few more events, I was helping Sean on his side of the club, then he helped me. And because he helped me out when I'd needed it, I stepped up and did a couple more nights working with him. The wave was rising.

We got into a fight one night and I did ok: Sean was happy about it. "You did good kid. I've seen that guy smash a few people up in the past." I hadn't done anything spectacular. I think it was more about having his back, having people's back being a fundamental part to working the door and to life. I did a few more nights here and there but I still didn't want to be a doorman.

Somewhere into '95

Now it was my pals Daz and Baz asking me to cover the door for them. They had new girlfriends or knock offs I wasn't quite sure but they wanted the night off to take these girls out. So again, they were my pals and they'd owe me one so I agreed. I was covering Daz and Baz, also covering lads I didn't know. I was working the club most weeks. So was I in the Zone? No. Was I a door man? No, nor did I want to be. As I've said, I didn't see the wave. I was more getting pulled down by the undercurrent.

The undercurrent. The second wave

The bodybuilding had hit a wall. It was 1995 and I had been told that I was too old to take part in the Junior (drug free) British Finals. I had gone over the age limit. My head was in bits. I wasn't looking great anyway, in fact, the more knowledgeable I'd become, the less I was able to hit top shape, the science of the sport not working for me. I was frustrated as you can imagine. Usually off the back of working hard and doing well came the popularity, the girls, the fun. But now everything had become tangled. I couldn't get to that fun zone. It's like I'd gone into a chrysalis in life; it was dark, everything was blurred and there was no sense to its being. Was I going to come out of this a butterfly, a creature of beauty? Or was I going to be more of a Gremlin? Some type of monster? I think it may have been a touch of both, to begin with.

I was hanging with a group of door lads and doing a lot of cover but still it felt like it wasn't for me. I figured I'd start going out again because my mind linked sober nights out with likewise people, to having lots of fun. But the memory was twisted this time. I wasn't happy with my look. I hadn't finished what I'd started because of the age cap on the bodybuilding show, so hadn't rebuilt the confidence I had lost. I had moral dilemma over females and friends. So before going back into the club scene where only the vain, the confident and the beautiful would survive, I wasn't equipped.

I was thickly set and looked ok but I wasn't ruling the roost. In the past I'd had it easy. The girls usually made their way towards me, but not anymore. I was going to have to work for it. It's hard being passed over and even worse when girls who have doted on you in the past are now seeing you like a second choice at best. Some didn't speak to me at all. So with all that looking pretty grim already, the worst was yet to come.

I started running into a lad I knew: His name was Big Tommy G. He was 6'4, tan, handsome, charming and muscular. He was like Ricky Martin with muscles. This fucker was living la vida loco. So we started hanging out. He couldn't do enough for me. He'd pick me up when I was working late, pay for my dinner if I had no money, advise me any time of the day and cheer me up when I was down. What a bastard, I couldn't even hate him.

A few years back this would have been a match made in heaven but not anymore, not for me anyway. We hung as a crew but I was never happy. Everything seemed like bullshit, I couldn't put on another show. It just wasn't in me anymore. I didn't like myself. I was angry at everything. The gym was the only place I was happy. I was doing everything right but there wasn't that spark. I was unsettled. I had morals and shit now. I really didn't know where I was at. With breakin', it was horse shit people pissing on me. With school life, it was a change in tide that I didn't want to follow but couldn't walk away from. Now though I was where I wanted to be. I wasn't drinking. I was doing ok with the girls and training. I was avoiding getting in any bother. My diet was mint. Everything was answered so what was wrong? Why was there no spark?

Bird burgling

The thing that would make me see the light would come from the dark. The answer to my problem was even darker: the undercurrent. When I was on nights out we'd get talking to groups of girls. Everyone was playing second fiddle to Big Tom. It was literally if the girls failed with Tom then they might give you a chance. Honestly, if these women didn't have legs, there'd have been slug trails when he was about. Tom believed the world was our oyster, that any girl could be got and that there were no limits. As much as this had been said to raise the mood, with the best of intentions, for me it was killing off the last bit of confidence I had left. I think I was looking for something real in life at the time; the love of a woman, a passion, just anything reliable. I wanted something where I could just be myself, be happy with myself. All the guys we were out with were posers. Tan, tattoos and tight T-shirts; everything I wasn't anymore.

I got talking to a girl one week and thought that I might want to see her again. Then one of the lads told me he got off with her and had bird burgled me. I laughed whilst secretly wanting to kick his face in. When the girl found out that the guy was a bit of a tool, she came back to me saying that she wished she had waited when I hadn't been out. Sorry love, doesn't work that way.

I found that when a girl fancied me more, the other lads would play up to it and try their best to get attention any way they could. It was like watching myself a couple of years earlier. Surely I hadn't been this bad?

Tom was good, he was all for me. But the fact that he

kept going on about no girl can't be got and then proving it, messed my thinking up all together: Women in relationships, sometimes with lads I knew. These girls seemed logical, moral. I thought no way but I was wrong. Many appeared at my house with Tom, swooning over him. Their character was totally transformed. Tom could paralyse women's minds better than Dracula. He had it down to a fine art. His take on this was that he was single and if the girls were in relationships then it was up to them to be loyal. Now how can you argue with that? Again, I would have said the same thing a few years back. He was right. I was looking for faith in others, meanwhile, these girls were shattering my every belief. I can't tell you just how badly it affected me.

Blasting off at the gym Christmas outing

1995 gym outing. There was a new crew of lads who had made their way onto the gym scene. One was called Matt Thomson and the other was Daz Desforges. They had been at our gym for a couple of years but this was the first time I had really got to know them as friends. I'd been out with them before but only when I was sober, and tonight, I wouldn't be sober. The other lads from the gym worded Daz and Matt up at the start of the night, "Watch him."

The night kicked off and we were off to a good start. All was well. Me, Matt and Daz were in the club, shots and what not. Everything was going down a treat. Around midnight I found myself roaming around the nightclub, not sure on what was going on. I was looking to find the party. I saw Matt. He had his pants around his ankles showing some girls his big legs. I heard one of them say, "Nice legs but where's your balls?" I laughed but didn't want to interrupt so I wondered off again. I ended up in the toilets when I heard some lads laughing, thinking they were laughing at me. I was now really drunk and paranoid. I started a fight with them but it was quickly broken up by a guy on our night out. He took me to one side whilst he apologised to the lads. He got me a glass of water from the bar, and told me to go outside for a bit to cool down, then pointed out where everyone was.

I was heading outside when I saw the young girl who worked at the gym talking to some guys, so I went over. She was called Kath. She was only 16 but she looked a little older. We got on well but I found myself looking out for her, knowing what guys are like. She was talking to the guys when I first imploded onto the scene. I was instantly aggressive and told Kath that it was time to go. One of the guys then stepped up, "Hey take it easy fella."

"You what?"

And bang. I'd hit the guy while his pal stood off; a raging inferno. I grabbed Kath's arm and dragged her through the club, then out to the streets. When we were outside, I looked for a cab, trying to spot if anyone else was about. Kath had gone quiet knowing I was on one. She hadn't seen this side of me before.

Before long, one of our lads turned up from nowhere. "Where've you been, we've been looking for you?" he started.

"Fuck off," I blazed back. Kath grabbed my arm and looked to me as if to say leave it. I pulled my arm forwards and walked off on my own, back towards our crowd. There were two young girls who had been hanging around the gym getting attention from the guys in there. I wasn't really keen on them. They came to where I was, and tried to be nice to me. "John, are you ok? What's up, John?" Their arms were around my shoulders. I was building up but it wasn't going to keep inside.

"Fuck off, you tramps. You don't know me. You don't even speak my language." At this point both Daz and Matt had come over to find out what was going on.

Daz: "Hey steady on John lad. What's up?"

"Who are you? Who the fuck are you?" I was venomous.

Daz carried on trying to reason but it wasn't going to work. I started jabbing him in the chest "Who the fuck are you?" I wanted a fight not an agony aunt.

Daz was doing his best but I could see he was losing his cool.

Wait for it... wait for it... Boom!

Daz had come at me like a bull. I was in the air, then sliding on my back. Game on.

We went at it for a few seconds before getting split apart. It was cold, dark and icy. Everything was a little difficult to gauge. I saw Daz with everyone trying to calm him down. He was going nuts. I had people holding on to me so I stepped back saying I was ok, but I wasn't. I was looking at Daz, planning a way to get to him. I got left alone for a second. Everyone thought all was well. Most people were over with Daz, so I made a move. Bang. I was back in it. Me and Daz battled, rolling up and down the street. Matt stepped in but we were in full flow. Matt took two from each side then slid on the ice. We carried on. We fought for a while but then I slipped onto some steps and cracked the back of my head. Daz was standing over me as I sat on the steps looking up.

"What's up with you, John? What's up with you?" I felt upset. I felt bad, but for some reason I wouldn't back down. I hurled some more abuse. Daz couldn't believe it. "Don't make me do this John," he said, fist clenched, doing his very best not to react. But I wasn't going to stop. He then bounced off my head with his fists.

I looked up, "Is that it?" He came at me again before walking off, totally tormented by my behaviour. I looked up to see my then training partner, Lee Ervine. He was the only one who'd stuck around. "Come on, John you dick head; let's go home."

"I can't". I got up and headed back up the street were everyone was. I wanted to make up with Daz but I would have preferred it if he'd knocked me out so I wouldn't have to face the rest of the night. Daz saw me and was on his way down.

As we got closer I stuck my hand out in order to make peace but I wasn't sure if he would see it. I hoped a little that he wouldn't, but he did. His demeanour instantly became forgiving. A big hug, his arm at the back of my neck, he smiled. "Fuckin' hell kid, what's going on?" What a guy!

Everyone came over. Daz saw me getting a little anxious, "Leave us a second. Just give us a minute." He took me round the corner out of the way. Matt and my training partner, Lee, were also there.

Daz: "What's going on John? What's up lad?" Lee and Matt made jokes trying to release the tension before stepping back. Daz was looking to find an answer. He was hitting certain notes trying to find the source to this type of behaviour. I was filling up. I was a child again now. There was nothing I could really hit on. I was lost. I had no answers.

"I don't know Daz. I don't know." Daz could see the upset so didn't push it any further. He told the others that we'd make our own way back. He then shielded me away so no one saw me upset and so I didn't have to talk to anyone. I can't think of many people who would have done this. St Daz (the angel of understanding).

Back in the gym on Monday I was the bad guy. Fair enough. A few people had a pop at me. The only ones that didn't were Daz, Lee and Matt.

Early 1996

I had competed that year but wasn't happy with myself. I kept getting told to work the door, especially after all the trouble I'd been in over Christmas. The bodybuilding scene had faded, replaced by stories from people working the door. The wave of bodybuilding had gone. The gym was now more about door life.

One night in early March, I'd finished doing a night on the door. I'd said I wasn't going to work anymore but now we were striking at the office, so I actually needed the extra cash. The wave made sure I couldn't go anywhere; the current pushed me back.

I was living with a guy; we'd been pals a while but had grown apart. We'd had a few arguments recently. He was part of the bird burgling scene; the club life. As I came in, there was already a drama. My pal was there with his pal. Some girl had stolen something and had fled. The other girl who was with her was upstairs in my room upset, actually asking where I was. I really wasn't in the mood. I went up to see the girl. She saw me and gave me a big hug and then we talked. The girl asked if I could walk her out (the lads were being arsy with her and she looked afraid). I was pissed off and tired so had a go at her about getting herself in this position. But I was madder at the lads for being on her case. She held my hand as we made our way downstairs. "She's coming down now, so just back off." Everyone went quiet.

I walked the girl out and saw her safe to her cab. As I got back upstairs, there was a note. 'John I've missed you. Give me a ring, we'll go out.' I'd known this girl a while, yet all the time I had just been nice she hadn't wanted to know. But now I was a little edgy and protective of her I was like the second coming. The letter went in the bin; same old shit.

Next week was exactly the same. A lad had belted his girlfriend so I'd gone at him. Everyone said to just leave it, it was ok. They liked the drama. It wasn't ok. I knew at this point I needed a way out, finally realising where that way out lay.

PART TWO
LEARNING THE TIDE

Chapter 1

I finally catch the wave

Welcome to Young Bloods night club

With every obscure sport I've been into, it's lasted around five years. Then everyone seems to disappear, even the sport itself seems to disappear. Then I lose my shit. Then I fall out with everyone, get wrecked and get into fights. Then something good starts to come from it, so here we are.

I'd been bodybuilding for five years like I had with breakin' and skating. It wasn't the trend anymore, so to speak, but it was my life. I wouldn't be quitting. Like after the breakin', the parties and the skating, this was when everything was at its best. So, we were all still training in the weights room and I kept being asked to work the night club; the party.

I couldn't drink, I didn't have to, but I have anger issues. I could get rid of all of that anger working the door. I might even be seen as a good guy for doing so. God knew I was naturally good at looking after people. This was a clear pathway to deal with every answer to every problem I had. God had been kind. It was time to get on the wave.

I was in the gym speaking with Baz. I told him I wanted a permanent spot working the door. He said, "I thought you didn't want to get injured."

"At this moment in time Baz, I don't care much even if I get killed."

It had got to Saturday night, I was with Baz again. "Hey

John, Doza's looking for a new lad Friday and Saturday night. I told him you are interested, so know he'll be watching you. Consider tonight your initiation." Cool.

As I got to the club it had felt different. I felt like I was a part of it. I was buzzing a little. I was in the zone, acceptant that I had to put in a performance but that it already felt right; something new to go at. First though, I was going to have to prove myself.

I was stood at my post when I was approached by a familiar face, Daz Desforges, (St. Daz). "Alright John, think you're on with me tonight, come on we'll have a walk about."

We'd been going through the club around 15 to 20 minutes. All was well. Daz then suddenly seemed to come alive. "John make sure you've got my back."

We flew in to a group of guys stood in an open booth. Daz threw himself in sideways at one of the guys. He'd obviously had previous issues with him. They were on one of the sofas. Daz was on top pelting the life out of the guy. After a short time, the guy managed to kick Daz off the seat, quickly got to his feet and was heading towards me.

I worryingly thought, "Ok. Now what" when the answer came to me rather blatantly: Daz, from out of the background, "Twat him."

Boom. I put the guy on his arse then dragged him back to his feet to get him out. The problem was, the adrenaline had kicked in. As I got the guy to his feet I started leathering him. I couldn't shut off.

A door lad named Ivan appeared at the side of me, "Whoa, whoa. He's gone for fuck sake. Just get him out."

So the night's started well. A little later on I get approached by a group of girls, all talking to me, when Baz came over smiling, "I've heard you've lost your cherry on the first night." He was referring to the fight. He started talking to the girls. We were all having a bit of fun then the girls said they'd see us later. When the girls had gone Baz said, "We also get groupies, they love us, right little fitties as well." We both laughed.

At the end of the night, when everyone was starting to

leave, I stood on the second tier over the stairs. All the other door men were on the same tier dotted around, but in view of one another. I was feeling pretty pleased with myself; it was a good first night. Unfortunately, though, the night wasn't quite over.

I was stood for another few minutes or so when I felt something hit my head. It was only a beer mat but still, who'd thrown it? I looked around and the only people I could see were a couple kissing each other, weird. I carried on looking out, watching everyone leave, when something hit me in the face; this time, a bottle top. I looked up and saw the guy who was with his girl snarling at me; the big I am. I figured he thought that because I let the bar mat incident slide, that perhaps I was an easy target but he couldn't be more wrong.

I realised I couldn't let it go; this was my initiation. If other door men saw me as a soft touch, that wasn't a good start. Plus, I didn't want to be pissed at myself, I had enough problems going on in my head. I headed up to where he was and, without a second's notice I was bouncing his head off the wall. I was pissed at him now. His girlfriend was crying, all upset, "It wasn't him. It wasn't him."

"Well it was definitely him giving me shit when I first looked up."

The girl was in tears. I still had hold of the guy but I was questioning whether, somehow, I'd got it wrong. Daz appeared, "What's going on?"

I start to explain, Daz interrupted, "Do you think he's done it?"

"Yes."

"Then he's done it then, fuck 'em." We grabbed the guy, took him down the stairs and into the back, gave him a quick kicking then threw him out the door. Job done.

When the guy was outside he started kicking at the side door whilst shouting, "You'll be getting buried, you dick. I'll blow your fucking knee caps off." Then walked away laughing. I got a little worried, thinking I might have just messed with the wrong guy, so I went to speak with Doza (the head man).

"Hey Doza, that guy I just had a fight with has threatened to shoot me."

Doza just smiled, "You'll hear that a lot working here pal. Welcome to Young Bloods."

Next week, at the gym

I was wearing a black top whilst training. Baz was training with Daz at the time and shouted when he saw me, "One proper night on the door and he thinks he's Dalton," referring to Patrick Swayze's character from the movie Road House. It was pretty funny.

The first big night

So I'd had my initiation, now it was time to get on board. At the start of the night, all the lads were stood near the door, pat downs and ID checks. A guy walked in; he was shaking everyone's hands, big smile and a little crazy looking. I thought, "Who the hell is this?" Everyone was smiling, obviously familiar with the guy. He was a pal of Doza's: Jay Barnes. He started telling a story about a fight he'd got into, but he was laughing furiously whilst telling it. The story was quite sickening; a more than vivid take of what sounded like a massacre. The guy rhymed it off like a comedy script; honestly though, you couldn't help but laugh. Jay had been a doorman at Young Bloods in the past but worked elsewhere now. He was in most weeks though; his presence was something you never forgot.

It was time to go inside the club to start the night. I saw an old pal as I entered the venue, a guy named Jay Cunningham. I'd always looked up to Jay. We had trained at the same gym a couple of years back. "How's it going, John?" He smiled.

"Good thanks."I then went and stood on one of the seats at the side of the dance floor, looking on. All the doormen were friendly looking, all doing a little jig to the music like I was. A load of dancing doormen! The atmosphere was fierce, great lads and great music. The place was busy and upbeat. I was feeling it.

The club filled up. The music was charismatic. I was relaxed but feeling a certain excitement. Girls were looking and smiling. I was thickly set but that belonged here; all the doormen had that look. still had issues but this was the best I'd felt about myself in a while. So now all we needed was a little action.

I was at my post, casually looking on, when out from the DJ box I hear, "Security situation on the top tier. Can all door staff make your way to the top tier!" Boom! The dancing doormen set off at it like gazelles."Shit, I'd best get running."

As I approached the top tier, everyone had already rallied in; body on body, everyone going at each other. This was it. Just as I started heading towards the fight, a guy stepped up from nowhere, pushed me back towards the steps and...Bang! He'd drop kicked me before I'd even managed to grab on to anyone. I was smashing down a flight of steps, landing on my head a tier below. What the Fuck. As I got back to my feet, it was going off on this level also. This time I saw a big guy. He'd just wiped some other guy clean out. Fuck. Now he was looking at me. Bang. The fucker had hit me hard on the forehead. I flipped backwards down another small flight of steps. I was in a crouch position on the bottom floor at the side of the DJ stand thinking, "Give me a break." I jumped up. I was still in one piece. Ok, here goes, third time lucky.

I legged it back up through the exit at the side of the back bar. The fight hadn't even got outside but everyone was going at each other. Baz was going at it like a wild tiger. The crazy kid, Jay Barnes who wasn't even working, was sat down on a step pelting a guy he had in a head lock. The scary part; he was laughing whilst doing it. I headed outside, finally able to get involved. I managed to crack a few skulls in the free for all on the car park at the back of the club. The lads getting a beating eventually decided to flee the scene. I saw Jay Cunners, Doza and Ivan, their arms folded and laughing, looking like they had just finished a round of golf, than of had a fight. I was seeing green, everything was a little blurry. My nose was pounding. I figured I needed to up my game, but I'd made it. I was still alive and, most importantly, I loved it.

A few weeks down the line, fighting had become the norm with four or five fights a night, two days a week, each one as rough and tumble as the last. I'd figured by this point that physical pain didn't hurt half as much as mental pain; your mind will batter you much harder than a kicking ever will, when not in the right place.

So I'd taken some beatings when I was fighting but it didn't matter, I wasn't getting hurt. But I did want to do better. I wanted to be a stronger part of the team, not just someone else's punch bag. I spoke to my pal Tom, and Tom being Tom sorted it for me. He had the keys for the boxing club he trained at and said we could train there on a Sunday, any week.

We went the first week, all was pretty good, a few guys interested. Any week then became every week with twelve to fifteen of us regularly turning up. An hour turned into half a day. I enjoyed the boxing this time around because everyone was upbeat. The Rocky sound track was blazing in the background. I didn't need pushing, I was all over it. I started sparring with a lot of the big guys. I did pretty well considering I'm only five foot seven and with no real reach. I was weighing in around fourteen stone. I took some punishment but always managed to get in tight. This is where I came into my own; my power and my ability to take the punishment set me up. I earned a lot of respect and in very little time. No arseholes. No egos. Training with a few laughs thrown in!

There were a few occasions during the week when we'd spar in the back street where Tom lived. His dad sometimes came out to watch us. He had been a boxing coach, himself, in the past. One night he shouted across, "You need to throw that bodybuilding lark out. You go at it like a middle weight Mike Tyson." It was a compliment I'll never forget.

After a session at the gym, one week, I decide to have a

go on the horse box. I flipped straight into the flares, up into a hand stand and then flipped off on to the crash mats. Everyone was like, wow. I hadn't practiced any sort of gymnastics or dancing since high school. My past skills were still pretty sharp considering the amount of time that had passed by. The other thing I didn't realise at the time was how my body could take all this punishment even though I hadn't trained for it. Or had I?

As I've said, God moves in mysterious ways. When I was growing up I'd spent five years break dancing, another five years bashing myself about on a skate board, boxing and now weights. God's wave had wanted me to look after people but I was never attracted to violence. So God toughened me up in a way that I'd get beaten harder than most fight classes dare to go, also in a way which fed my Life Addict addiction, the feel good factor. Every one of those factors now relative to the other, the plot thickens. I was doing well with my boxing. I'd been smashing my body all over since I could walk. I had been biking, skating, breakin', body conditioning at its best. So now I just needed to add the skill factor and away we go.

I started doing some training with a lad named David and a guy he trained with, Pete. The two of them did ninjutsu and started teaching me. I'd been in a lot of fights so I was a little sceptical about what would work and what wouldn't.

Training on mats is totally different to fighting in clubs. I needed a format, something not overly complex but something that would consistently work.

They taught me about head control (ragging the head down, even pulling down at the arms to diminish your opponent's strength). I had the power and the body weight so using the technique of grabbing behind the attacker's neck and pulling down whilst keeping my arms in tight, worked. Once people are tucked down, they can't throw anything, kicks or punches. The body follows the head so this puts you in control. You can manipulate the head into a guillotine then let them up whilst throwing a few punches off. Alternately you can spin them about with the aim of getting them in a Nelson hold or choke hold. It's also about speed and keeping your opponent off balance. I worked with it until perfected and while of a decent size, it worked on several occasions whilst I worked the clubs and bars. Seven-eight months down the line, I'd be confident in my abilities.

Just to back track a little...

I'd met a girl one night while I was on the door. At the end of the night I got talking to her and her friend. Bear in mind, that at the time I didn't trust anyone and hadn't liked what I had seen recently when it came to women. I thought of them as disloyal, liars, morals when it suited and in general full of shit. I'd found it odd that the initial girl who came over talking seemed cool about her friend now chatting to me. What happened to jealousy? This girl truly was something out of the ordinary though; very attractive with liquid blue eyes and blonde hair. She could really sell herself. I was already trying not to like her!

I had linked party girls to bullshit. I didn't want to know, but I kind of did (if you know what I mean?). She asked if I wanted to go to a party. I told her I couldn't, that I had training in the morning. "You can't break me with those sweet blue eyes," I stubbornly thought. She started going on about being cold. I even took that the wrong way. I thought this was her way of calling me frigid because I wouldn't go back with her. Even writing this makes me feel like I'm demented. "Stop looking at her," I tell myself. "Just go home. Not for you John." So a quick peck on the lips and off I popped; moody and nervous, head like a time bomb.

The next day after training I told Tom about the girl I'd met. I was negative, saying stuff about her just wanting to use me and her being too confident, that she was too good to be true. I was making excuse after excuse not to phone her.

Tom:"just give her a call. Don't get caught up with it, a few fun times, keep it light." He was right but I'm past all that. It was either all or nothing. I needed to just walk away but I couldn't. I rang her that afternoon. She wasn't in. Fuck it, angry kid comes to mind. That night I couldn't get my mind away from this girl. She wasn't what I needed. I needed a librarian not some hot model type.

Later that night I heard the phone go: "Hello, is John there?" Her voice was so soft. When she wasn't in a club atmosphere there was an apparent transformation from party girl to sweet girl. She sounded lovely. I came off the phone, the world was my oyster, sceptical yet childlike. I was like the Grinch when he suddenly realises he still has feelings!

In the gym the next day I saw a couple of the door lads training in the next room. "I heard you've robbed Reggie's bird," one of them said.

"She's a head fuck. Watch you don't get played," another.

Christina had previously been out with one of the lads I worked with. This was how I found out.

"Here we go again," I thought. "Same shit, different day."

That Saturday, Baz was at my house but I'd lost my keys and couldn't get in. I wanted to work. Baz told me that he had a spare shirt. I could scrub up my old boots a little, but I still needed some pants. So it was the case of head first through the shed window looking to find a pair. Luckily I found some. They were a bit scruffy looking but what the hell, I'd made the effort right, so on we went. I was a little anxious about what had been said in regard to Christina but then I just thought "fuck it". At least Doza was always sound.

We got to the club. "How's it going Doza?"

He looked me up and down. "Couldn't you have polished those shoes? And what's going on with them pants?"

I was fuming. All the effort I'd put in just to get there. "Fuck you," I said, but only in my head and safely enough away just in case he could read my thoughts.

I go into the club. This was when the fun really began. The lads were standing over with Reggie, I'd said hi but it was obvious that I was the talking point and not in a good way. One of the lads had said that Christina was only using me to get to Reggie. Ok, so no one liked me anymore, but I'd sensed that I was part of things. I know this sounds strange, but I still wanted to be there. Glitches and setbacks I was used to but I knew I wasn't going anywhere. My sense of something good to happen lay here, it was just a little blurry at the time.

Christina came into the club a little later and asked me what was wrong? She had noticed me being a little quiet. I didn't say anything at first, but then I asked her about Reggie. She got a little uppity about it and started going on about him cheating on her. I then say "Well they've said that you cheated on him" to which she said "No, I finished him because he was cheating on me."

"Ok," I angrily replied. "Fuck it, let's just leave it."

"Fine" she fired back and off she went. Two minutes later I got paired up with Reggie, of all people. Brilliant.

So we'd walked around a while then I decided to drift off on my own. A guy who was stood with his friends came over to me. "Hey pal, stop walking around like ten men. You don't need to have that attitude." Bang. I'd head butted the guy and put him on his back, the icing on the cake.

I headed upstairs. I was stood at the side, looking over the dance floor when a girl appeared then started dancing behind me. I thought of Tom's words: "Just enjoy it. Don't get caught up with it all." He was right. A few minutes had passed when I saw Christina walking by. She glanced at me slightly then carried on walking. She was stood at the side of the dance floor, around 15 yards from where I was. The place was packed but she'd stayed in sight. I got a sense that she wanted me to go over. I got the sense that she actually really liked me.

I looked at the girl I was with. She wasn't the one. I really didn't want the drama. I honestly thought this couldn't end well but I really liked this Christina girl. "Fuck it." Without any explanation I moved out of the grips of the girl I was with and over towards Christina. I was stood at the back of her, slightly cradling her. She knew I was there. "Is that your girlfriend?" she asked.

"No," I murmured. Nothing more was said. I gave it a second then took her hand as we moved away from and around the dance floor. I was looking on, not knowing what to say. I then turned to Christina. She was already looking at me.

There was an innocence that shone from her eyes, a sparkle. Whatever may come of this, I wasn't sure, but I knew this was real. The way she was looking at me was real. The feeling was real.

As I looked at her there was a track playing in the background: Children by Robert Miles. It was inviting, melodic. It took us into the moment. There was a deep gulp, the clash of eyes, the track to our first kiss.

The room spun. Magic happened. Words weren't needed.

I knew this club was the place that something good was going to happen. So here I was for the first time in my life, falling in love.

As time went by, people became more accepting of mine and Christina's relationship but I was always a little worried about what had been said. I was hearing stories week in and week out, of various exploits. I figured something must have been said about Christina in the past but when push came to shove, nothing had.

I was sitting with Reggie and some of the other lads. I had tried avoiding him but he was blatantly open about nothing ever going on between him and Christina. He said she'd just messed him about. I told him I still hadn't got anywhere with her either but that I preferred that to someone who's been everywhere. Until now, I had disliked Reggie, but I realised he had just been looking out for me. It seemed like some of the other lads looked to be trouble-shooting, or perhaps they were just looking out for their pal, maybe even me. After a late night conversation over chicken at Billy's place, we all had a much better understanding of one-another. It was a brotherhood on the horizon.

In the early days of working the doors I'd had to battle with self-doubt, anger, emotions. I knew there was a place for everything but I couldn't figure out how to get everything in its place. I was like Neo in the Matrix: I knew somehow I belonged. I was finding my feet but wanting answers; still trying to find a clear pathway through the drama. So if I was Neo, who was Morpheus?

Chapter 2

Ian Cardoza (Doza): The doorman's answer to Morpheus

I know I've mentioned about the pants and shoes incident with Doza, but this was Doza being Doza; no favourites and professional. Exactly what he expects from his door staff would be what he was willing to do himself, and then some. He wasn't out to control you. If you didn't want to do it his way and to his standards, then you could opt to work elsewhere. No harm, no foul.

Military equivalent

I had served in the Royal Fusiliers from 91-93. I'd done well on the training side of things; assault courses, shooting accuracy and running with a rifle and Bergen but the honour in soldiering was never there for me, despite finishing near the top of the grid. I was mouthy with officers when drunk, I'd been locked up for fighting and I was called out on numerous occasions because my uniform was never ironed nor were my boots shined. I remember saying to a commanding officer, "Why do we need shiny boots and ironed pants if we are in a war zone?"

"Good point," he replied.

For this, I was told to help disassemble all the netting from the assault course. We finished at one a.m. the next morning. I didn't question much again after that.

In my first book I talk about my fusilier initiation, then go on to explain how I earned my feather and beret. A friend of mine and former fusilier, Dave Holt, had a dig at me about the feather story. "It's called a hackle. Men have died for the honour of wearing one," he'd said. I didn't get a sense of honour from the army though; my honour lay elsewhere.

Ian Cardoza had served in the full time armed forces prior to him becoming a door man. His pride in his own leadership was very much the same as that of a commanding officer. Doza was a leader by example rather than demand though.

Once I had pride in wanting to be part of Doza's team, it meant everything to me. Unlike the army though, I always shined my boots and had a perfect pleat ironed into my pants. I wore my blue plastic jacket like a soldier wore his beret. My hackle was my clip-on brown tie that I wore with pride as being part of Young Bloods door team. Doza was our Sergeant. My position on the team held my honour and these guys were my platoon.

After the first couple of months of working with Doza and the team I was getting tagged in a lot of the fights that went on. The sides of my forehead were full of gashes and holes. The fact that I ran head first into every fight really didn't help my case.

Doza was always giving us little talks, wording us up on what was happening, who might be trying to kick off, well known families and whatnot to be aware. He gave us a regular instalment of self-belief speeches about this team being able to win against anyone. There wasn't a better team to take care of things. I really loved the talks. I felt enriched, being part of the incredible team he was talking about.

There was one little problem though: When I worked with my little pal Col, he would always be taking the piss about me getting clipped. It wasn't anything major, it just messed with my pride a little. I was getting irritated by it and I think Doza caught wind of it. He didn't directly say anything to Col, instead he subtly worded something at the end of one of our team talks.

"I don't ask any of my doormen to do anything I wouldn't do myself. I'm not asking for anyone to be the best fighter in the world. All I ask, and what we have, is eleven lads who will jump in on any situation and have each other's backs, regardless of any outcome." I was stoked. This was the reason I had started the extra fight sessions. Doza had belief in me, maybe not in my abilities as a fighter but certainly in my loyalties towards him and the team. I now wanted to be better.

If I was working the upstairs and a situation arose, the first thing Doza would do is ask how I wanted to deal with it. He instilled that we were all good enough to be head doormen ourselves, able to make our own decisions. He always backed us on that decision. He dealt with everything fairly. I really wanted to get on this wave.

Learning by example

Doza's set up:
Every lad who worked for him mainly trained at the gym. They were well mannered. They didn't do drugs. They didn't drink on the job. They were always clean and well turned out. There were no egos. We were a team. You could tell there were a few cheeky Charlies, those who, without Doza's influence, would have strayed. When you're part of the A Team though, you don't want to be anywhere else. Everyone was on the natural high. Doza was selective but everyone was warned well in advance. There was many a tale of lads doing dodgy dealings as a side line, popping a few pills or failing to get involved in the fights. Doza knew and told them the script. If they didn't listen and carried on, thinking they were clever... Well I think you can guess the rest.

There were a couple of early incidents I'll never forget. I hadn't been there long. There was this little angry doorman working with us. He was having a go at his Mrs at the top of the foyer steps when Doza tried to intervene. The guy asked Doza to back off so he did, whilst keeping an eye on the situation. Thirty seconds on the guy had cracked his girlfriend. Doza stepped in and slapped him. The guy didn't just fall down the stairs; Doza hit him that hard he flew seven feet up against the wall behind the stairs. The guy hit the deck, broken ankle, game over. I'd never seen a guy fly upwards before.

I remember getting into a fight: five or six lads were all going hell for leather at me. I was lashing out whilst getting mashed. I saw Doza and Jay Cunners running in from the corner of my eye. Seconds later there were just bodies everywhere. My eyes were squinting, fully blood shot, and I could feel the blood running from my nose into my mouth. Jay came over with a big grin on his face and gave me the rookie pat on the back for giving it my all. Doza was looking on while trying to hide a smile. I looked like road kill. "Good effort, pal. Now go and get yourself cleaned up." Those guys were unreal.

Doza wasn't just all hard and mighty though, he was also one of the most courteous and open minded people you could ever meet. When I first started working for him, I'd been driving without a licence for a couple of weeks. When he found out, he worded me up about what would happen if I was caught, then said that he passed my house on the way up to work and would give me a lift. He did that for the best part of three years. He even came to watch me compete. Like with everyone on his team, he just seemed to make time for everyone. His ways, I really admired.

When we drove to work together in his car he seemed to have the answers to all of life's questions. As well as feeding the passions of all his door staff with self-belief, team spirit, and a sense of honour, he was also available for the small stuff. I obviously had certain issues ringing round in my head, but didn't want to make it known. I was always very locked up when it came to talking about personal stuff. Doza had a good opinion of me so I didn't want to just suddenly start coming out with all the ridiculous shit that was going on my head, even though I knew he would have the answers.

I kept asking random questions in the 'I'm asking for a friend' type of way. Doza laughed sometimes. There really was some random shit going on in my bonce at the time. He answered the questions though and gave me perspective. He opened my mind to aspects of people's personalities; why a certain thing may have happened. He gave me scope, almost like a forgiveness, an understanding to a situation but on a wider plain. He really helped me to understand, to see a bigger picture. I didn't have to agree with everything he said: it wasn't about that. It was more about weighing up the possibilities and how to think more for yourself.

By just taking a little bit of time to get to know me properly, Doza had helped to build me up to both my physical and mental best. He didn't go out of his way to do it as such. This was the way he was with everyone, how he still is today. I say he's like Morpheus but in this situation he was more like Moses parting the Red Sea, giving clarity in my head from the blood lust I hadn't managed to shift. Now the sea of blood had parted, there was once again that clear view; the high tide of happiness shining through.

Chapter 3

On top of the big wave:

Love and loyalty

1997: The world was my oyster again. My training was going great; I was in my best shape and had learnt to handle myself well. I was enjoying my day job; the sun always seemed to be shining. I was happy in my skin. I wasn't arrogant or egocentric, just confident this time.

The club was rife with girls but I knew that was just a smoke screen now, that wasn't real. I'd asked God for that one person, the person who would like me when I didn't even like myself. I'd prayed for that so I appreciated what I had. Christina wasn't just any girl; she was the girl. I hadn't had to settle for what I could easily get. I went for someone I didn't think I'd be able to keep hold of; someone unobtainable. I worked my hardest at making it work. God had showed me the darker side of life when it came to women, a reminder to look after the gift I'd been given.

Staying loyal

Staying loyal was never a problem for me, despite being surrounded by some very obviously welcoming ladies and Jack-the-lad doormen. Doormen at this time were a good commodity for the young girls; the doorman being the catch of the day back then.

The girls were wild. There was a guys tops-off contest

once. All the lads had to stand in a line. None of them has much meat on them and the girls were the first to let them know. Like animals, they were throwing glasses and bottles at the guys on stage, shouting about wanting some meat up there. Unfortunately, I had been stood at the front of the event, "Come on you, get your kit off. Get up there." They started to rag my pants. Other girls then joined the hunt and I found myself in the firing line. My shirt was partially ripped off. My tie was gone. My pants were coming apart and I was holding onto my belt for dear life. That was scarier than any fight I'd ever been in! Luckily help was on its way. Doza suddenly appeared. No, he didn't start tearing the girls off me. He'd seen the bigger picture: the girls wanted flesh. He stepped up on stage, shirt off and into an array of double biceps and lat spreads. I was left to make my getaway. The beasts had new meat to prey on. Madness.

Women and violence

There were some madcap women in the club also. I remember a guy named Ian Lomax showing me were a woman had smashed him in the head with a stiletto shoe. He said to me, "When it comes to domestics, leave 'em to it." He was trying to help the woman escape from her abusive partner when she had turned on him.

The story I most remembered though was when Ivan was carrying this big girl across the dance floor. She was going absolutely nuts, kicking and butting him with the back of her heel and her head. Ivan was bright red, "Fuckin; help me!" I saw him and headed over. We both managed to get the girl to the front door. She was like a friggin' banshee. Ivan let go of her as I pushed her out the door but instead of going through the door she slightly detoured, smashing her head against the wall. Tony Waldren (the older, nicer doorman) wasn't happy. "Fuckin' hell John, you could have done that a little better." Tony reached down toward the girl, "Are you ok love?" She didn't take his hand though. Instead, she bit a big chunk out of it. Tony's airs and graces soon went as he cracked her on the back of the head and slung her out into the street. Everyone was in stitches as Tony returned. He was serious for a second, still a little pent up, but then just started laughing. "I've sent her to the kebab shop, cheeky cow." It was piss funny.

Doormen and women

Most of the doormen were, pretty much, women mad. There was one guy named Ralph, who would spot something strangely perverse nearly every week. I remember once, he told me to come to where he was. A girl was dancing on one of the podiums but he was looking down instead of up at the girl. "Look at this," he said. It was a mirrored podium, so when he looked down at the mirrored base he could see directly up the girl's skirt. "I don't think she's got any knickers on either." Jees, how long had he been working on that one?

I remember another time; my pal had promised me a lift home at the end of the night but when the time came he had appeared with a couple of girls by his side. "John, I'm just going to drop these off first."

"Ok, no worries," I thought. When we arrived at the house without a word said, everyone piled out of the car and into the house. I waited a few minutes then got told to come in. By the time I was in the house, my pal and one of the girls had made their way upstairs to one of the bedrooms. Whilst the other girl was making us both a drink, I could hear the noises: rocking, bed springs, then bang, bang, bang. I knew this was going to be awkward so I quickly pretended to fall asleep to avoid any unpleasantness. It was the longest thirty minutes I'd ever known. When they finally came down stairs, I had to pretend I had just come too. Everyone was looking at each other, obviously I was there to make a four. "Are we going now?" I said while pretending to look dazed.

Another problem that kept emerging was that there were always groups of girls wanting to party with us come the end of the night; they wouldn't go home sometimes. There was this one time, when this group of Irish girls were all sat around wanting me to go partying with them. The door lads kept coming over, "John, those Irish birds are waiting for you. They won't go."

So I was steering clear, when I saw Doza. "Ian, them girls keep hanging about." He looked at me like I was demented.

"Get over there."

He saw me dip my head and quickly realised what I was really trying to say. "Ok pal, there's the chains. You lock the doors up; I'll take care of the girls."

As I've said I'm a shepherd; I'll lead by example, rather than follow a crowd. I see the bigger picture now. I've a long term memory of knowing how I felt when I was yesterday spaghetti. The girl I was now with, way out-classed any of the other girls looking to just party or only want you when you are on your glory waggon. Was I finally growing up? Yeah, definitely a little bit.

The wave was, again, at its highest:

Fighting had become fun. It was a place where potentially I could get killed every week, yet never been badly injured once. I was more at peace than the Dalai Lama sat on his mountain. I remember the music, our shiny Ellesse boots and blue shiny jackets. Pleated shirts, square jaw lines and broad shoulders. It was the buzz of every Friday and Saturday night. Loved up with the Mrs; late nights at mine, only needing the love of one woman. Like breakin', like skating and the early bodybuilding but no ego, not needing to be the centre of attention. I had a clear mind; loving life, no drink, no drugs, looking after people with like minded friends. The world was my oyster.

The wave was at its highest. I'm a life addict, so here we are again. I'd finally found my way through the matrix, Morpheus by my side.

God had put me at that place. I was, once more, indestructible. The devil was powerless against love and, at this moment in time, I was loving everything.

Chapter 4

Band of brothers

Life on the home front was at its highest. I was living next to my parents. Everything was good there. Things had been a little sketchy when I had first moved out. Like always, there were group of kids around: Greeny, Shawn and Gary. They were painting my garage, my dad's, building dens and helping with the gardening. The neighbours were great and my friendships were great. Every day was sunny, magic almost. I proposed to Christina. She said yes. I was a very happy man.

Like everything I'd ever done, sooner or later it came to Bury. This time it was the full Young Bloods door team. Everyone was training at Silvers Gym; all of us training together but separated up into groups. We wound Doza up whilst he was under the squat rack, calling him a pussy when he was on his biggest set. The bar went down, "I'll show you who's a pussy." Mint. Life couldn't be any better.

Killing the ego

All was still well working the door but because I was winning so many of the fights we'd been getting into, I had begun to get a little cocky, that ego was starting to creep in. This time it wasn't about how I looked, my physique or relationship. This time it was about my ability as a fighter. I was never a bully. I never started a single fight, that wasn't the problem. I'd learned some fancy locks, big kicks and was moving well. No one was getting hurt but I knew how impressive this stuff looked when it was carried out properly. I started to go a bit over the top (too many Van Damme and Bruce Lee movies!). Rather than just sticking to what was needed, the Lazarus effect, perhaps. That ego always found its way back; somehow, some way.

One night in early autumn 1997

It was the night I got back from my holidays. Doza rang asking if I could cover a shift because he wanted the night off. I told him I'd be an hour or so late but I'd cover. It was a good night. We were a couple of men down but the night was going quite well, good atmosphere, everyone in good spirits. It was one of the first nights nothing had happened at all. It seemed too good to be true. And it was.

A fight suddenly kicked off on the top floor where I was working. There were bottles, tables, the lot. A lot of people were involved. It was mainly me and a guy named Ian Lomax that were hauling arse. Lomax usually worked the downstairs. We were ragging anyone and everyone to the fire exits, then down to the concrete steps. Punching, throwing, grappling; whatever it took. Even though a ton of people had been launched down those steps, up until this point, no one had been seriously hurt. I'd taken a few trips down them myself.

We'd been fighting a while and we were down to the last two. Lomax threw his lad down the stairs, job done. "Last one," I thought. "Smash in a few round houses, then finish off with a spinning kick." Stupid really, but hey ho, it just seemed like a bit of fun at the time. Both the lads were wiped out at the bottom of the steps.

As I went inside, Lomax was stood there with his missus and a couple of their friends. They were all taking the piss, calling me Karate Kid and standing on one leg like in the movie, I just laughed. Two minutes later I step back outside and see the guy I'd kicked still lying there. His feet were twitching but there was no movement; Apollo Creed in Rocky IV sprang straight to mind. Oh shit. I walked back in then closed the doors. Lomax was still laughing, messing about before going downstairs. Meanwhile my insides were rising up into my chest.

I didn't even feel like I was in the room. A wave of anxiety clouded my mind. A few minutes passed and Old Col (Young Col's dad, who also worked with us) came flying over.

"What have you done? Police are everywhere," he said as he grabbed onto my collar. I didn't say anything. I was scared to death. "Go back to the door and wait there," he instructed.

As I got outside the back door, I could see Young Col waiting in his van. "Get in, you daft cunt," he smiled. "What have you been up to now?" As we set off away from the club, police and ambulances swamped the scene. It was a nice feeling as the lights and sirens started to fade into the background. That night I got no sleep; every light that passed the window had me on edge. The morning couldn't come soon enough.

The next day, young Colin was on the phone. I asked him what had gone on. He said all the doormen had stayed stum when being questioned by the police. One of our lads had come in his civvies and was undetected when the police were about. He'd gone into the video room, popped the video under his jacket and walked straight out again. Old Col had phoned Young Col to take me out of town. I wasn't down on the rota to work so it was like I was never there, job done. Talk about everyone pulling together, unreal.

The next week when I was in the car with Doza I asked about the incident and how the guy was, if he'd heard anything. "I don't know anything pal. You did your job, that's all that matters." Obviously, it was just another day for Doza.

I ended up calling the police but nothing had been reported. I saw the kid bouncing around the club a few weeks later.

I calmed down a little after that. God protects you when you're fighting for the right reasons; vanity and looking good are not any of those reasons. I'd got the message: back to basics. Apart from this minor demise, the only place that ego never really got in, was working the doors.

My partners in crime

I met a lot of good people whilst working this door. There was Stu, a South African guy; we watched each other's backs and were like a tag team when it came to anyone coming on to our women, a great lad. Then there was my pal Col; I'd had to help him out on a few extracurricular events away from the door. As a pal though, he was always there. Col was a boyo but knew his stuff. He'd drag me back when we were face to face with smack rats, holding their needles. "Leave them, John, let them finish. You don't know what other diseases they have." He saved my bacon on a few occasions

There was a big fight once. I'd just been hit in the head with a glass, it was mayhem. I was wiping the blood from my eyes and still trying to fight, when I saw a guy with half a bottle coming under my ribs. Col was in, bang, bang, game over.

When we were working together I always ran to the middle of the fight when it had first kicked off, being the bigger lad. Col picked them off from the side lines. We were like the dynamic duo. In the back room where we did drug searches, Col would put on some polythene gloves if he had found a small stash on one of the lads. Sometimes he'd tell them he had to do an internal search. I saw some proper worried faces. I reckon a few changed their minds about wanting to be wheeler dealers after that. We'd start pissing ourselves midway through. The lads would be thinking, What the Fuck. But they were always relieved knowing we were only messing about. Lesson learned.

The door in general though was known as the best: it really was something. We even made the papers for the amount of drug busts we did. The police were sceptical. They thought Doza was running his own little racket. They couldn't be more wrong. For the time in which we had all worked together, Doza had made us immortal; we were brothers.

I remember a track playing out from the DJ booth, in the autumn fall of 1997. I was stood overlooking the dance floor from the middle tier. The track was playing: "Forever young, I want to be forever young. Do you really want to live forever? Forever young." I stood next to Stu and my pal Col then looked down to see Christina smiling up at me from the dance floor. Doza was smiling over from across the way and the whole world just sort of felt as it should. I did want this moment to last forever and in my heart and when thinking back to these times, I'll always be Forever Young.

Chapter 5

When Dad steps up

In April 1998 I was in my house talking to Christina on the phone when my sister, Karen, came into the room. "John, Dad's going off on one. He's going down on to the estate on his own to sort out that rough family from off Fairfield."

I told Christina I'd have to go as Karen started telling me about how some kid had battered my little sister. Mum had been down to the house to talk to the parents and their Dad had come out and told my Mum to fuck off, then called her a slag. My Dad was known as 'Mad Mick' for a reason back in the day and my Mum was my Dad's favourite person on the planet. Like a red rag to a bull.

We all jumped in the car. The whole family headed down to the estate. Apparently, this family had been bullying the whole neighbourhood for a while. We arrived at the door and a big lad opened up. Bang. My Dad had belted him before a word was said. We headed inside looking for their Dad. I ended up cracking one of the lads; he'd come through a side door holding a bat. My Dad was battering another two lads in the front room. I joined him and wiped the lads out. Then I stepped out into the hall and saw their Dad, I quickly had him pinned up against the wall. I was ready to go at him, when I heard my Dad's voice, "John, leave it, John."

I turned round and he had hold of this little girl, comforting her. The rest of the family were obviously arseholes, but this little kid couldn't have been any sweeter. She was upset, crying for her Dad. I think the room melted and the fight came to a halt. The guy I had hold of, although a prick, was still this little girl's hero.

As we walked up the street on the way back nearly every neighbour on the road was stood in their front gardens. There were a few nods of approval. There was a line of kids sitting on their bikes looking at us like we were heroes, like an old wild-west movie. In the weeks that followed we were given a few death threats; the family were coming our way in full force but it never happened. They soon moved on and no one got bothered again. One of the kids who was there that day, Jordon Herald, still reminds me of that story to this day; how we had helped out the neighbourhood. I still feel quite proud about it. This was another example of that one person being able to make all the difference, that person being my Dad. Or 'Mad Mick' as he was on this day.

Chapter 6

The last days of disco

Trials and Tribulations

Being your best seems to come more easily when you're in the company of a positive influence. It's when the influence leaves, that you find your true metal. I know some of the doormen, after parting ways with Doza, reverted back to how they would have gone if they hadn't met him. There were other people who felt empowered just by being in his company.

The thing in my mind after working with Doza, wasn't how I could follow him to the next port of call, or mention him as a guy I'd worked with in order to get recognition; my only question was, would I still have the guts to man up and follow through, to do the right thing, even after we had parted ways? With every question there's a yearning; it's not a prayer as such but it's similar in the way that it's something you need an answer to. Closure, if you will. People hope for things but when the answers to your wants, your cravings, arrive it's always going to be much more of a task than you first imagined. But you have to keep remembering, deep down, you asked for it.

1999

The world had pretty much been my oyster for some time. Me and Christina were living together. She was in training to become a midwife. We didn't have much money, in fact I was working my days off as well as the door, just to tide us over. The house had no pictures on the wall. We had a TV which had a big hole in it (it was my Dad's TV; he had thrown a glass at it because he was sick of seeing Peter Andre on the telly). I was helping Christina with her studies and she was training with me at the gym. I was looking and feeling pretty much my best. The wave: a steady high.

Working the door had also been good but like with most things, they start to change. The tide turns. Doza had left Young Bloods and gone to work in Bury with some of the other lads. Others had gone on to work different places. A couple of the lads had picked up criminal records so couldn't work anymore. So like everything else I've ever done in life, when I was at my best, I was on my own.

Old Col took over as head man but slowly started to lose interest so bit by bit I had started covering his post. I didn't see myself as a head man. There were guys working with us who really looked the part but when it came to the kick-offs they were running to me asking what to do. I hadn't got the leadership skills Doza had. I was pretty happy just working my post, but it wasn't going to happen. The kick offs became more intense, the fights were lasting longer, I was getting tagged again; the cavalry were too slow and not very efficient. I felt the deficit. These guys thought I was something but I wasn't feeling it at all. I didn't have a niche for the leadership nor the responsibility as yet. I hadn't questioned the other doormen I was working with; I just knew that I couldn't rely on them the same way. I realised just how good Doza's team had been. I still enjoyed the job though, despite the changes.

Whilst working the club one night I heard a ruckus on the dance floor. As usual, I stupidly ran in on my own. I get to the middle of the floor and see a big, coloured guy. He had just wiped out two lads. No other doormen nor the DJ had seen me. My power, strength and skill had done me proud so far. I had confidence in my abilities, so in I went.

We started fighting. Instantly his strength out-powered

mine. I didn't dare grip him, I knew he was too strong. It was going to be a fist fight and the guy was powerful. I was covering up but this guy was rocking me even with my guard up. I tried firing off a few shots, nothing. We were hitting each other hard but I wasn't winning. Where's the fucking cavalry? We'd been going at it a while. Then, it was almost like his hits seemed to stop hurting as much. I sensed the fucker running out of energy.

I first played it safe, letting him burn himself out. Then I was in. Bang, bang, bang. I grabbed his throat and forced him backwards off the dance floor. I had him lent over one of the booth tables. He was leant backwards but was still facing me. I looked around, still no one about. I looked back, smash. The guy had grabbed two glasses from the table and had double slammed me from either side. A tumbler and a pint pot, one in each hand. He'd won.

I was standing, but I didn't know where I was. I couldn't see anything. I was holding onto him, trying to stop his punches. He was just a shape; I couldn't make out his face. I was glaring aimlessly when I faintly heard a scream. The guy stopped punching. The scream got louder. What was going on? My sight suddenly returned. "Grab him John," one of the lads shouted. The guy screamed as we ragged him out the doors. I was still a touch frantic as we kicked him out into the street.

As we headed back inside I was still wondering what was going on. One of the doormen was laughing but I was still none the wiser. He pulled out the spike that held the entrance tickets from the club. I started laughing. "Right up the arse," he smiled. Brilliant. I wiped away the blood and picked the glass pieces from out of my face but there was a clear gash on one side with a dark, thick flow of blood. The door lad came over, holding the same needle, "I can stitch that up if you want mate?"

"No thanks pal. Thanks anyway!"

I went into hospital that night: stitches in the right side of my temple, I lost part of my hearing in the left ear where a piece of glass had gone in and had a face full of small holes and gouges to top it all off. Was this the test I wanted? Yes, partially. The main test though, wasn't that outcome; it was about coming back the following week and the week after that, to do the same job and just as well.

Another test: A lot of gangs and 'not-rights' wanted to take over the club, to have their door staff selling drugs and what not. I had several threats and warnings telling me to get out of Young Bloods. I knew the guys making the threats and thankfully they had respected me enough not to take over the club whilst I worked there. I was proud knowing I didn't leave the club until I was ready. There were no drugs or gangsters that took over the place whilst I ran the door. I didn't really know what I was doing; was it bravery or stupidity? I didn't know how fucked up these people were but I knew Doza wouldn't have fled. I kept telling myself that, every time I turned up to do the next shift.

Chapter 7

Failure to acclimatise

October 1999, my days at Young Bloods were over. God had made me man up to the rigours of what had been plaguing my mind. He did this whilst helping me to help others; fighting, but fighting for what was right. The tide had turned once more; five years of build-up leading me to this point. The next point of call: a nice place, a place with manners and addressing situations with resolve rather than violence. The happy ending if you will. Hold up, no one said anything about resolving dispute without violence; what's all this?

I started working for my old pal Tom. The venue was smart with good, classy people. What could go wrong? I'd spent the past five years handling situations pretty much hands on. In all honesty, I still had very little in the way of negotiation skills, it just hadn't come up. The lads on the door were all smartly dressed, looking the part. Then there was me; bomber jacket and black pants. No problem, so to speak, the first couple of weeks. I found it strange getting paid for just smiling. I was bored, I wasn't used to this.

My first noted wrong doing: One night I spotted an argument going on, on the upper floor, a stone's throw away from where I was. I think the protocol was just to go round and disperse the situation. Sorry, I didn't get the memo. I jumped up, grabbed a guy by his neck, ragged him over the rails then started to go at him. Tom's brother, Pat, was with me. We gave the guy a hiding then put him out onto the front street. Pat smiled, Tom wasn't as pleased but didn't make a problem of it. It went off a few more times. I was like a bull in a china shop and Paddy was my new partner in crime. We'd both been hauling a little arse recently. Tom wasn't happy, but honestly, I didn't realise I was doing anything wrong.

The other doormen enjoyed my old school way of handling things but it wasn't what the place needed. Tom took me to one side, "John, it's not like working the club. You need to bring as little attention to a situation as possible. I know you've done it differently where you last worked, but just back it up a touch. Kill 'em with kindness." Argh, the penny dropped. So I become on board with Tom, being nice, walking people out, getting to grips more with this mellow approach to working the door. Tom had been great. We worked up to Christmas and into the New Year without any problems. We brought in the millennium together and Tom even paid my parking ticket, knowing I was a bit stuck for cash.

The new millennium: All's pretty good. I'd started getting used to the nice guy doorman thing. I'd started to acclimatise. One usual night at work, Tom had asked me to work downstairs in the club part of the pub. Christina was out after having arranged to have a few drinks with Tom's girlfriend. The night picked up; a full house, everyone was dancing. I was stood on the side lines, quite content, when a kid, who was dancing with a group of lads came towards me. "Hey pal cheer up. Give us a smile," he sniggered.

"I'm ok pal, you enjoy your night."

He drifted back off but then five minutes later, he was smiling at me again, taking the piss. Normally this was my limit. "Tom's given you a second chance here John, don't blow it." I half-heartedly try and smile. "That should do it." I stood for another minute but then he came over again. He grabbed my face into a smiling position this time. I pushed him back. He then sniggered at me when back with his crowd.

I was fucking fuming. I was doing my best but I knew that letting this kid walk out in one piece wasn't going to be an option. Sorry Tom. As he came my way once more he started to smile then licked his lips to blow me a kiss. Bang,

bang, bang. His head was through the door. Another kid jumped on my back and so got a few elbows. I attacked like a wild ape. The group of lads were all out on the street. Pat was first on the scene and had managed to calm the situation. I think he knew the kids from the boxing club he'd trained at. My own staff had to talk me down because I wanted to carry on the fight in the street.

At the end of the night, everyone was laughing and joking. A kid called Doc said, "That's how you do it. None of this namby pamby shit." The club owner, Kev Clark, was going mad. In my rage I had bent the exit door off its hinges. Pat had tried covering for me. I saw Tom's face: I'd let him down. It wasn't intentional, but I'd let him down.

I turned up for the next shift the following week. I was stood by the door when I see Tom. "John I've got you a job working near to Manchester. They've been having a lot of trouble. I thought this might suit you a bit more. I think this place is a little too quiet for you."

Not long after a bright blue BMW screeched to a stop with its music blaring. A guy got out wearing shades. He had a Manc accent and obviously wanted to be seen and heard. "Are you the guy?" he cockily asked.

"Yeah," I offer.

He told me to put my coat in the back of the car. I hadn't even started taking it off when I noticed there were guns in his boot. I guess I was supposed to be impressed. What a dick.

When we arrived at the venue it was how I'd imagined it would be. The place its-self was pretty smart but the lads on the door were a sight. None of them were actually standing on the door and the head man was sat at one of the tables on his phone. The crew looked weary. They could hardly fill the jacket they were wearing and their people skills were non-existent. No one even acknowledged my presence. I stood on the door. I did the job I was supposed to do. I was polite, in sight and vigilant. And so the first couple of weeks went by.

From the start I'd known these guys were largely involved

in drugs. The head doorman was on the phone one minute, a couple of lads go missing the next but I didn't get involved. By the second week of working there I'd struck up a mutual respect with a guy I was doing a bit of cover for. They called him Para Dan, as he had served in the forces as a paratrooper. He didn't work at the pub but he ran the night club that wasn't too far away. I worked his club after I worked the door at the pub. He had very little time for the other lads, he just needed the staff at this time. He had no fear of Marko's boys, as they were known. He was a tough kid, you could see he'd been about and was definitely no angel. He was fair though. He'd see and treat people for what they were.

Into the fourth week, the door team seemed anxious. None of them were leaving the pub. I could hear whispers but none of them had told me what was going on. During the night I heard a ruckus in the pub. As I turned, it had gone off. Everyone was going hell for leather. I smacked a guy and he instantly hit the deck. Almost straight after, I got thrown through a table. I was on my back getting my ribs kicked in. One of our lads hit the lad who was stamping on me. They started fighting each other, leaving me to get back to my feet and back in the fight. I had a good run after that and, as a team, we won. Although fucked-up washed out looking mother fuckers, the lads were all decent scrappers. This was the first time I got acknowledged.

A night to remember

The following week I turned up for work. There was no big conversation but I got a few nods of acknowledgement and even a thumbs up from the main guy, who never usually looked up from his table. The night was going ok until a group of lads walked in. They caused a little uproar but it didn't break into a fight. They then left. I got a sense there was a tension though. It seemed to be serious. The phones were on the go, hushed and hidden conversations but by the end of the night nothing had happened. On to the club.

The club was nicely tucked away down a country lane. I had taken my usual post, on the upper floor but not long after, Dan appeared. "John can you work the front for a while? A couple of the lads seem to have done one."

"Ok, no worries." As I got to the front door, I noticed a couple more of the lads were being picked up by their girlfriends and were also leaving. I started to get a bit dubious. Then we got a call to the side fire exit, it was going off with quite a few lads involved. It broke into a fight but we managed to get them out of the door. I then went back to the front. We were all a little black and blue but nothing more was going on so we decided to grab a coffee whilst we were stood outside.

Next, a taxi arrived with a group of concerned looking girls. "There's a massive group of lads running over the hill." I went to take a quick glimpse from the corner. I couldn't see them as yet but I could hear them. Then I saw one, then another. Oh sh t!

We safely ushered the girls in. Then we dimmed the music and asked all the punters to stay inside the main hall. Me and Dan were the only ones left, except the older doorman who was keeping everyone in the venue. We literally had seconds. Dan grabbed the chains to lock the door. The glass had steel mesh on the inside which we hoped would hold up a while. Dan grabbed a pole from the cloakroom and I grabbed the umbrella rack.

It was like an army of zombies trying to smash through the windows and the doors. The initial attack was the scariest thing I'd ever seen. The glass was getting split from the rocks. There was a sound like a gun shot. The mesh in the glass was giving way. I was smashing at anyone, anything that popped through the glass with the umbrella stand but the glass and the meshing had finally started to come down. I could sense the worst possible outcome: if that glass went, we weren't going home.

They were getting through. A few more stood on the ledges and they were getting much harder to fight off. A few more seconds and it would all be over. I was frantically hitting out then... sirens.

The police arrived in full force. That sound and the sight of their flashing lights were the sweetest thing I'd ever seen. The noises quickly lessened, the windowsills cleared, a few more rocks were thrown before there was nothing but the sound of sirens fading away into the distance.

I slumped down on the floor, layered in sweat and full of anxiety; my body was a palpitating mess. Dan looked over, "Why didn't you run?"

"Why didn't you?" We both laughed. After a few minutes, I headed to the bathroom to clean myself up. When I was out of sight I had a sense of panic; the 'what if' factor. I started getting a little emotional then my legs started to shake uncontrollably.

Being a passionate, adrenaline fuelled person doesn't necessarily make you tough. You put yourself through things because the afterthought of nearly getting killed will far exceed the headache of being seen to be a coward. Now how fucked up is that? But it's true.

I made my way back outside. Dan hadn't needed to sit down, he was a tough kid. But as we walked back through the main hallway we were seen as the same; on this night we were heroes.

The following week was payday. Dan picked me up and we went to the pub for our wages. We arrived first with all the pay packets laid out with everyone's names on them. Dan asked the bar manager where Marco was. He shrugged. Dan was eyeing up the packets. "Tell Marco I've took all the wages. Tell him it was Dan that took them." He was on one. He grabbed all the pay slips then we walked outside. "'Ere John, take half. Fuck 'em." We laughed. "Flee the scene for a while John. I'll call you if anything decent comes about. You don't want to be part of all this. You're a good lad, I've enjoyed working with you."

As limits went, this was mine. I was happy knowing I had stayed, followed my initial intention; to look after the people inside the building. God loves a trier.

After this, the wave was set for a slight diversion. I

couldn't go back and work for Tom. The rumour was, his brother, Pat, went on a rampage after working with me, fighting with half of Bury. I did the odd night in Bury, working for Doza, but it didn't feel right us just all stood there having coffee and messing about. I couldn't acclimatise. We had been like the army of the 300 Spartans in our heyday, or so it felt.

The wedding

The five year wave of love and romance had finally led to the big day, our wedding day. All the lads turned out, my old school pals, work pals, the lot. It was the best day of my life.

I sneaked Christina off at the end of the night do. All the work lads were yelling, "Jonnie, bum by A. Jonnie, bum by A," as we left the building to go to the honeymoon suite at the Bolholt Hotel. Christina thought we were just going home. It was magic.

The following morning, we had breakfast by the lake while Drew Barrymore's The Wedding Singer played on our TV. In my grand plan to whisk Christina off, all romantic, I'd forgot to pack her any shoes. I had to carry her back over the thresh-old and back to the car.

Two weeks in Italy followed: a day and night in Venice. Smooth as you like.

Chapter 8

When the tide is right but you aren't:

The final lesson

2001

I walked away from the doors to embark on something different, something new: the Commonwealth Games were coming to Manchester, security staff were needed. It was the next big wave. The stadium was brand new. It was spectacular but for all the greatness and magic surrounding it, nothing had been tried and tested. On the first major event, the bridge leading over the athletes' pathway had become sodden with the recent bad weather. Even though I was only a guard I trialled the idea of using rails to form a new pathway while the athletes were on the field. When they were ready to come off, another guard would let us know so we could move the rails back, that way keeping the punters to one side.

The plan worked a treat. The 'so called' supervisors were nowhere to be seen and left me to it. During the break I was approached by gold medallist, Steve Cram. He asked me about the bridge and how I'd managed it. We got to talking, when the head of security, Grant, appeared. "Well done, great plan. Where's your supervisor's jacket?"

"I'm not a supervisor."

"You are now. Come and see me after. In fact, do you think you can handle the full section?"

"Yeah, sure."

"Great stuff." He and Steve quickly headed off elsewhere.

True to his word, the next week, Grant had got me running a full section. In one day I'd gone from steward to guard, guard to supervisor and from supervisor to section leader. Promotion had never been easier!

I had a team. I had the freedom to be wherever, whenever I wanted and at any event. I headed a string of events, always right on the side lines, watching the main athletes. Luckily enough I got to cover the men's 100 meter sprint. I thought I'd place myself right at the starting grid, to see just how quickly they set off. As it turned out, it wasn't such a good idea. The starting gun fired and by the time I'd turned my head, all of the sprinters were more or less over the finishing line. They were rapid.

The last day of the ceremony was definitely the most exciting. At the end of what had been of one of the biggest events to take place in England for a good while, came a moment I never thought I'd see. The Queen had been at the event. At the final part of the night, her car drove around the stadium, then through the middle gates. I got an unexpected radio call. "John, stay with the Queen's car as it leaves the grounds." As the car pulled out, it was just me running along its side, leading and guarding them to the exit. So there you go, I was the Queen's guard for the best part of a minute. Awesome.

I'm not sure whether it was during or just after the games but I got a call asking me to work the door at a big indoor stadium in Manchester. I'd still get the higher pay rate even though I'd no longer be a section leader but I would get the heads up as soon as something came up.

I'd done my initial couple of shifts when I got my first break. The team of lads who were supposed to be running the pit hadn't been showing up due to other commitments. It wasn't uncommon but the fact was, they needed someone to take over the job. The pit was right at the front, the gap between the stage and the barrier. It was the front row to the stars and possibly the most important job to manage. So of course, I said yes.

The first big gig I covered was no other than Morrissey, one of my all-time favourites. I was a foot away from where he was singing. I was a bit hands on with the crowd surfers at first. I got a thumbs up from the side lines to say well done for how quick I'd dispersed the situations but then got told to be a little less aggressive. I was all over it.

When a crowd surfer approached, I'd stick my shoulder beneath them and carry them out of the pit and back around to the side of the crowd. I got an idea to throw out some bottles of water to people in the crowd who looked like they were struggling and to pull those out who were getting crushed against the barrier. The team followed suit and the night flowed smoothly.

At the end of the night I got a well done from the section leaders as well as the event organiser. I got promoted on the spot to run the pits while the other team were elsewhere. I ended up covering for a few more well-known acts around this time.

The kids I was teamed up with were quite young but after a little time spent, they knew how to get into the zone. If I saw a lad who was on the chunky side, a little less than confident, I'd big him up as a big strong lad and put him in a prime spot. He may have been a little under confident when he started out, maybe he'd been taunted at school, but when he was referred to as a big strong lad, you'd just have to sit back and watch him come alive.

I felt good about this job and how I approached it. Maybe God had wanted this to be my next big wave. Perhaps, I did kind of hope for it, but like everything, there's always that test. Or was it just the usual, having to deal with the undercurrent of humanity?

It was summer and the world was once again, my oyster. I'd won a string of big contests both in stamina strength as well as bodybuilding. I was a reputable doorman, I was confident. I had a beautiful wife and loved my job. The world was a sunny place; top of the wave.

There were a few big acts coming up and I'd got used to my unofficial role of helping to run the pit. We'd covered the Ricky Hatton fight a few weeks earlier. I'd also ushered Triple H at one of the big wrestling events.

As the bigger acts were being lined up, the official team came back to run the pit. I'd managed to keep my spot when they first returned but then got told to go back to door security. I'd really enjoyed my time in the pits so thought I'd try and sneak in one more night.

Everyone congregated in the backstage area when I get spotted. The head of their team shouted over, "Hey pal, I've told you, you aren't on with us tonight. We've got the staff. We will call you when we need you. We don't need you."

I was in one of those moods, a dark stubborn anger. I had run the big events when these idiots where nowhere to be seen. I had no comeback but I didn't move. The guy came over, he was on one also and tried to push me out the door. Although I didn't hit him, I pushed him hard and in front of everyone. I had made a big mistake. I got escorted out, then and there.

I got a call the next week: apparently the guy was pressing charges, even though he was the one who had pushed me first. If I leave quietly he'll leave it, he'd said. I was advised to take the second option.

So the test here was to step back or to have sorted a working position before the event. Pride had clouded my vision. I'd failed.

I ran into one of the supervisors, somewhere down the line. He said that particular crew had dispersed. "Would have been yours that, pal. They went after that gig. You would've got Madonna if you'd stayed." Gutted.

2002

My bodybuilding life had run into some troubles. Some of the guys I'd been training with had put a huge negative spin on my training and my relationship.

I found a new, higher wave though. I left the gym I was at and all its negativity.

God was happy, I didn't try and get revenge, I just walked away. I aimed for the British title I so wanted. And I got it. God had tested my want over obstacles faced. I had passed. The key to happiness: stick to the path and don't let the negative noise deviate. It's about getting over the obstacles, not running at them. God takes care of the rest.

2003

I was still hearing various threatening rumours even after I'd walked away from all the meddlesome bullshit at my old gym. Their gym was running a stamina strength show. I wanted to show 'them' that I had no fear, that this 'word on the street' shit didn't faze me at all. I should have really just walked away like last time but I didn't. So for the first time in my strength training career, I wasn't trying to win a show, I was simply competing to prove a point.

More so than ever, I've seen how the tide of life works. I had sensed God forming the path I had chosen. I knew that stepping back was the key to moving forward. Unfortunately, I still wasn't grown up enough to just live by my senses.

I did the show. I set out and proved what I had wanted to prove but it was a stupid decision and one that would cost me. Within a few days my chest had swelled up and was on the verge of a tear. Worse than that though, the back of my arm had massively separated from my shoulder; I'd already had a warning earlier on during training. I was taken into hospital and had biodegradable pins shoved into my arm pit to hold the muscle together. What had I done?

The best job I'd ever had was out the window. I couldn't train due to injury. The problems leading up to the contests had also put an enormous strain on my relationship. The world as my oyster had once again been ripped from my grasp. And because of my bad choices, the undercurrent of humanity had left me gasping for air.

So then I went out and I got wasted. I just wanted to blow off a little steam while I was injured. I got full of drugs and drink and woke up full of bruises but couldn't remember any of what had happened. I thought I'd be able to handle letting loose a bit better by the age of 28. All I wanted was a few laughs. I didn't realise that everything I had built up could be torn down so quickly.

It wasn't what had happened or what had gone wrong that was the real problem; it was the undercurrent of humanity; that was the problem. I was known for being a pretty handy lad but now there were stories about me getting a kicking. I was known for being a clean living lad but now there was gossip about me being full of drugs and drink. I was known for being a decent bodybuilder but now there were rumours that I was finished. People just love to talk; they don't see the bigger picture or maybe they just don't want to.

There was no break in play, I couldn't get away from who I was. There is no way out. God obviously didn't want me drinking or doing any drugs but what was his real reason for this?

Well, drink and drugs affect the memory, I couldn't have written this book without that. God wanted me to build my soul and to do both things. You need to have a working mind and a strong memory, not that I knew this back then. Was the reason things were going so badly because I'd ignored everything God had done for me? I knew there was a path that God wanted me to take. Maybe he just couldn't waste any more time with me always fucking up. Was this the time I'd have to walk life's path alone and unguided?

I know I've learnt from my mistakes and for the first time, I wouldn't be making those same mistakes again. Even though I only touched drugs and drink as a means to let off a little steam from time to time, I never touched them again. I stepped back in order to move forward. Unfortunately; I was going to have to hit a lot more rocks in the undercurrent before finding the next big wave.

After passing my exams to be a personal trainer and

nutritionist, Christina and I decided we wanted to emigrate to the USA. We sold our house in the hopes of everything moving along quite quickly. However, due to the incidents surrounding September 11th, Christina's qualifications as a midwife were not on the list of contributing professions that the USA was looking for, so we got refused entry. We found a house to rent that looked really good on the surface but after a while it turned out to be a breeding ground for lice and mites, mould, you name it. And we were tied into the contract so we couldn't even move out. And to add insult to injury, someone smashed into Christina's car within a week of us being there. I got into a battle with the boss at work and ended up getting suspended without pay. Then I was moved to work in Bolton during the investigation. When I finally returned, at the end of the year, I was under a five year suspended dismissal notice.

It wasn't over there either. I got a bad infection in my arm which lead to me nearly getting septicemia, I was training to compete at the time.

In summer 2006 Christina and I were just starting to see the light at the end of this dark tunnel and had decided to start planning for a family. Unfortunately, she suffered two miscarriages and wound up extremely depressed.

So yeah, I had a right fuckin' laugh in this particular couple of years, all off the back of a few arse holes and a couple of bad choices.

Now I could see the big picture. God had given me plenty of warning when it came to drugs and drink. He'd now kicked my arse from all angles. I think it was mainly about building and keeping my soul. Well I definitely got the message this time.

Chapter 9

Getting back, giving back

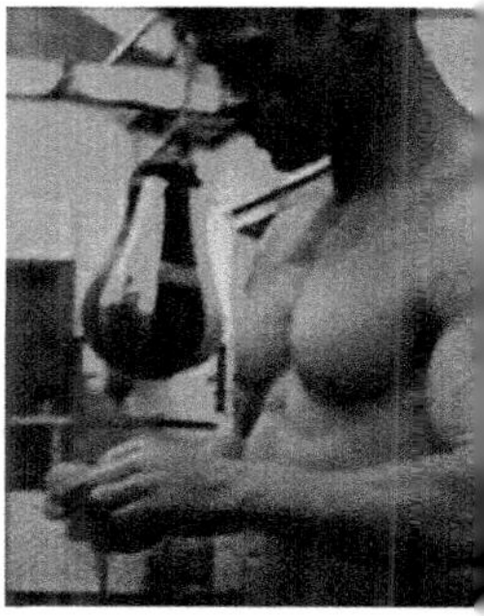

So 2004-2006 had its set-backs but like anything you have to the find the positives. Although my bodybuilding had been difficult, I managed to bag a couple of decent British titles and take my first positive step: competing at an international level. I moved from 9th in 2004, to placing in the final 6 in early 2006. On the surface all seemed well. I was well received around the gym, always the person to go to. The kids all thought a lot of me, like when running the youth club only the kids were in their late teens and early twenties this time. Another place where all seemed to be going well was back working the doors.

I started working the local, slightly more-classy, night club in my home town. By March 2004 I was enjoying the door life once more. However, due to past happenings I'd seemed to have lost a lot of my self-confidence.

I'd be working with a guy called JB. When we got to talking, it turned out we were going through a similar patch. He, too, had got himself injured, as well as having home life problems. He'd got off his face and had got into a few fights that, on a normal day, he would have won, but because he was under the influence, he hadn't performed at his best. His home life issues involved young kids and people saying he was a bad father, always off his face. None of us are perfect but it's always the voices, the side line undercurrent opinions that cause the most damage. JB was a good guy and a good father. He just blew off from time to time. It was good therapy for us both talking together; we saw each-other's problems through the same eyes.

Despite all of this, the confidence I once had just wasn't there. I hadn't hit a bag or done any fight classes for around two or three years and apart from the pissed up fights I seemingly lost, I hadn't had a fight since around 2001. When working at Young Bloods we were in it every week so after a while your confidence soared but it didn't take long before you started questioning your own abilities. I had a great reputation around the gym: the kids in there thought so highly of me it was untrue. There was a decision to be made: I could either bury my head and shy away in a bid to keep my reputation or I could man-up and become every bit of that person everyone thought I was. For me there was never any real choice. If things are meant to be, they are meant to be. This was definitely one of those times.

Omar's fighting emporium

In between weight sessions I'd started making my way into the bag room. It was a slow process to begin with. It was a little hard to get momentum and loosen up my arms and shoulders due to allowing myself to have become quite muscle bound. I was around fifteen stone, lean and very strong around this time.

A few weeks down the line I was starting to use my power quite well, coming through from the back foot for the big shots and the front foot for the hooks and upper cuts. There was a new TV show that had just come on called Contender, presented by Sly Stallone and Sugar Ray Leonard; two guys I'd always admired. It was about a group of boxers who faced different fitness challenges. At the end they fought each other in order to get to the next round. I found the boxers on the program, as well as the program itself, very inspirational. I started taping it every week, taking tips for when I was in the bag room. Then I got fixated by another guy named Joe Calzaghe, a world champion boxer from Wales, and started buying and taping all of his fights trying to learn more. I have always learned best and quickest when I am watching people who inspire me. A few months on and

I was moving pretty well; happy with my self-progression, starting to feel confident again, like I could actually do something if I wanted to.

One day, whilst training, this big Asian guy walked in. We'd always had the banter around the gym but still, I didn't know him all that well.

"Hey kid," he smiled. "I didn't realise you did a bit, you're pretty good. I thought you were just a big weight lifting carpet fitter. Didn't even realise your arms could move." We both started laughing. Then I watched him kick the crap out of one of the bags and realised he, too, had a decent talent as a Thai boxer.

After a couple of weeks, we started doing a bit together. I'd never done Thai boxing before but thought I'd be pretty good with the kicks. However, due to battering my legs in the gym all the time, I'd lost quite a lot of agility but I liked the head locks, the knees and how to block using my shins, as well as the foot work and the elbows.

A couple more weeks went by and more people started paying a little more interest. There were five of us, then ten, up to fourteen, then fifteen of us. It was a regular Wednesday night thing. The class started at six and sometimes finished at nine. I was also doing a more technical bout on Sunday mornings with a kid named Mark O'Beeb. On my days off from work I'd do some sparring and extensive body conditioning with a pal of mine named Baz Smart.

A few months down the line another kid turned up to the Wednesday class, a guy called Mikie Borg. The sessions reached a new climax.

By now the sparring was blood thirsty; open noses, smashed mirrors, mid sections had purple, yellow and blue bruising most weeks. We weren't even holding pads anymore; we were taking near enough full pelt shots to the legs, body and head. In a way it was kind of sadistic yet somehow still fun. Earlier on different people would attend the class and keep coming back, but now people coming in at this later stage would last a week at best.

The crew was immense, all bringing different styles to the

table. It was MMA but before MMA was known to most people as being a sport. I was good at take downs and the boxing but I excelled when it came to conditioning. The punishment I could endure at this point was something else but, like I've said, physical pain doesn't hold a candle to mental pain. Building myself physically would also lead me to good mental health and peace of mind. The ultimate goal.

At the start of the sessions was the warm up: sit ups, press ups, shuttle runs and shadow boxing. Omar would then have us all lying in a line on our backs before, literally, running over our stomachs. I'd shout some abuse at Omar as a means of fun. He'd try not to laugh. "It's like that then is it our kid?" He'd either jump up and down on my stomach doing the running drill or alternately it was 50 press-ups or squats. The mood was always positive and the sessions, however hard, were always fun.

My old pal Sean joined in with us on the first couple of months. A couple of guys I'd known a while, Mark Holland, Rob Lions and Pete Jones also did a bit. It was always the politest people who got the most stuck in. There were a lot of empty vessels not making much noise after these sessions. We'd beat the life out of each other for hours but by the end we always felt like we were on a high. Although the experience was barbaric, it was also euphoric. You actually felt loved up by the end of it.

Looking back, I guess this was a bit like self-harming; proving your worth to shut out the pain of feeling deflated or having no worth. Self-harmers are stereotyped for cutting their own skin, usually in a bid to hide a much darker pain that lies deeper within. It was the same scenario for me, only I handled it a little differently. I put myself amongst like-minded people, all taking and giving a kicking. My confidence was re-booted with the progress and acceptance of coming up through the class. It was about how much you could take and still be able to smile. The final outcome was new skills that would never leave, amongst people you'd never forget. The confidence I had needed to get back on that wave.

Like similar to working with Doza, all those many moons ago, this was never about who was besting who. We all had our strengths and our weaknesses. If you won a good bout you'd get a pat on the back. If you didn't do so well, you'd work on your flaws then get back at it. It was all in good faith though, I can't remember anyone ever getting offended. We had a great team.

As time went on, I started struggling to raise my game. I couldn't do the head kicks anymore and the Thai fighting style was so different to anything I'd done in the past. Omar could see my frustration, "Hey kid, you're not getting to grips with your timings. I'll tell you what: come with me every night for the next three or four months and I'll have you moving like a champion."

So every night after training weights I'd go and train with Omar for forty minutes to an hour. "1,1,2, 1,1,2. Stop dropping your guard. Come on kid I'm going to slap you harder every time you drop those hands." He stuck with me and I did get slapped, but all of a sudden everything came right. I was blocking using my shins, I could see everything coming, my low kick was strong and my stick and move was relaxed. My punches were still more like a boxer's but hey ho, here we go. I was through the matrix again.

Moving on

The club I worked at was a decent place. There wasn't much trouble but it did go off from time to time and when it did it did. All the young kids from the gym regularly attended, as well as the more mature and cooler end of the social spectrum. The door team was divided so I just tended to stick with the odd team player I knew to be reliable: JB, bullet proof Andy Marshal, John Turner and the head doorman, Andy McKenzie. I also had a tendency to just deal with things myself. Because of my reputation around the weight room, in the bag room and on the doors meant I got to run the door a lot more leisurely.

When I say this, I'm thinking back to my first door where

Sean Patrick just had 'that way with people' and how easy he made it all look. Well that's where I was now. I'd put in the time and been right with everyone whilst on the way up. The club I now worked was full of people from my past and present; I'd already earned the respect. When the odd fight did occur or someone I knew was in trouble, that's when I stepped up. At this stage I was very confident in my abilities and I could wrap someone up like a sandwich and put them out nicely or the alternative; if they mistook my kindness for weakness, they'd get a glimpse of the darker side that I was capable of, although that didn't happen too often. There is one fight though I can remember quite well...

There were a couple of young lads, I'd see and speak to them most weeks. They were related to a lad I'd hung out with at school, I think that's how we were introduced. The kids were always pleasant, however they looked to have been doing a little heart breaking. I'd had to sort out a few minor incidents on their behalf. Anyway, one week they must have really pissed on someone's chips. A girl had come into the club. She had a group of big aggressive looking guys trailing behind her. She's then pointing at my two young heart-breaking pals whilst sifting through the crowd. I spotted the ruckus and where it was heading "John, help. John! John!" The two looked proper up against it so I quickly headed over. I started trying to reason with the aggressors, putting myself in the middle of the argument. The big guy nearest looked me up and down, clearly pissed that I was stood in his way. I kind of knew what was coming... This wasn't going to end nicely.

The guy went for me but I quickly ragged him into a headlock and pounded a couple of shots into his face. He sounded in pain but he took it. As I was smashing him, he was slowly getting out of my headlock while punching me in the back of the head. I had to think quickly. As soon as he was nearly up, I let go of his head as it shot up. I then span around from my front foot and cracked him with a good upper cut, forcing him into the middle of the room. Everyone was looking on; I had seconds. I hit out a straight left, then a slight move to the side then square on the chin with a big right. The big guy dropped like a sack of potatoes. Game over. Everyone was stood watching with their drinks. They all cheered as the guy hit the deck. It was mad. I then caught JB from the corner of my eye: he'd just dropped the other guy. His confidence was back and he was glowing with integrity. The fight had been a belter. We grabbed a hand shake and a big hug. This fight had been the answer to our self-doubt. It felt good to have fought so publicly and to have won.

Back in the gym on Monday I was telling Omar about my 1,2 bonanza. He laughed but, honestly, he'd helped me out massively.

So my confidence was up, my training was going well and I was happy with how I looked. There was still the undercurrent ebbing away in my home life, but I was more focussing on what was going right. The most positive thing was how much time and help I was putting in with the kids at the gym.

There were under confident kids, and kids looking to better themselves as bodybuilders. There were kids who were worried and misguided on what they were taking in terms of muscle enhancement and kids who weren't quite ready for fight class but still wanted to learn a little. I made time for all of these people, one by one, quietly and without embarrassment. I'd been in every place they were at so I was happy to help raise their confidence. A lot of them went on to be fighters, bodybuilders, bouncers and power lifters. A little time and effort can build a great foundation. I've learnt this all too well. I was proud of the influence I was able to have.

There were some kids, though, that couldn't be helped. They were great kids and they'd always appreciate that you tried. But some kids had to feel the flames to know there's a fire.

Chapter 10

Big Rick

Going back in time to around 1984:
Our family had moved on to Dicky Bird council estate, or Dicky Bronx as it was also known. As I've already mentioned, the estate was a touch rough, according to Google it was one of the most deprived estates in the country. Here's just a few of its traits; couches in the street, smashed windows, open nappies thrown against fences, overgrown gardens, and the odd murder here and there.

Kids would play out late, sometimes waiting for their parents to be heading back from the pub so they could share a bag of chips as they rode home alongside them, on their bikes. There were a couple of dysfunctional mother fuckers, smack rats, glue bags and a paedo that was always knocking about, called Franky Wankey. Other than that, it was a friendly enough place!

I remember walking to the nearby shops once, when I spotted a group of kids throwing stones against the butty shop sign. The butty shop was called 'NIBBLES' but one of the 'B's had been broken away, making it look like a 'P'. The kids eventually knocked the bottom of the second 'B'. The kids as well as the passers-by were all laughing. The shop once known as 'NIBBLES' was now seen as 'NIPPLES'. I couldn't stop laughing either. This was Dicky Bird mentality at its finest.

On to the story

I was in my back garden when I spotted a couple of kids playing next door. There was a young kid called Wayne who immediately struck up conversation. With a big smile, he asked if I wanted to play so I hopped over the fence and away we went. Whilst playing I noticed his little brother, Dean, playing at the bottom end of the garden. He'd been digging holes then after a while we spot him running towards us with something in his hands: "Worm, worm," he's saying. Seconds later he was eating it whilst smiling, obviously chuffed about the catch of the day. Their Mum, Viv, came flying out." Dean, stop eating those bloody worms," she shouted, whilst trying to hide a smile. She then brought out some drinks for us all.

When I got home I told my Dad about the neighbours and how their Mum said she knew him. My Dad then starts telling about Viv's husband, Tony. According to my Dad, Tony was a well renowned scrapper. My Dad said he was huge with a wide neck and was known for being the toughest guy in Bury.

We went round to their house the next day to see Tony. True to what my Dad had said, he was massive. He had a big, dark ginger moustache and short ginger hair. He was carrying a fully grown Alsatian that he'd just brought back from the vets. She was called Kim and he carried her like a baby with absolute minimum effort. As he walked in I clocked the neck, it was like a bull terrier but wider! I'd had an expectation of how Tony should sound and act, like Bernard Hill's Yozza Hughes in Boys from the Black Stuff; the type or character who had a short temper and was always aggressive. As he started talking though it was plain to see he was anything but what I had imagined. He pulled sweets from his pocket and passed them to Dean, Wayne and me, then started to show us some videos.

I'd never seen a video or a video recorder before, not many people had them. He started showing me and my dad how it worked, like a big kid with a toy. Then he pulled a little bit more magic out of his hat; three black video tapes, the Rocky movies! "Watch these three films. Watch this one first," he said as he pointed to Rocky 3. "Then watch this one, then the second one." So we watched the films, all arse about face, in the order in which he thought was the best, to his least favourite. He said to my dad, "They star a guy called Sylpster Stallon. He's really good." He obviously meant Sylvester Stallone. He was so down to earth it was untrue. It was only when I saw him wipe a guy out at a do we had all gone to, that the stories became reality. Tony was a renowned tough nut and the hard man of Bury for around 10 years. To know him, though, he was just a really good guy.

Around 1991

I was at the gym in the foyer, where I regularly sat. I loved being around the gym, especially with the older members who always made the most time for me. I'd been talking to this older bloke for some time, he knew my Dad and was part of the Maudsley family. He was called Ted Oddie.

Later I was talking with my pal Big Lee, and guys named Walt Duckworth, Dave Holt, Clive Ashton and a few more characters from around the gym. Conversation moved onto Ted: apparently he'd also been the hard man of Bury back in his day, and was known as One Arrow because that's how many shots it took for him to knock a guy out. So I got to thinking that this must be Tony's dad, fighting must run in the family. To my surprise he turned out to be Viv's dad. It left me thinking that at least one kid from this family will turn out to be extraordinary at some point.

History lesson over: back to the story

I was under the squat rack at the gym, when two young kids walked in. One was shorter with dark hair and a smiley face. He was called Lee Layton and his nervous looking, tall and slender, curly ginger haired pal was named Rick, Rick Maudsley. "Hiya, you know my brother Wayne," he talked with his head dipped, barely making eye contact. "He said to speak to you, that you would help me, to get me into training." He was really shy but seemed nice, so instantly I wanted to help him and his little mate.

In the months that followed, Rick and Lee started to fill out and had developed a good sense of humour. After a while I started putting in a couple of workouts with Rick when Lee was working but it almost seemed like Lee had started to get jealous but only in a fun kind of way. He started calling me to Rick and calling Rick to me, hoping that we started having a go at each other. It didn't work though; we were onto his little scheme. So we started making "sssssssss" snake noises when he was in the gym training or when he tried to speak to us. He laughed but was none the, wiser. We carried it on for a while then changed tactics and blatantly started calling him Snake Boy. It didn't deter him though, he carried on with his little wind ups. He liked being the snake.

A few months later I ran into Wayne, who told me that Rick kept getting into trouble with people having a go at him and asked if I could keep an eye on him. I felt a little deflated. Rick was coming on a treat at the gym and was lots of fun to be around so I couldn't work out why everyone was giving him a hard time. Obviously my answer to Wayne was yes, I'd help.

Rick came out to the club one night when I was working. The poor kid stuck out like a sore thumb, looking very nervous. He was with a group of girls but it seemed more like they were looking out for him than anything else. Not long into the night I caught a few guys making a line for Rick. I stepped in to ward them off but they were really on one so we had to throw them out. It seemed really odd that both Rick's dad and granddad was such tough nuts but here was Rick, the most placid guy on the planet. Even his brother Wayne was a renowned scrapper, it seemed the family genes had skipped him? I started spending a lot of time with Rick to try and build his confidence and get him bigger and stronger. He was too nice a kid for this kind of thing to be happening to

After a while Rick and Lee seemed to disappear from the gym and no one seemed to know where they'd gone. A few months had passed when I spotted Lee on his own training.

I went over to speak, "Not seen you in a while pal."

He looked subdued "Have you heard about Rick?," he asked.

"No?"

"He's in prison." He went on to explain how Rick had put his fist through a Range Rover window, dragged the guy out of it, then battered him. Then he'd battered some other guys who'd had a go at his Mum. Then somehow, he'd got caught up in an armed robbery while he was still on the run from the other two incidents.

"What the fuck? His brother told me he was getting bullied and asked me to look out for him, and what about those girls who used to look out for him?"

Lee just looked at me like I was dense. "Those girls were with other guys; he'd been having a threesome with them. And Wayne wasn't worried about Rick getting bullied, he was trying to keep him out of trouble because he's a fucking nut."

"Ahh." The penny dropped. I'd inadvertently helped build this frightening 6'8 monster with fists as wide as my head, a neck like his Dad's and an underlying anger issues. Shit. I really didn't see this one coming.

A few years later Rick bounced out of prison, larger than life in both personality and build. He was around twenty-two stone and it took a few seconds just to scan his shoulder span. Most people do time and come out realising the error of their ways, wanting to make life changes and better their attitude or approach to life. Rick was talking about going back inside; he ate well, he trained well, he'd got stronger. He'd have put this prison ahead of any Butlins holiday camp of its time. Madness.

Back in the gym, Rick had freak-like strength. It was like he'd developed a super power or he'd been worked on in a lab like a Marvel character. He was going around making a lot of noise and bigging himself up: "I'll lift this. I'll lift that." He made sure half the gym was watching. It was ridiculous but the fucker lifted it. So the Ted Oddie, Tony Maudsley creation had arrived: twice the size, twice as dangerous, and also twice the fun. He wasn't creeping to me anymore. Instead, the banter was rife. He referred to me as the little dwarf. If I ever managed to beat him on anything it was only because I had little arms and didn't have to do much moving. He gave everyone shit but he loved the comebacks.

One day he was going on with himself, loving the sound of his own voice when I cut him short, "Rick there are thousands of skyscrapers everywhere. They are quickly put together, not very pleasing to look at and are easily forgotten. Then there's places like the Vatican, St Paul's Cathedral, The Kremlin: they aren't that massively built, but are hand crafted works of art and millions of people flock to see them every year. They are buildings you never forget." I was of course, referring to our different physiques. It actually came off even more smoothly as I was saying it.

"John, you're a cunt. I'll give you that one. That's fucking brilliant!" A big smile and a big hug. Great times.

Ricky was the renowned tough kid of Bury. With very little training he went on to become a UK MMA fighter. He went up against the best lad in the federation and was on the highest bill of the night. He managed to batter the lad for two rounds straight. It was only in the third round when he ran out of steam that the result was a draw. He was an exceptional kid and someone I'll never forget. His strong point wasn't how big, strong and tough he was though. Rick had that thing where in the gym, or anywhere, he could take the piss out of a full room and never offend anyone. He pushed buttons but always stepped back if he thought he'd hit a nerve.

People like myself and Big Rick, people who are proud but not too sure of themselves, we like to take the time to learn how to have fun without bringing people down. We do it in such a way that everyone gets a bit of stick but no one ever gets truly offended and everyone goes home laughing. Sure training was important, but the banter played a significant role too. It helped shape character and we usually ended up training better because of it.

You'd never see or hear of Rick on a downer. He wouldn't

let you. He wouldn't tell you about the shit lonely nights in the cells or how he felt in there, if it scared him sometimes. No, he turned everything into a comedy show. It's a coping mechanism; you want to get as far away from the bad stuff as possible. That is, unless you're craving sympathy. There's a certain image to uphold, a pride, an ego even. We battle our inmost thoughts. We deal with our deepest scars. And we do it alone. So when we've recovered all you will see is our smiles, our pride and the image of how our friends like to see us.

Rick has been the big fish of Bury around the gyms for some time now. I guess this was the passing of the baton. I was glad to have spent the time and had a little influence on such a big character. And we're still great friends today.

Chapter 11

From demons cometh the angels

As you know, 2005 wasn't really my year. I'd battled septicemia whilst going up to a contest, rented a house full of bugs and mites, got a five years suspended dismissal warning against me to do with a violent, aggressive act whilst at work. We were refused entry into the USA and our car had been written off while we slept. My relationship with Christina was struggling.

More time needed

After trying to get our relationship back on track, and moving house, myself and Christina decide to start a family. Although it seemed a little hasty, once we knew we had a child on the way, it really did seem to put the sunlight back into our relationship.

After much excitement, Christina and I went to our twelve-week scan to find our baby had no heartbeat and had died. The comparison between the magical feeling we felt as we were approaching the hospital versus what we felt when we left, I can't really put into words. I think a part of Christina died there and then.

A few months later, Christina got pregnant again but it was short lived. After three or four weeks the baby passed, like a pebble of blood, while we were at home. Christina shrieked as she held onto me. I knew, then, that she couldn't go through this again.

I tried to do right by Christina and stop the bid to start a family at this time. I genuinely cared for Christina and this was for her sake. The babies we'd lost didn't quite hold the same weight for me as they did for her though. There's something deeper for a woman; the attachment, the sense of duty and motherhood that is embedded since being a girl and playing with dolls. By 2007 I was losing Christina and I didn't even know it.

When I think of God at this time, this is when I suppose I could say, what the hell? What are you doing to me, God? The answer I have today makes up for this initial thought. Yes, I'd lost two babies but again, God has seen the bigger picture. It was me who wasn't ready. The pride, the obsession, the ego, that hadn't gone; not enough for me to be a good father. A child and this, selfish, bodybuilding was never going to work out well. That was the big picture. I just couldn't see it.

Away from God's green earth, we've found so called' progression: power lines, TV, riches and false personas. The world: a manmade illusion of how you are supposed to live your life. Since I was a kid I've had a pre-perceived image of heroism in the image of a bodybuilder. God knows the strength that comes from training protects others and feeding the mind with the correct nutrition is important for many reasons. However, the competitive side of things, the ego, the pride, the harshness of the diet and training all contribute to cutting off human senses. It doesn't really help anyone. Even the competitor himself faces a less than healthy danger.

The dedication and pride I had invested in bodybuilding was massive and at this time in my life it was ridiculous. I was in a vicious predicament. If I quit I'd never become the me I needed to be, for myself. But If I carried on I was going to lose the most important person in my life.

I competed, I went out with my friends, I didn't include my wife. If I was a real man I'd have been at home helping her through her trauma. Instead, it created more distance between us. Christina was hitting out. She had accused me of having an affair with a girl at work. She told me to break contact, but I didn't. It wasn't the girl that was the problem; I was the problem.

My mindset was saying: keep yourself happy, don't quit on your friends. I tried to get Christina out and about but it wasn't working. I didn't want to end up in a negative rut but I couldn't see things from her perspective. She'd lost two children but I couldn't see the fuckin' problem.

At this point whilst writing this book I don't have the answers to everything I should have done right but I'm hoping by the end, the answer will come to me. Like everything, there has to be a positive come from a negative. Everything somehow happens for a reason. Unfortunately, after many arguments and fights, Christina and I decided to part ways towards the end of 2007.

The year wasn't a complete write-off; I'd done some good things, mainly for myself. I'd won two back to back UK titles. I think this was possibly one of the only things keeping me afloat when my divorce was going through. I'd worked doing some night time security for the council and saved an old woman from a fire on the job, as well as putting out the fire. I think there was a little write-up in the local paper about it. I also worked with my old pal St Daz at a bar in Bury called Lilly's.

After splitting with Christina there was an instant lull of unpleasantness, a distinct distance between me and the world. I was looking for the wave. I'd throw myself into anything rather than go out and get wasted. This was the difference when I was older.

In hindsight, I probably should have stepped out of the bodybuilding arena for a longer period, but I didn't. I started dieting down for yet another show the following summer. My pride and ego wouldn't let divorce get in the way of what I thought I should be doing. In reality, what I should have been doing was making things right with my wife. I turned negative, plagued by my thoughts. The divorce, my loss, the pressure of the contests, the diet, and all the shit that goes with that started to take over. I was a raging mess; a black void of the person I once was, unrecognizable in manner.

2008 was a horrendous time. Losing my wife affected me in a way I never thought possible. There was no wave and I didn't see any undercurrent. If anything, I was the undercurrent. Even my friendships took a hit. A pal of mine, Johnny Walton had come to see me at the time. He described it to me later. "You weren't rude or nasty. I don't know what it was, I just knew you wanted me to fuck off."

I had three accounts of assault pending against me. I didn't actually start any of the fights, that's the truth, but I was quick to finish them. I lived mainly out of my car, some shitty places in-between, finally renting my pal's old house. I did get the odd offer of company here and there but, in all honesty, I wasn't fit to be around anyone, that much I knew. I didn't see much of my family. I didn't feel sorry for myself and wasn't on the verge of suicide. I was, plain and simple, angry, lost and soulless. I had a couple of violent outbursts at the gym and I was even horrid with the kids I normally helped out down there. If people wanted advice, I'd tell them not to bother me and I trained with a 'fuck off' attitude.

I smashed my car up 'accidentally on purpose'. I'd bought it from my pal Kenny Buckle whose reaction was, "What the fuck have you done to my car?". I explained the situation to him.

"You need to get it off the road pal." I was in a dark place. I didn't want help, I wasn't seeking it but my cousin, Phil Rose, just seem to step up from nowhere to act like my counsellor. I'd always looked up to Phil, possibly the only reason why I let him in.

The wave of Phil Rose: The angel of optimism

Phil Rose was one of very few people I know, who did in life exactly as he set out to do. As a kid he always dreamed of owning a Porsche and being a millionaire. Phil had also been through similar to what I was going through at this time.

There were also children in the equation but he worked it in well. When he saw the state I was in he made an instant effort to be there and kept making regular arrangements to meet up.

Phil had a straight forward attitude to problem solving. There was no name calling, no aggression just a job that needed to be done. I was at his house regularly. One night I didn't turn up; I hadn't wanted to talk to anyone. He appeared at my door, "Where were you? I waited for you." This was his way of letting me know he was there for me as long as I needed it but not to mess him around. Phil was the only float I had, the voice that could save me from the undercurrent. There was no one else that could get through to me. For me, there was nothing left to cling to, a definite sense of oblivion.

Phil was different to most people I knew; he wouldn't back down on anything he wanted to achieve. And he knew that I was exactly the same. He ignored the creature I was turning into, the psychopath inhabiting me at the time, and appealed to my better nature.

To relate life like riding a tide, I was riding a huge wave over a massive undercurrent. There were rocks and sharks below. The water was way too deep to resurface if I fell. Phil didn't tell me to come down from the wave because he knew there was no way down. Instead, he came up on the wave with me and guided me long enough until I was safely back on shore.

I can't be sure if Phil ever believed in a higher power but I know for a fact that he knew he had a path and on that path there were tests, failures, victories and lessons learned. Phil worked hard, was a good father and became successful. He made his dreams a reality.

God can see what you really want over what you think you want; the bigger picture. He also appreciates work ethic, honesty and doing things for the right reasons.

The Wave of Phil Rose

Originally, Phil had wanted to be a police officer but there weren't any vacancies at the time he was looking. He would never have been able to have the life he truly wanted if he'd been a police officer. While he was waiting for a vacancy to open up, he got a job as an office boy just to tide him over. God's plan for what Phil really wanted. Phil then gets enthusiastic as he realises his potential at the place he worked. Then his charisma, drive and willingness to get his head down, year in, year out, sent him straight to the top. He became a chartered accountant and then was made partner at the firm. Later, down the line, he left to set up his own business which he expanded to five national locations, becoming a high roller in the financial investment industry.

Even the job itself is positive. He sees businesses that are doing well, then he tells his clients where to invest their money. Obviously there will be set backs, but in general, he takes a company that wants investors, that makes the company more money, then his clients also make money by investing in a growing business at the right time, so it's a win, win for everyone, magic.

Phil started getting me out at the weekends knowing it was the most difficult time. He warned everyone not to let me drink though. He knew I was on a spiral; he also knew what a fuck up I was when I did drink. So although I wasn't ever tempted, he had taken away the temptation for if I ever was. I'd offered to drive at the weekends. I turn up to Phil's house and I'd spot his Porsche shined up on the driveway, then he chucks me the keys. "Because you've offered to drive I've said to the lads that we will sort out your meals and drinks. And if you want to borrow the car through the week just let me know and I'll have it ready for you." He knew I had little money. Phil never offered sympathy, or looked down on me in any way, he crafted everything really well. All I ever got from Phil Rose was optimism.

Phil was the man with everything, everything but the one thing that money can't buy: Love. He was a charmer with no shortage of women knocking on his door but he'd never met 'the one'.

Phil had seen me safely back to shore. Christina and I were briefly seeing each other when 2011 sprang a little surprise on us, the best accident to ever happen; our son. Phil was at the hospital after Michael was born. We chose him to be Michael's godfather. He was there every step of the way. Phil didn't want anything from me, it was a selfless act. Apart from buying him a really neat T-shirt at Christmas, which read: 'I love girls that love girls' there was very little else I could do for him. So if all that's good comes back to help, then where was Phil's thanks? How would God reward the man who had helped out one of his fallen disciples?

The gift

Phil was out one night with his pal Chris Yates. He'd seen a girl and had a plan. She was standing on the opposite side of the bar when Phil sent her a glass of wine and told Chris to tell her who it was from. He stood waiting with a cheese dick smile on his face. The girl's friend turned to Chris as he passed on his message, "Your mate's got no chance."

"You don't know my mate," Chris smiled.

The girl drank her wine only to find it wasn't wine, it was water. She laughed and they got to talking. And the rest was history.

Her name was Becky Walker, then later in 2017, Becky Rose. As I moved into fatherhood, Phil had found his soul mate, his gift from God.

The darker side of me: The dark angel

In my earlier memories of Ms Right and the aftermath that followed, it was my parents who were my guardian angels. I wonder if, even then, my mind or God himself began to wonder 'if I'm ever in this position again, what happens when I get to a point where asking my parents for help isn't an option anymore?' But I'd been in this position before, during the time that followed the break dance era, when I was fighting and not allowing myself to be a victim of bullying.

Being angry as a kid could cause some real problems in the future because you're not mentally prepared for how to deal with it. As you approach adolescence this is more complicated by the body starting to produce testosterone, which can act as a confidence booster or a catalyst to aggression. However, when it's used for its true purpose, it can be the key to rising up and facing the challenges that life throws our way. For some people, something else has to happen first before this natural defence side of testosterone will kick in. It could be the result of the stress our bodies have been under, oncoming dangers or just being backed into a corner. So how do we deal with our battles? I guess some people don't, they walk away or just take the brunt. Not for me though. If I'm in a jam or backed into a corner, there's a fear inside, that's me. Then there's a darkness of mind that instantly acts to protect. It's an impulse, one our bodies have learned through evolution and survival of the species. It's a lot stronger than the everyday you and it often acts without thought. It's the part of you that defends your soul, that preserves the good natured part of your spirit. It's a fire, a fire that doesn't back down. Its only goal is to protect you. Then it vanishes, allowing you to get back to who you are, when the job is done.

Some people are naturally aggressive. Some people can fight without breaking a sweat or getting mad at all. They are the lucky ones. I wasn't really one of them. The most passionate people, those with the biggest hearts, are the ones who usually have this fire or Dark Angel, as I call it.

Primal instinct is to kill or be killed. This is the law of the land; lions, insects, in fact most living creatures live by these rules every day, but in our own 'controlled', supposedly 'civilised' environment they lock you up and you become the bad guy regardless of the circumstances or outcome. God is part of the primal part of your mind; Jesus is humanity. We act with good will towards others in order to keep our primal instincts at bay.

So what happens when the demons won't go away? What happens when you can't get out of a rut? How do you keep the Dark Angel from taking over altogether, and how do you know that this angel won't be tempted by demons? What happens when you are no longer in control? What will God do then?

Back to 2008

My world at this point was a dark void, even with Phil Rose playing my counsellor. The void plagued my heart and my mind. In a fight my reaction was barbaric and without remorse. I was that fearless that fear itself didn't even cross my mind anymore. I could break up a fight on the doors with just my presence. My cold, derelict eyes and relentless eagerness for more darkness were all too evident. I was a dark, empty, soulless shell; the better part of me, well and truly hidden.

The miracle

In July 2008, I was driving back from yet another contest. It had been a rough trip, the plane had nearly crashed on the way and had made national headlines. And I was only good enough to get 6th place at the contest. My worries of what was coming next were alarming; what would I become? The only thing that had kept me on any sort of path was bodybuilding. How much more was I going to change? How dark was it going to have to get? My Dark Angel was working overtime. Meanwhile I didn't know who I was anymore or where the true me had gone.

The drive home was late and I was tired and agitated. I'd just got off the slip road from the services, after picking up a coffee, then running to a standstill within a sea of traffic. I sat there in the dark peering into the queue of lights, when I noticed drips of water bouncing off my T-shirt. Then I realised it was coming from my eyes. It wasn't tears, it was flowing and warm. It was as if God knew exactly where I was heading and had to intervene. It was like another baptism but in my own tears, in order to save my soul. Picture The Incredible Hulk turning back into Dr David Banner: that basically sums it up. The anger, the pain and the aggression was draining from me with every drop that flowed. People may say it was a wild panic attack or some kind of breakdown. Maybe it was. But I prefer to see it as God stepping in. It was the hand of God squeezing the callousness out of me and leaving behind the better part of me; the Jekyll to my Hyde. I was practically euphoric in the aftermath.

After the incident my Dark Angel seemed a lot less active. I became more placid, forgiving and less violently reactive. But this was merely consequence, not reason; my heart didn't work the same way it used to. The passionate person, the better side of me, the child that needed protecting had vastly disappeared. There was nothing much left for my Dark Angel to protect anymore.

I still got that sudden surge of upset, rage, emotion but it never escalated beyond a point. The ability to fall in love, the energised drive, even the cocky confidence, it just never rose to any kind of level, although I still had the pride of a thousand men when it came to setting my goals and rising up to challenges. It took a good few years for the old me to totally re-emerge.

I'm the angel now, no longer dark. As even though a lot of my feeling had been taken down, I yearned to help the open hearted. I didn't want what had happened to me to happen to them. I could also take a better route for my own problems, having a much wider perception on how to deal with things. In this way it has become a gift. I love seeing people happy, their heart on their sleeves. So I choose to use my gift well, a gift that may have saved my marriage if received earlier.

I've questioned myself many times on how close to hell I actually was and could a good soul truly turn to devilment? As the song suggests, I was on the wrong side of heaven and the righteous side of hell, yet I know that, deep down,

I'd always protect what's good, despite being laced with demons. Just like, my antithesis, the guy with his big smile and nice guy persona, possibly wanting to be better. If he's the devil inside, that will never change. You'll soon recognise each other and in the long run, you'll never stand side by side.

My Dark Angel still exists but its appearance is few and far between. My Dad is very much the same. He's nice guy Mick to some, but Mad Mick to others.

Chapter 12

The Three Stooges

August 2008

After the hand of god incident on the motorway, I was a new me. It was like I'd been set free from prison. For the first time in 12 months I had peace of mind, I wasn't back on the wave but I was safely back in the water and looking for a bit of fun. I was working for my good pal Big Tom. We were now in Bolton. I'd worked on and off for Tom during the previous year and even though he'd had to move me around due to temperament issues, he'd stuck with me. Of the three doors that I worked, I warmed to the big club the most. I wasn't sure why this was and the existing doormen there didn't seem to like me much. Tom seemed shocked that I wanted a permanent spot there but he got me a full time position over the weekends.

I heard there had been a meeting amongst the door staff. Tom had told the head man, Jimmy that I was going to be starting on a full time basis at the weekend. Jimmy wasn't happy. He wanted his own brand of Boltoners. "It goes off a lot in here. He doesn't look like someone who's going to get stuck in."

"Well, if there's anything I do know about John, it's that he will get stuck in. That's not a worry," was Tom's reply.

First night

When I arrived, Jimmy, Tommy and Billy were all stood there, The Three Stooges. Not one of them let on. "I'm just going to use the bathroom before I get started," I mentioned. As I walked away I could hear Tommy mimicking me in a stupid posh accent, "Oh, I'm just gowing to use the baarrrthroom." Jimmy was laughing. Then I heard Billy: "Why is he going in the men's?" As I came out, Jimmy was waiting, "Right I'll show you what you're doing." He walked me inside and we headed towards the side fire door. "This is where you stay. Don't let anyone in or out. Make sure the door stays closed, unless you have to throw someone out."

"I usually walk about and make sure everything's in check," I offered.

"Not anymore. You stay there." Then Jimmy walked off. The three stooges hung outside while I was stuck inside on my own.

The atmosphere was good and the place was bouncing as the night went on. I was still on my own unless the other doorman, Garry, who was floating around, joined me, but that was a job Jimmy didn't want me doing. Eventually a fight broke out and it was straight in with fists; these Boltoners don't fuck about. I'd hit a guy, then his mate had come at me, launching a bottle which I'd managed to duck. The other doormen had soon run in to help disperse the fight. As I'd turned I noticed that the glass, which was meant for me, had hit some other guy and had torn half his face off; a sight I'll never forget.

It was a messy scene when the ambulance and police arrived. None of the doormen asked me anything about the incident or even how I was. As soon as the drama was over, they all headed back outside. At 1 a.m. Jimmy came over, "Right you can go and work the front gate 'til close." Once I was reallocated, the other doormen went back inside or up into the courtyard and left me to it again. I'd gone from dealing with all the shit inside, where it was boiling hot, to freezing my arse off outside and dealing with all the pissheads leaving or trying to get back in. This went on for weeks.

Even though the place was a bit messy and dysfunctional I liked the atmosphere and always got talking to lots of the punters who were all of good character as well as a few of the girls. Some of the girls had asked The Three Stooges about me but Billy, the weirdest of the crew, had apparently told them all I was gay. I found it funny, even if I did think they were all a bunch of dicks. The women at that club were something else though, not backwards about coming forwards you might say. If a fight had broken out and I was clearing the space after the event they'd be grabbing at my bits and anything they could get their hands on. It was a pretty scary scene! However, it was the Bolton girls who, when push came to shove, would be my initial back up when it came to working the club.

At the end of one night I was working the gate, as usual. I'd been talking to some of the local girls. They hadn't liked me at first. They all seemed to have the same story; the nut-case ex who battered or raped them, they worked hard to support their kids but liked a drink at the weekend to blow off the cobwebs. They all smoked like chimneys, which isn't my thing, but the conversation was always fun. Considering their backgrounds, they were all seemingly good hearted and generally nice girls. Most of them looked quite nice but were just a little too rough around the edges for my liking.

On this particular night I'd been having a bit of trouble with a kid at the gate. He was being an arse about not getting into the club. I was trying to talk him down when he pushed me to one side. As he went past, I grabbed him. He went for me then grabbed me by the throat. We wrestled off the walls. Then I spun him out through the gates and on his arse. He was up on his feet but wasn't advancing. I could see he was a horrible kid though. "You are getting fucked up. I'm going but I'll be coming back and you'll be getting fucked up." As he left, I thought he probably wouldn't come back. I couldn't tell the other door staff that I might have needed back up; this is obviously what they wanted.

I stood for another couple of minutes, talking to the girl posse. They were asking if I was ok. I was, but I was a touch on edge. After a few more minutes I saw the lad coming back up the street with an entourage of five or six other lads. I was standing my ground at they started to get close. My first thought: I don't think I'll be winning this one. They were in my face. The kid pushed, I pushed back. His whole pack then came at me. I heard a crash of glasses and bottles coming from behind. Before I'd even managed to step forward the girl posse had come up in front of me, armed with broken glasses and bottles and were at the lads' throats "Get away from him."

"I'll fucking kill you if you come near him."

"I'll stab you in the fucking throat. Now fuck off."

The lads were gone seriously. The girls just laughed "I think we need another drink, girls."

"Stick with us love, you'll be alright."

So that was my end of night door team sorted then. What the Fuck!

It was another few weeks before I was in the firing line again. This time I'd gone in and Jimmy and Tommy were in my face saying I'd grassed on them to Tom. At the same time, weirdo Billy was at the back of my neck, sniffing me and chanting under his breath, "Gay boy, gay weight lifter." It was an odd situation. I knew what had happened but couldn't be bothered explaining it, "Say what you want, I don't give a fuck, but I haven't grassed on anyone." It started getting a bit heated, I think I was about to get lynched. Tom came over and managed to disperse the situation.

One of Tom's lads had worked with us the week before. He'd picked a fight with a punter and got filled in. I was the one who got the guy cut and had helped the lad. But Tom's mate had then seen his arse and gone crying to Tom. I didn't go into detail because I knew it wasn't going to make a difference, it was just the fact that they didn't want me there.

After a few more weeks the three stooges were still leaving me to it but I was proving my worth. I'd fought my corner and not backed down, even when I worked on my own. Tommy, the little boxer, had started hanging around a bit more. He didn't say much, in fact he usually just growled as he walked past, but he kind of smiled from time to time. If I'm trying to sum it up it was like that movie, An American Werewolf in London, the scene from the Slaughtered Lamb Inn. Jimmy was like the Brian Glover character and the other two were like the weirdos in the bar. It was that 'greater good', small village mentality. That's the only way I can really get it down on paper.

The next week started the same but there was a fight inside. It looked like a small affair at first but within seconds there were ten or eleven people involved. I was in the middle of everyone going at each other, hitting and getting hit myself. Someone belted me in the side of the knee and as I buckled someone punched my head against the metal pole which ran around the outside of the bar. I didn't lose my shit; my Dark Angel still wasn't there. I definitely felt this one. The whole side of my face was numb. I was frantic but still had my wits about me as I pushed the fight into the courtyard. I expected the cavalry to arrive once we got outside but there was no sign. The fight luckily took itself out of the gate and into the main street. Tommy and Jimmy walked in a few minutes later. "Where have you been? It's just fuckin' gone off." Once I had their attention I frantically told them I expected them to be there once I'd got outside. It turned out that the fuckers had gone looking at couches. My eyes were bloodshot and my face was practically purple. This wasn't the way I wanted to earn their respect but things did change after this.

Once I'd earned my stripes, The Three Stooges turned out to be good characters. I guess they were just sceptical of people letting them down. It certainly wasn't the open door appeal. Jimmy was a former pro wrestler and renowned hard man. He was somewhere in his fifties now. He still carried a lot of respect and was well known and liked in the area. He was always trying to be there for his family and often held on to the day's worries whilst talking through his problems. I think that working the door allowed him a bit of give and a chance to be a bit daft. Once he knew I wasn't going to let him down, he took me under his wing. We had the crack as well as the back-up. Billy was the weirdest, it took him around eight or nine months before he even spoke to me. When he did, he was surprisingly intelligent. We actually had a lot in common. He even came training with me on a few occasions. He had served in the army at a decent level and at some point was a competitive Thai boxer. Even when I'd got to know him though, he was still the strangest man I'd ever met and that still hasn't changed!

I'd say Tommy was somewhere in his early 50s. In his heyday, he was a British boxing champion. The story goes: He was on his way to becoming an Olympic athlete and possible world boxing champion. Around the same time, he's got into a fight with some bully from the estate he lived on. He'd ended up beating the guy in a street fight and although he didn't get sentenced, his fighting licence was revoked. He too liked the fun of working on the doors and even in his fifties he was still very reputable and could put young lads to shame when fighting them in the street. He was a likable rogue. He loved the wind ups and even though he'd always kept an eye out for me, his way of character building was always going to be tough love.

Once we were all on the same page, that's when the fun really began. Tommy started coming into the club a bit more. He'd come over and ask how I was, whilst glaring. Then he may lay on a little head butt. "Always be ready," he'd chuckle. If it wasn't a butt, it was a jab "Where were you". One week he butted me right on the nose.

"Right that's it," I started. He put his hands up to start a fight and before we knew it we were bare knuckle fighting in the middle of the club. I was annoyed but I knew it was only a bit of fun.

He was like Kato from Pink Panther most weeks, always ready to pounce. I got more black eyes, bust noses and ripped jackets from fighting with Tommy than I did in any of the door fights. I kind of looked forward to it though, even if I rarely won. He'd always come to me with his big roguish smile. Then pounce. It got to the point where punters thought it was real and Jimmy would get called in to sort it out. It drove him mad. "You two again," he'd laugh and walk back out. Once, I managed to put Tommy out onto the street and locked the door so he couldn't get back in. I heard a few of the doormen across the way ask if he was ok. "I've just been thrown out by Mr Muscles," he laughed. He had to use the other entrance to get back in. I thought it was pretty funny but I knew Tommy by now; I'd got the better of him so he was going to come back the week after like a fully loaded pistol.

Sure enough when next week came, I was stood in the kitchen making a coffee when the side door opened. Wham. We were seriously going at it, throwing each other about the kitchen. Pots, pans, knives, everything was flying everywhere. We had a lot of fun.

I struck up some good friendships with other doormen we worked with also. Their names were, Garry Mcainey, Phil Booth, Andy Conroy and Ian Harrison. There was also Bobby, the manager. The place was rammed, the atmosphere was upbeat, rough but fun. We worked well as a team and everyone got stuck in.

During a big fight nearing Christmas, Tommy's back gave out half way through. I had to step in and help him out. The fight was a blinder. Tommy grabbed me by the collar, shortly after the fight had ended. He was all pent up, his face in my face, "You're one of us now. You are one of us." The guy was nuts but this was Tommy's way of telling me that I had passed my initiation, that I had earned my stripes. Proving my worth on merit had always meant a lot to me. This had been a tidal wave of fun. 2009-2011 were two very positive years.

Chapter 13

The thanks for decisions made

So I'd lost a few things over the past couple of years; my wife, my friends, my home, my sanity and worst of all, a big chunk of my heart, part of my soul and the person I was. I was ready for the next wave, a tide to take me away from all the hurt and turn this plaguing time into a gift. I'd followed my own code of conduct on what was right and what was wrong so where were the good times I'd missed out on? These thoughts coming about at the time I'd just started working with the three stooges.

Throughout the full marriage break up, I had never tried getting back at Christina. I actually moved away from my home town in order for her to be able to carry on, so even if she moved on and met someone else, we wouldn't be in each-others' faces. I also never posted stuff over public media containing anything that would hurt her feelings. Nor did I call, or try to say anything in an underhanded way relating to our relationship. In fact, I actually posted some old pictures of us together because, although we weren't together anymore, I still had fond memories of her and didn't want them to be destroyed just because she wasn't mine anymore. It didn't mean I didn't love her anymore or wanted anything bad to happen to her, but neither did I want the beautiful memory of when we had loved each other to ever be forgotten.

Like I do with the dead, I remember them for being at their most alive and happiest. Once you start looking at everything as a loss, then, I reckon you could start yourself on a depressing spiral. I had toughened up, but I had also become much more forgiving; it kept me moving forward whilst putting aside the negative and keeping the good times alive. I was becoming the perfect me; absorbing the good while diminishing the bad.

Unfortunately, Christina and I weren't quite on the same page. She sent texts calling me a psycho. "How could you be so nasty? Why would you put up pictures of us on Facebook?" Apparently there were a few people who thought it was quite tasteless. Her friends were obviously part of the reckoning. Following this I got more hate texts, texts of wishing I was dead, wishing she had never met me, all good stuff! No matter how negative those texts were, I just saw them as upset. I reckoned she still thought a lot of me and in some ways I actually felt bad for her. I couldn't see the negative anymore; I had truly changed. My response was simply this: "If you hate me so much why have you kept my name now we are divorced?" After that, the texts stopped.

So the first gift I'd received was total forgiveness. I didn't need to belong to anyone; I didn't need to hurt someone I couldn't have or someone who didn't want me. I could be happy in the knowledge that I'd experienced love, and love at its best. I would always see this as a gift, knowing many won't have come close. It was a great gift.

Now the fun stuff

For the past 18 months or so I'd been mostly living out of my car. For a lot of people this could be considered a nightmare. Women, especially, like to come home to a clean house where everything is in its place. My clothes were hung up in my car. I'd shower at the gym and make my weekly feed at work. The contents of what I owned were a little here, a little there and a little everywhere but I still had a clean house. By this I mean my mind. Now that it was running free it was happy. It didn't matter if I had a slate roof over my head. I had a lust for life. I'd drive to a nice scenic spot at the night time with a small flask of coffee. I'd sit looking out over God's great garden whilst I swilled the heavenly brew. I may have been sat in a car but my mind was in the clouds, my dreams were a definitive. So when on my own, I was once again at my best.

My house wasn't mine anymore, I'd lost the love of my life and I couldn't really afford to live anywhere but what I did have, and all I really needed, was peace of mind. This gift far outweighed any other, especially at this point in time. I shouldn't have had it, but God had been kind. I had no bitterness towards anything or anyone. The world was a great place. It was time to find the next big wave.

Let the magic begin

I had got myself back into acting. It was a little Monday night set-up. I thought it might be my next step after finishing with competitive bodybuilding. Like with everything I've wanted to do though, I didn't just think about it, I got straight to it. I did one, maybe two sessions every week.

There was also a breakdance event coming to Manchester. A couple of the old school 'Rock Steady Crew' were going to be there, so again, I started to think 'what if?' I didn't want to miss a passing chance of dancing with those guys, so I started practicing two or three short sessions a week. I was buzzing over lots of things. It didn't matter if nothing came from it, it was just enough to believe that something could. It was the excitement that comes from working up to something that could be so spectacular. I had already, lived and visited that scene in my most vivid of thought' almost a childlike excitement.

The first big positive came whilst working the doors. Tom had hired two more lads to work the door. However, these two decided that they came as a team. Tom honoured this by getting them work on the club but not thinking, he'd over manned the venue. I'd been told that there was plenty of work but I'd have to go back to doing a little here and there for a while. I wasn't happy about it but I didn't make a problem out of it because it wasn't, at least, not compared to some of the things I'd been through.

When The Three Stooges got wind, they hit the roof and went to see Tom. I got told all about it from Bobby, the manager. They were bawling at him, saying I was the best lad they had and that I guarded that side door with my life. I honestly never saw it coming. Anyway, within a few weeks I was back on my door and we became, The Four Stooges.

This was the first time in over fifteen years in which anyone had fought to get me back working on their door. It was the ultimate compliment. And the last people I'd ever expect to have fought my corner were these guys. Sometimes the biggest hearts hide behind the roughest of exteriors. I'd gone with my gut rather than judging a book by its cover. Water had turned to wine, the rough seas into a great tide and another lesson learned.

After working the actors class, I got a walk on role in an independent movie. Not long after, I landed a decent role and got my name in the credits of a Brit flick starring Michelle Holmes (from Rita, Sue and Bob too) and Paul Hurstfield (from Dead Man's Shoes). The movie played in a few cinemas so I was lucky enough to see myself on the big screen which was another dream I'd always kept.

When it came to the breakin' event, I'd practiced all the way up to it not knowing if I'd get my chance, but I did. I danced with some of the original Rock Steady Crew at the after show party at the Lowry Centre in Manchester. It was a touch of luck. The lad I was with, Paul Morris, knew one of the dancers and got us the after show invite. This was the first time the old crew including Paul Burdacci (now Morris), Steve Rammy and Louise Burke had all got together since the 1980s.

At the end of 2009 I placed well at another international contest. The whole experience this time, including the lead up, was a much more pleasant experience. After the contest I went across to the USA and got involved in a bodybuilding photo shoot for the 75th anniversary of Muscle Beach. I trained at all the major gyms and was the muscle on Muscle Beach. I spent an hour after the photo shoot taking pictures with punters looking on and taking snap shots. These had all been such big dreams to me whilst growing up, it was all massively surreal. So you can understand my reason for praying!

While I was there I covered a thousand-mile road trip including Santa Cruz (used as San Carlos in the movie Lost Boys), San Francisco, San Jose, San Andreas, Californian beaches and open mountain ranges, Alcatraz island and the Golden Gate Bridge.

The trip landed me back on Venice Beach where I managed to live the dream of skating with a couple of my old pro idols from back in the day, Christian Hosoi and Jesse Martinez. I skated Dog Town's main bowl, goaded by the two pros, as well as the lesser known skate fans. I grind the top of the 12 feet dish; a dream I had kept since 1989. I'd brought my old skate board along just in case, and, just in case just happened to happen. It was absolutely magic. There had never been a bigger wave.

When getting back from the trip I managed to get my own place and without it costing me the earth. The location was Ramsbottom; rolling hills, steam railway, picturesque rivers and countryside, this was it. I had my Rocky picture on the wall, plenty of books and little all else. Perfect.

I'd been having an on, off relationship with my ex-wife. It was like, we couldn't be together but we couldn't be apart either type of thing. I was training up to a world bodybuilding competition, (this would be my final show), when Christina announced she was pregnant. We didn't get back together as such, but with a child on the way we knew there was a fresh new horizon for us both. We were together as parents, knowing that something special was about to happen, even if we weren't quite together as a couple.

I finished bodybuilding at the top winning my class on the world stage. I had trained for twenty-five years and had competed for twenty-one. I had managed to get the look I had always wanted and more importantly, however straining it may have been on my body, I had enjoyed the whole experience; getting it right, as well as the build-up. It wasn't quite the Arnold Schwarzenegger version of the Mr Universe. Still, it was of a great standard and it stretched me to being the best I could be, and more importantly, it brought me the closure I needed. It was a great way for me to be able to leave the sport. There was very little aggression involved this time, it was a very secluded yet beautiful affair.

So between 2009 and 2011 I'd skated Dog Town, danced with the Rock Steady Crew, seen myself on the big screen, I'd been the muscle on Muscle Beach, then reached my ultimate goal in bodybuilding. To tie it all off I got some modelling work for some sports companies and appeared on a few posters and catalogues advertising for them.

I was on the biggest wave I'd ever ridden. I was in control, the sky was blue. I was feeling blessed and very much at one with God. I hadn't turned to bitterness after my divorce. Even when I lost my shit for a while, I never started any of the events that had been the catalyst for sending me over the edge. I did get mad, but I never thought to get even. I worked through the problem, rather than fight with it. I fought through my own battles, my own rights and my own wrongs and I won. I think I'd done God proud this time.

Every answer to every want I've ever wished for, I'd received. There was never a clearer path to what was coming next, the next big wave; fatherhood. But unlike some of the waves I couldn't quite get to grips with: this one I wouldn't be messing up.

Chapter 14

Michael

For the first five or six months through Christina's pregnancy I wasn't really on board. I'd been training towards my contest. When we talked about it I was very matter of fact in explaining that I would be distant in the lead up to the show but I was explicit that I would be 100% on board when the show was over.

The day of the birth: 6th of April 2011

It was a seven am till seven pm day and all systems were go. I was with Christina the whole time, steady and progressive to start with then boom! Around 6pm we were having a few complications and Christina had been shot up with numerous injections. She was surrounded by her midwife friends so I knew there was something wrong when I see them whispering to one another. I was getting irritable watching her go into a coma like state. When she came to she was still in agony and all I wanted to do was yell for her friends to do something but I knew it wasn't going to help. A lot of the girls had actually come in on their days off just to oversee and help out at the birth. I had to help get Christina into stirrups as well as control the venflon machine. Christina was like a little girl, holding my hand and wanting it to be over as she tried to be brave. We were pushing again. I was still aware something was wrong but I was holding on, looking after Christina whilst praying inside that this baby came out in good health. "It's coming."

I promised myself that I wouldn't watch the birth from a lower angle but I was so anxious I couldn't help myself. I had to see.

This little purple looking Easter egg looking thing suddenly made its way out and into the doctor's arms. Still very close to the birthing area. I thought, "Why aren't they moving it?" Then I see where the problem lies. The umbilical cord was wrapped tight around the baby's neck. I was frantic. My baby had turned totally blue. Everyone was on board, a few panicky moments as the slow process of trying to dislodge the cord came into play. It was an anxious time as the cord finally broke. I was staring at this little blue alien like object, praying for it to start doing something.

Slowly but surely, blue had gone to purple and as purple started turning into pink, the little Easter egg-like shape opened up, arms and legs kicking. The scrike of a healthy, now normal coloured baby had emerged. It was absolutely mind blowing.

Our first talk

Unlike most births where the baby is usually placed with the mother, Christina was completely out of it so the baby was quickly cleaned up and handed straight to me. As I looked down at his little face, the bond we shared was instant and unquestionable. I couldn't believe what I was witnessing; the gift from God was selflessness. There wasn't a thing I wouldn't do for this little boy. If they were suddenly to say this kid needed my heart in order to survive, I would have given my life for this child to be able to live his, there and then. I still can't get over the feeling!

I don't know why, but I found the need to go over to the quieter side of the room, to be able to talk to my son, to introduce myself properly. His eyes were sky blue. They never veered once from looking up, despite not having full sight at this time. It was like he was waiting for me to speak, all content and quiet. There was an elevated radiance between us, I can't really explain it. "Hi Michael, you don't know me yet, but I'm the one who's going to take care of you. I'm the one who's going to keep you laughing. I'm the one who will always keep you safe. No matter where life takes you, I'm always going to be here for you. I'm your Dad." I talked a little more before finally lifting my head. As I looked up there was a room full of teary midwifes who had all been listening in. Christina had come round a little and in her eyes there was a sparkle. It told you this was a moment she had wanted for a long time. This was honestly the greatest, most honest moment of my life. I knew for the first time I was actually not such a selfish prick after all. I knew just the amount of effort I was going to put in, in keeping this little boy happy. It was so nourishing. I didn't think there was such a love. It was the tide of a new life.

We named him Michael John (MJ), after my Dad, and also after Christina and mine's favourite pop star, Michael Jackson.

That night

It was getting late and Michael was passed out on his little cot trolley. Christina was resting and I was starting to nod off on the floor next to Michael's trolley. Shortly after the midwife attended the room and asked if I wanted a bed for the night, but I didn't really want to leave Michael's side. Later on, around 4am I'd passed out on the floor and Christina woke me to tell me to go home and get some rest.

The next morning was sunny and I took it as a good sign. I decided to pick up a McDonald's breakfast and head straight to the hospital. When I arrived Christina was already awake with Michael in her arms. It was such a beautiful scene, her smile held a real sense of radiance. I had a couple of calls that morning, wishing us the best. A string of people attended the hospital including my sisters Debra and Karen, my cousin Phil, his daughter Charlie and my favourite auntie, Cynthia. It was like a high spirited game of pass the parcel. It was the sunshine that would make you instantly forget about the worries that had preceded the day earlier.

That night, and the weeks that followed

At night, and for the first couple of months, I spent a lot of time asleep at the side of Michael's Moses basket, or having him tucked under my arm on the settee, or lying on my chest. Myself and Christina weren't officially back together but for some reason it didn't seem to matter. We now realised that the petty hearsay of he said, she said, and having to know where the relationship was heading had as much meaning as it should have had in the first place. None of that stuff even mattered anymore. I didn't have to be at the house every night but after the gym, I found myself just wanting to be there. I'd always stay until Michael and Christina were asleep before enjoying the late night drive back to my apartment, always looking forward to the next day.

After a while, I was spending that much time down at the house that I eventually moved back in. It was more of a natural progression than anything else. This little miracle seemed to have made everything right.

Bonding

Bonding was never a problem. After around ten months Christina returned to work, regularly working nights up at the hospital, which basically left me looking after Michael the majority of the time. I'd get up with Michael whenever he woke during the night, which was at least three or four times. In the morning, I'd get him ready, sort his feed, wash and always put a little time aside just to chill or play. Then I'd drop him at early nursery, start my day at work, grab a workout, then head back to pick Michael up and the rest of the night was, food, getting him ready for bed, then mainly playing before passing out on the couch. Christina tended to work long days on Sundays also, so that became Dad and Doosh day, when we tended to go here, there and everywhere.

From 2011 into 2012 the tide of life became more like a

calm sea. I had faced the cruel undercurrent and was then able to rise up and ride the greatest tide of life. Now I'd hit a calm, a time to reflect, to appreciate where I was and who I had become. It was a nice time in life, where I had become the person I always wanted to be. I'd gone from athlete and door man, to a doting father. I was able to switch using the same passion and drive I had used to nurture my own gains. Now I was looking after the better part of me that had come from it all.

There are always certain questions in life we ask ourselves: What could I have done better? What would have made my life a little easier? These are questions that I never had to answer. Whatever had gone right or wrong in my life brought the very second in which my son was conceived. There is nothing about my son that I would want to change. He's everything I ever wanted. A moment later, a different event and my son would have been someone else; that's how I know I've done everything right. All the training throughout my life; physical perfection, vanity, pride, ego, whatever the reason was. I think that was mainly to help me be, the me I needed to be for him. It brought me peace of mind, helping me become a good father, to appreciate just what I now had. That in itself was a kind of re-birth. You always have to find the positive out of the negative in order to create the most positive future.

Moments

When they say it's the small things, they aren't wrong. I could be sitting with Michael and just him putting his hand around my finger was enough for me to feel totally tranquil. For a guy who always had to be moving, I figured that this little bundle of joy must be my new passion as everything else had very little meaning to me at this point.

One of my greatest memories was driving home one night. I remember glimpsing back at Michael sat in his little seat. He was looking right at me. I could tell in that moment that he knew that I was his Dad and that he was happy about it. A warmth and depth of feeling that can't be matched or properly described.

He was always excited. Nappy times I remember all too well. I was changing his nappy (something I thought I'd never be able to do), his eyes lit up and his legs started kicking, an excitable shake, fingers twitching, anxious and happy. In our earlier nappy sessions I pretended to fall to the wall as he kicked me so he did it even more, all excitable. So I carried on making the nappy change into a play session. Once he was clean we'd play even more. He remembers this and links nappy time to play time. I hated changing nappies to begin with but it became the time we had our best play. I might take forty minutes before we returned down stairs but I was in no rush, nothing should be a chore. I figured, even the dirty jobs should be greeted with fun, like every second I was with him had to count.

I loved his little squeaks but when they became his first belly laughs, well I must say there were few little tears of joy building in my eyes. My soul was back at its brightest. As I've mentioned before Michael would wake regularly through the night. The nights when he was quiet though, I'd end up checking on him anyway. I'd make sure his cover wasn't near his face and I'd wait to hear him breathe before I returned back to sleep. I'd be happy sometimes just watching him sleep. I got to savour a lot of little moments like that.

One of the best moments I remember was a Sunday morning. I could hear Michael rattling around his cot. That was the usual since he had learned to climb up the bars and to his feet. It was the norm for there to be little noises and for him to let us know he was ready to get up, but on this particular morning it was more than just a noise. "Daduur. Daduur. Daduuur. Daduuuuur." Michael had said his first words, testing the different tones. I reckon he was pretty happy with himself. I sat and listened gleefully, my soul once more aflame. It was just such a joyful moment. I'd realised that the best things in life were truly free.

I was there to witness his first steps on 11th June 2012, the same date as my sister's birthday. We were all on holiday in Cyprus for my sister's wedding at the time. I taught him how to dance at a Greek night in Greece the year later. I taught him to swim in Florida USA in 2017 then taught him how to ride his bike in 2018 near the river not far from where we live. We went from park to park during the summer time and over the years my son became my best friend. If there was anything I was naturally good at, it was being a kid and looking after other kids. Like everything, God had prepared me for all this many years earlier when I was growing up. I'd enjoyed my childhood massively and had helped to create and be a part of so many other kid's childhoods too.

Did I ever mess up? Of course I did. I was a cheeky kid, not a model student. I always tended to let Michael stay up a little late. Sometimes if I wanted to watch the odd horror film, I'd just presume that Michael was asleep but without really checking. I was pulled to one side by Michael's after school teacher, Mrs Webb. She asked me about him watching horror films. I d said he only watched the PG rated ones. "That's funny," she said "because he's been running around frightening all of the other children, shouting, "Hi; 'I'm Chucky, wanna playyy?" Ah, no comeback with this one. So there were still a few things that my lesser responsible side needed to address here and there.

There was also the time where Michael had told me he had got told off for kissing a girl in the school yard (he was five at the time). He said they'd had to be separated and put into separate classes. "Seriously, just for kissing?" I asked him. "How the hell did you kiss her?"

"Like that Dad," then pointed to James Bond on the TV. Ah, another one to leave alone then. The fact that I laugh at some stuff some parents may frown upon probably doesn't help my cause. Like when he tells me about girls he's chasing at school and how he's working on winning them over. Perhaps I shouldn't laugh but to me, this is growing up, having fun, falling in love and breaking a few rules all part of it.

I like to engage more than I discipline and Michael is always complimented on his good manners and caring nature, which is the most important asset to any person.

I think myself and Christina put so much in, as we know that sooner or later this will all end. This is my gift. I see what's coming next so I really try and pursue what's happening now to its limits. The good part, Michael is very similar to me in the fact he's enjoying where he is, so is in no rush to get to the next chapter in his life. He's all for staying the child, being loved and happy. We are all working hard to keep what we have. This is the wave of no boundaries. If everything else in life is on a downer I won't let his wave be harmed.

There are some days when I pick Michael up from school and see him in the playground playing. I remember once driving up to school and pulling into one of the parking spots. I saw Michael but he hadn't seen me yet. He was just spinning around, arms out, head towards the sky on the sunny day. When he'd finished spinning, he laughed to himself because he'd made himself dizzy. He then fell over a few times, laughing; just him and God doing their thing. It was so simple yet so amazing.

I've slipped forward a few more years in my eagerness to discuss Michael, so I'll just back up a touch:

2011 was a fantastic year. I witnessed the birth of my son and was working on getting my relationship back on track. I did some modelling for a sportswear campaign and I'd started a new martial arts class, Kempo Jujitsu. I was back with my old pal Sean Joyce and another pal named Anthony Hall. I was smashing it about four or five times a week, mainly training with the black belts in the class as well as our sensei Alan Wolfenden. I was still enjoying the gym also.

Chapter 15

The Wild Bunch:

The final brotherhood

The only thing that didn't seem to be going right throughout this year was working the doors. The place I had loved for the past three or four years had now lost its appeal and a lot of things were changing.

By the end of 2011, largely due to the recession, people weren't going out as often or their nights out were starting later and they were pre-drinking more at home. The pubs and clubs were emptier longer which meant less need for staff. We went from nine door staff to six, then six to four and Big Andy just came across from over the road to help us at the end of the night.

The change in tide

It had gone off in the club and I'd had to run in on my own. It had ended up getting very messy. I'd taken a hammering. Jimmy returned once the fight had dispersed. He looked flummoxed, "John stop getting stuck in. We haven't got the manpower anymore to be able to get to you in time. Fuck 'em, let 'em fight. Just drag 'em out when they've done." He seemed upset having to use his own words against his beliefs, a sinking ship feel to his persona. Billy and Gary had already adopted that attitude but it was short lived and they lost their jobs because of it. In the end, after many a disagreement with the bar owner, even Jimmy and Tommy finally got sifted out.

The new punters were not-rights but the bar needed their money. We started much later and to add insult to injury, we finished much later too. The atmosphere and the character of the place had been stripped to the bare minimum. At the same time, Christina was back at work, so no matter what type of night I'd had or what time I got in, I'd have to be up and ready with Michael the next day. That meant sometimes getting in at four and waking at six, best smile on and away we go. It was all getting too difficult. Tom asked me and Andy to take over as head men, to run the club and the two neighbouring pubs he ran. It was a compliment, but with Tommy, Billy and Jimmy all sticking their necks out for me, it didn't seem right. I decided it was time to leave while I still had a lot of good memories of the place.

I'd only been out of work for a week between Christmas and New Year, when I ran into a lad I knew whilst in town; Ryan Wallwork. I had known him from the gym and like so many others, had helped him a little with his training when he'd started out as a young lad. Like a lot of the lads who had come on the gym scene in the mid 2007-2008 period, he had gone on to work the doors. Ryan was now head door man at the Four Barrels Inn in Bury.

We got talking and I told him about calling it a day in Bolton. Then he mentions that they need someone at his place as one of the lads had been suspended. He said it would only be for a month on Friday and Saturday nights. I started thinking: The rates of pay were good, the place was local and I knew most the lads I'd be working with. Once Ryan saw my eye brows start to twitch he was on a rampage trying to sell me the gig. I thought, "If I do two nights a week for a month, then I can take a month off to decide what I'm going to do next." I knew the place was never overly crammed and figured it probably closed around midnight so would be able to have more of a day with Michael and the extra cash would always come in handy. So I agreed. The wave again was keeping me in the loop, like this is my calling, working the only job or hobby that I'd always been called to do and been seen to be good at.

When I arrived at the venue on my first Saturday night I was pretty stunned to find that they had six door staff running the place. As far as I knew the place didn't get that busy and it wasn't of any great size. I couldn't have been more wrong.

This was what I had missed: The two clubs that ran up the precinct had closed down. The pubs for all the mad heads and the young not-rights had also closed down. All the other pubs in town were only licensed 'til midnight or 1am. The Barrels was the only bar in town that had a 3.am licence. So that basically meant, this was where the young and old, the good, the bad and the sometimes very ugly would venture to come the end of the night. So yeah, it got busy, we also got every crowd from every walk of life.

So the line-up of doormen were all early to late twenties with most quite new to the game. Confident enough to want to get stuck in but not knowledgeable enough to know how to run a door. The initial line-up consisted of, me, my then training partner, Phil Vyas, Lee Smith, George Lindsey, Adam Walton and a few helping hands, Woody, JP and Sam. Then there was Ryan, the youngest of the crowd, the wildest and madly enough, the head door man.

The door was quite gung-ho from the get go. It wasn't as brutal as the Bolton doors but when the pub was pent up, you aren't going to be relaxed while working there. At the end of the first night a kick off occurred. Being the most experienced, I saw the trouble as it emerged. I ran in and grabbed the aggressor out of the fight but then the whole crew were over my shoulder like wolves wanting a taste of the flesh. I got more smashed by my own doormen than from the incident. Wild punches and overly gallant behaviour, I could sense there was a lot of energy wanting to let loose.

At the end of the same night a guy came at me out of nowhere. I brought him down with a quick rising forearm. All the doormen and this rough looking tattooed kid named Woody were smiling, "Go on John boy," Woody yelled. I wasn't sure at the time how he knew my name; it was another new venture for me but everything would soon be explained.

At every club or pub I had worked I'd had to earn my stripes, so to speak. It was never, "Here's John, this guy's good." It had always been quite the opposite; I'd had to get my head down and prove my worth every time. I always walked in the rookie and left being recognised as being a good lad. But this time it was different.

Everyone had known me from working the doors since way back when. Most of the young lads working the doors now were the ones I had helped out in their earlier, less confident days. When Silver's Gym had been in its heyday, I was the one running the martial arts class, lifting the weights, winning all the bodybuilding shows. I was the one involved in a lot of the big fights whilst working the clubs these kids were at when they were younger. I often helped them out of trouble. I didn't really know just how well known and well regarded I was. This was the first time it was becoming apparent.

When life imitates art

As a kid, I never gravitated to door work. However myself and my good pal, Sean Joyce, must have gone and seen the movie Road House around five or six times as kids in the mid-eighties. The main character Dalton, played by Patrick Swayze, was the cooler and better negotiating part of the door team. He had a good reputation for cleaning up the doors on the rough clubs. When people saw him for the first time they looked him up and down then came out with the statement, "I thought you'd be bigger."

I guess that was what it was like. I wasn't the head man but Ryan, who was, liked me running the show. He had me on every shift because he liked how I worked. The other guys I worked with also had a certain respect for how I did things. Everyone was standing around, not really knowing the ropes then the next minute everyone seemed on the ball, vigilante and wanting to be the best version of what they could be as doormen. They'd gone from messing about to being at their posts, I never veered from mine, I was always looking on. I think it was Ryan that took my lead, then everyone else just seemed to follow suit. Once established, we had a strong team. A bunch of good hearted nutters is the only real way I can describe it.

At the end of January 2012 a young lad approached me at the start of the night. He had blond hair and intense blue eyes and reminded me of a young Rutger Hauer (who had stared in the original Hitcher). "Hi, are you John? I've heard a lot about you." I looked at him, not quite sure where he was going with this. "I'm John Bakewell, the guy you took over from." John was coming back after his month's suspension. He looked me up and down, "I don't know why, but I thought you'd be bigger." And so it begins.

John was a reputable Thai boxer at the time. I think he'd had about eight or nine fights and had won them all. His brother, Andrew Bakewell, was also a top notch fighter and British bare knuckle champion so I think fighting must have been in their genes. John was known as Angry John due to his fearsome temper, but underneath he was a good kid and whilst working together, we were like a tag team.

I was initially seen as the character Dalton, but as time went by I was more like Dad. Everyone liked the way I did the job. I was pragmatic in my own circumstances, usually calming situations really well, but when my crew of young gung-ho doormen picked their fights, I was also in there, backing their bad decisions (in more than hands on way). The lads were quick to come to me with their problems but tried to hide what was going on behind the scenes. Ryan was the worst. His transformation from what I had seen in the gym to how he was on the door was a world apart. The amount of people who he knocked out for little and next to no reason was mind blowing. I think he liked me being there, I actually think he wanted some guidance, someone to channel him in a better direction. The team was rife with drugs, drink, ego and close competitive rivalry, which initially wasn't too noticeable but as time went on started to show more.

On the first night I worked with John Bakewell an incident occurred. There were three lads being shitty with a few of the door staff. I knew the outcome so as I always did, I tried to appeal to the lads better nature to try and get them out of what was coming next. After talking with the lads a while, they'd accepted that they weren't getting back into the venue and were about to set off on their way. As they turned to walk away I heard the biggest of the three, "Now we can't get back in, I reckon we should go and scratch a few of the cars up in the car park." They knew it was the car park that the doormen used. They persisted to walk, key in hand, to the side where all our cars were parked.

These lads had made me look the fool by trying to protect them. I was angrier than anyone now. Lee was the first to address the situation, "Fuckin' wankers are trying to scratch our cars." He was straight in. Lee threw a punch but missed as the lad got out of the way and Lee fell through the side gate. I saw the lad and put him down. I was that angry that he had taken the piss out of my kindness, that I decided to rattle his head off the gates a few more times. I was fuming. As I turned, another lad was close. Bang; a drop kick then a steady right. The lad was wiped out on the floor. At the same time the last lad was coming at me from the side. I'd not seen him. John Bakewell swooped in like a falcon; bang, bang, bang, speedy kicks and body blows. All three guys wiped out. Myself and John had our first moment, it was the start of a beautiful yet very violent friendship.

There were many fights, everyone at the helm. We even had trouble with our own friends and lads who lived on my post round or who went to the same gym as us. This was the problem working your own town, you were always going to be around the people you have problems with. If you do the job properly and fairly though, most accept what you've had to do and are willing to swallow a little personal pride here and there.

I was also pretty good at getting my, not so agreeable, counterparts out of sticky situations. There was many a morning after, that I was tapping on doors trying to sort through an aftermath, with my friend's health and interests at heart.

I always enjoyed the start of working nights. I'd go in the back and sort out a coffee, referring to them as Bad Boys; a strong thick black coffee to raise the senses. Within weeks everyone was on it. All the lads liked helping out with the coffees, the start of the night ritual. We'd stand watching day turn to night. This was where most of the conversation took place, where we built our initial bonds. John and Ryan were the ones I spoke to the most early on. Then after all the fun and frolics the evening brought, the last song of the night was always Mr Bo Jangles. Woody, the tattooed kid, loved the track.

I was pretty confident in my abilities around this time and liked how calmly I dealt with everything. It was the best of both worlds for me; my fighting ability and how fairly I addressed each situation. The guy who ran the bar was also happy with my work. He had told my cousin Andy that since I had been there I had helped to clean the place up massively. In all honesty, though, there was still a lot of work to do but I figured as long as I was fit and healthy and my home life was good, nothing could go wrong. Unfortunately, my health and my home life were going to take a turn for the worst.

The work situation

I had been on the post for around nineteen years and had always loved the job and knew everyone on the round.

After around six years of being on this particular round, there was a big shake up in the work place. For me, and most others, rounds were being changed and made into much bigger routes. The length of the routes had been massively mistimed and we were out for up to six hours some days. There were no place to use toilets and no time to go even if there were.

It didn't take long for my stomach, legs and arms to start cramping. I was losing more than a normal amount of weight and after a few months, me and my working partner Col

Jones went off sick. Myself, Colin and a guy named Tony were all at the hospital with blood disorders and internal problems.

When getting back to work I was still on full rounds but on my own this time. Fortunately, there were toilets accessible so for the time being I had solved the problem. It wasn't an overall fix though. I was visibly slimmer, I felt weaker and if overly exerted I would cramp up. No one could really tell me what the problem was, doctors just mentioned that my kidneys may have been affected by the dehydration. I was steadily improving but whilst working an active door I still saw this as a weakness, both in size and strength.

The holiday situation

In June 2012 I was still off work recovering but I was training and had gained size. I was looking and feeling pretty healthy.

Without going into too much detail, the whole family had gone on holiday to celebrate my sister's wedding. I had shouted at a kid for knocking my 14-month old son over. Michael had smashed his head on a glass window and a metal chair. Half the family fell out with me over the incident. There were two more family fallouts shortly after (which I wasn't part of) and by the end of the holiday no one was speaking.

Back home

Christina was working most nights as well as long days on Sundays. Deb was out most weeks and the rest of the family wanted nothing to do with me. I was up with Michael every morning. I'd drop him off at nursery, work all day, train, pick him up and look after him most nights. I worked the club Friday and Saturday nights. Sunday, I was up at whatever time Michael woke. We'd play, go to various parks. When he slept, I slept. Whilst working the club I was hiding a kidney disorder where everyone thought I was immortal. The door team was the only family I knew, the only place that felt like home and my only real sense of belonging.

The arrest

A couple of weeks after the holiday, I was back at work and back on the door. I had a lot on my mind but working the Friday and Saturday nights with the lads took me away from my home-life and illness worries.

The team was at its best. There were many fights but very few a loss, good comradery and a band of brothers in full flight. The summer nights were lasting longer, the atmosphere was great and The Four Barrels was definitely the place to be. It had that, almost celebrity door team feel to it; an adrenaline that everyone wants to be a part of.

The fights usually started inside then broke out onto the main street where the punters had their cigs and talked to one another. It was where everyone enjoyed the fights between the door staff and the riffraff.

One night in early August, a group of about 13 thickly set lads came strolling into the bar. I think they had just come from a nearby MMA show. Most of them wandered over to the dance floor, but a few of the older ones stayed back leering at Ryan and Lee. None of us really wanted any trouble from this particular crowd.

John had told me what had been going on so I came into the venue then headed towards Lee and Ryan. The lads were from Bolton. One asked if we were the ones who would throw them out if they made any trouble. I politely answered, "We are the ones who will try." The same guy then tried my patience a few more times but I had him in knots. I basically killed him with kindness.

We got talking about Bolton and I told him where I last worked. He asked if I knew Big Andy and after I'd said I'd worked with him for around five year's we then got to talking about what a hard bastard he was, then the conversation drifted on to his boxing career. The situation was dispersed and boxed off nicely. They stuck around for a bit longer before going on their way.

Not long after, a ruckus started up. I saw Little Tommy from behind the bar. He was frantically motioning for me to go over. John and I were first on the scene. When we arrived all we could see were a couple of big built girls hanging over the bar trying to serve themselves. They weren't happy with the drinks they'd been given; it wasn't what they'd asked for apparently so they thought they'd help themselves. We moved them away from the bar but it was obvious that they weren't going quietly. While they were arguing I whispered in John's ear, "Whatever you do, do not touch them." As we guided them away from the bar, I made it clear to the girls that they wouldn't be getting served by the bar staff and they wouldn't be getting another drink. We slowly started to guide them out.

I looked towards the door. John was only a few feet away. I caught his face. He had the Bakewell angry stare. He was about to blow. He managed to hang on for a couple of seconds but when I looked back, him and the girl were going at it. He'd picked her up to get her outside as she brutally laid into him. She was going hell for leather by the time he got her outside. I stepped in to help but as I pulled her back she fell backwards onto the cobbled street. It soon became apparent that these two girls were out with the big lads from the MMA show.

I didn't see anything, I just felt it. One lad had side winded me and was laying into me. The girl on the cobbles was up on her feet and smashing her stiletto shoe into my head.

Everything was happening too fast. I was very aware that I was getting a beating but saw an opportunity to grab the lad by his throat. He was going for it so I knew I couldn't waste a punch. "Think John, think."

I stepped back quickly and hit out with a perfectly straight jab. It landed. The lad was shaken but still upright. I needed the same line, just harder. I stepped out of my block position and thrust a speedy, powerful jab landing in exactly the same spot. The lad's head spun around, legs went from under him, K.O'd on the cobbled street. I looked around to find the whole door team kicking arse. They had their hands full but they were winning. I got involved to help with the clean-up.

The fight came to a standstill as the lads sifted into the large audience of onlookers outside the pub. I got the team back on the door then started dispersing the crowd. As I walked through the crowd telling people to go back inside or move on, I passed some of the lads we'd just been fighting with. I told them to call it a night and be on their way. Some pent up anger was still in flow but they seemed to be stepping away from the situation.

As I carried on through the crowd I see another of the big lads, this big stretch arm strong looking mother fucker. He glares at me.

"Come on pal, let's call it a night."

His glare intensified, "You what? You little fuck. What're you going to do?"

I looked him up and down; he was massive. The side of my face was still feeling paralysed from when I'd first been punched. The back of my head was hot and itchy where the girl had stuck her heel into my skull. I wasn't giving this guy the benefit of the doubt. Fear mixed with aggression had brought my Dark Angel back to life.

"Fuck this," I thought "I'm not taking another beating." The rage, fear and adrenaline luckily took over. Abruptly, I started smashing him up. I don't think he was expecting it. He was already in a guard position. I couldn't stop and the guy was in total defence mode. After a few seconds I was in full flow. I'd blown.

Out of nowhere I felt hands grabbing on to me, trying to pull me back. I assumed it was his crew so I lunged forward and flipped one over my shoulder and kicked one in the leg. I was still going at the big guy even as I was being restrained. I broke forward again, elbowing someone in the face. Arms started appearing everywhere. They hauled me up in the air and quickly dropped me to waist height. A group of hands, dragging my wrists together, all wearing black jackets: something wasn't right.

It was the police. All the arms, all the hands; I hadn't seen them. "You're under arrest." I was cuffed and dropped on my back onto the cobbled street. I could see the troublesome girl. She'd slipped in through the police and the crowd.

"See how you like it," she glared at me. She lifted her foot in an attempt to stamp on my face. Luckily John had seen and swooped in behind her to drag her away. He looked over reassuringly, "I've got you, pal."

I was taken away and locked up for the evening. I'd seen this before, but not for a good while. In all honesty, I felt a little embarrassed. I was gutted I missed the celebrations with the door lads at the end of the night after that fight. I was also worried about the grilling I'd get from Christina when I got home. One small consolation was that I knew she wasn't working so at least Michael was taken care of. I sat awake for most the night, proper pissed off, shouting and bawling on either side of the cell.

When they finally let me out of my cell the morning after, I got taken to the front desk to tell my side of the story. I was polite, trying to show I wasn't a thug. The story I had to tell was the truth so I had no reason to feel bad. The fact of the matter was, though, I'd assaulted five police officers.

The officer behind the desk turned out to be a good guy. He could see my predicament. He said my story checked out and that all the others involved had carried on with the police after I had been taken away. Most of them were in the cells sleeping it off. However, the police had to deal with how violent and aggressive I had been towards them and worst case scenario was that I'd be inside for two days. If the police I'd assaulted decided to press charges, then I could face up to three years behind bars.

When the interview was over the officer told the guard not to take me back to my cell. He explained that I might have to go back later depending on the outcome but he could clearly see that I wasn't a criminal and that the situation had just, unfortunately for me, got out of hand.

I sat for ages at the front desk area, hearing the phone ring and various conversations but one was unmistakable. Christina had managed to get through and was in battle mode. I could hear her chanting away to my officer friend. "You can't keep my husband locked up. We are decent people. Why don't you try catching real criminals? I'm in the medical profession and my family are of a good sort."

"For fuck sake," I mumbled to myself, head in hands. I heard the phone click down and looked up at the officer with an embarrassed smile. "Sometimes I can't tell if she's my mum or my wife. Sorry about that." He just laughed.

After another hour or so, a guy approached the officer and they started quietly talking. Minutes later the officer called me over and took me to one side. "None of the officers want to press charges. You really don't know how lucky you've been. Everyone's checked footage and your story accurately corresponds with what you've said. I can't ignore the violence and aggression though. Plus, I now have two officers off sick because of you."

I received a £200 fine and a year's suspended sentence. I couldn't believe it. I felt like dancing.

I signed the agreement and release forms and got on my way. I walked out of the building completely dehydrated and washed out, my legs were tight and forcing a limp. As I got to the foyer I recognised a few faces in front of the police station; the lads from last night. Quickly I hid the limp. I left the building looking confident and unscathed.

All I could think about as I wandered home was the bollocking I was about to get off the Mrs. As I walked into the house, all eyes were on me. Christina peered up from her seat but Michael broke the tension. His legs were kicking and his eyes were bright; excited to see his Dad. I picked him up and we started to play with the Lego. Christina still hadn't said anything. I figured she'd be mad.

When I'd finished playing with Michael she looked across at me. It wasn't the glare I was expecting, instead, I could only see the young open hearted girl I fell in love with all those years ago. I'd not seen her this upset in a while. Before she gave me a long speech about responsibility; she whirled up to me like a scared child. She was shaking as I held her and tears started to appear. She became inconsolable. All the worries of me not coming home from the night before had taken over. I didn't see this coming.

I hadn't considered us as a couple since before Michael was born. I still wasn't quite sure if we were actually together or not. It was clear at this moment though that she was still the same girl she always was, still as much in love with me as she had always been.

For me words mean little; people break their promises all the time but actions like this can't be faked. It was all very real.

I hate to see people cry but knowing Christina still cared for me was worth the night in the cells. Like they say, God moves in mysterious ways.

I spent the rest of the day with my family then later popped into The Four Barrels to see what had been said. All the lads were there and this was the first time my wife had met them. Ryan and Lee had freshly shaven heads. JP had a black eye and Woody had more ink on his face than today's newspaper. They all sat swilling beer in the middle of the afternoon. "Ey John boy," I heard as we walked in. Christina's face was a picture.

Back on the door

The following Friday night I walked in to the DJ playing Return of the Mack.

"John your song's on," Lee shouted. John then stepped in. "Fight fire with fire in it John."

"You fight fire with water you dick head" I replied. We all laughed.

From that day forth, if I was ever trying to tell the door staff to keep their calm, there was an ongoing joke: "What, like you did when you got arrested?" Adam particularly liked it.

Throughout the summer we struck up a good bond. We

fought many a battle and backed one another's play.

In August Ryan decided to do his HGV training and had to come off the door. He wouldn't be returning until October and asked if I wanted to take over as head doorman while he was away. Of course I said yes. Fish, the man at the top, was happy with the outcome. So from August to October, until Ryan's return, there was barely a fight that took place. I kept all the shit at the door. Everyone was on the ball, the ship was sailing smoothly, everyone was happy and the place was always packed.

Ryan's return

When he returned in October, Ryan asked if I wanted to keep the position. I figured it was his door and I was hoping to get a few days off here and there for various things so I was quite happy to hand it back over. The job of cleaning the place up was done. All we had to do was keep it steady.

Team confidence was at an all-time high, but the team had quickly become prima donnas. Ryan was drinking on the job then most others followed suit. Aggression was on the rise. Ryan was a good lad but had a few issues at the time; still a touch young and definitely too wild.

The door staff started going out after hours again. They formed new friendships but with old enemies. Their bans were lifted and they were back in the club. One bad scenario led to another.

Even the steadier members of the team were lashing out; after hours drinking, relationships were struggling. It was ego o'clock.

As time went on the trouble and the amount of people turning up to the pub escalated. I didn't know who the people were. It was Lee that seemed to be the authority on every criminal in Bury. It was like a game of 'Top Trumps' listening to him go on about it. I was always the opposite, like Doza had taught me; it doesn't matter who anyone is, trouble is trouble so you deal with it. It was obvious with this new growing crowd though that sooner or later things were going to get really messy.

The after hours incident

It was another loud and busy night. Lee had worded me up on everyone in the venue. "He's shot someone. This guy always carries a knife..." and so the list went on. Later into the night, we'd already had to sort out a few fights and I'd moved to working the inside rather than the door.

As I was doing the rounds I saw two guys arguing quite aggressively so I headed over to the scene. Just as I got there, one guy butted the other. I dragged the aggressor to the side door and we had a bit of a fight outside. I had him down, then Ryan and another guy I knew (but not part of the team) appeared saying it wasn't the guy's fault. I was little confused but the fight stopped and the guy went back inside. I went out to cool down. Ten minutes later, the same guy was outside having a go at George. I caught John's attention and motioned for him to keep an eye out, knowing that he was aware of the incident. John relieved George. Bang. The guy head butted John and they started going at each other. I legged it over and grabbed the guy by the neck and dragged him up the street out of the way. When the guy had got back to his feet he didn't seem to want any bother with me but it was a different story for young John. The guy shot him plenty of death threats and said he'd be back later. Ryan was apologetic about making the wrong call earlier but he told us that the guy was well connected and John, especially, would have to watch his back.

By the end of the night we'd had a little bit of trouble with everyone. From small time gangsters, armed forces to smack heads and gyppos in the parking lot – it was a fun night to say the least. Most of the lads had popped off for a drink, leaving Ryan, George, John and me to have our little end of night sit-down. We'd sat for around half an hour and were about to wrap things up when we heard a loud knock at the door. We kind of already knew who it was. John got up but we told him to stay out of sight. When Ryan, George and me opened the door, it was worse than we thought. There were four big lads with hoods half covering their faces, coming from a white Range Rover. Another two were on their way. I saw one lad had a wrench, hiding it up his sleeve when getting out of the vehicle. I noticed one of the guys stood near us had his hand held upright; he was obviously concealing something similar.

We went outside waiting for someone to make the first move. We were badly outnumbered but still needed to stand our ground. We pushed at one another but as one of the lads went back I thought I recognised him.

"John?" I looked up, still not sure who he was. He flicked his hood back and I realised it was a big kid I delivered to from off the estate. We would always have the crack when we got talking if I saw him on my round. "What's happening John?" We both just looked at each other.

"Not sure what you've been told but it's not what it seems. I'll pop in and see you through the week but I think you'll find it's just shit that's got out of hand. Worse case, you can come back next week." We both laughed.

At this point all the lads looked a little puzzled as the big kid turned to them, "John's sound. Come on, we're going."

They all piled back in the car and drove off, job done. Young John was off the hook.

So manners, negotiation tactics and being a friendly postman had won. There was a touch of God and a splash of good fortune. But there were always those nights though that no one could save.

When all hell opens up

I was glad I'd cleaned up the door to a respectable standard, I'd been that one man able to make all the difference, but it wasn't my door anymore and I welcomed that change too.

Throughout that year I'd spent a lot of time looking after my younger sister. The upset of the family fallout had affected both her and her husband quite badly. Myself and

Christina tried adding positivity to the negative situation and spent a lot of time being there for them, at their house most weeks. Her husband Jody was on the phone to me often. So I'd been a kind of life line to the two of them. But the negativity of it all was starting to affect my mood. Work was also hard especially with me having this cramping and kidney problem as well as looking after a manic door team, an energetic child as well as a few out of control friends.

The lads on the door were also going through either home life, work or relationship problems. The club was filled with more not rights than ever so at least our negative anger had somewhere to go, and for once, was necessary.

We had a staggered team and some new faces. Most lads were in the club even on their nights off. The car park, the cobbled street as well as the pub was rammed busy. The police were always about trying to torment the doormen, or causing problems for the pub. The Four Barrels soon became the roughest pub in town.

Our tempers were soiled and everyone needed that way out, the right frame of mind at the right time. So like the Kurt Russell line from the movie Tombstone, I was coming and hell was coming with me.

Some of the lads were getting fucked up on cocaine at the start of the night. Some were being shot up with steroids, and most were knocking back shots throughout. I had my black coffee and water. I liked being on the ball.

It was time to embrace the chaos.

The nights were chaotic and we fought like fuck with everyone. I got stabbed with a glass and ended up in hospital, but still couldn't wait to get back to the door the following week. We sometimes argued amongst ourselves but we battled hard, we were battle scarred and by the start of the next year the trouble had stopped coming back. The end of the night fun lasted longer, and the band of brothers was at its fucked up best. I'd envisioned a happy ending lay in a bed of roses but I'd still have a good time sometimes just rolling around in the dirt.

The young, the old, the good the bad and even the very

ugly weren't coming back. The Barrels went back to being the drinkers' pub it once was. There were tidal waves and Hurricanes. Everyone let off steam and luckily no one got killed.

A little like the story of Noah. We had to clear the place for it to be able to start a fresh. Although inadvertent, it was the only way to be able to get the pub back as it was when things had gone too far.

When all turns out

Stepping back to December, the varied behaviour within the team hadn't changed much but I was always happy to see them. I knew this would be my last wild door so I wanted to make the most of it. There were a lot of egos but behind each of them was a good heart. It was just their time, when everybody felt like somebody.

It was the morning of my son's christening. I'd invited all of the lads but didn't expect much of a turn out, knowing their nocturnal, after hours antics.

When the christening had commenced and everyone was gathering in the church, I noticed a lot of my family orientated friends hadn't shown up. I noticed who had turned up though. The full door team, including the Vyas brothers, Walton brothers, George, John, Ryan, Lee, Scouse, Woody and JP were all there. Each of them was suited and booted, looking pristine with their own families. I couldn't have been more proud.

On this day, all the fuckups that went on were forgotten. This door team had been like family and when I'd most needed it, something I'll never forget.

Working this door wasn't a dream I had wanted, it wasn't a wave I had chased. But the wave came all the same. It gave me the admiration I had for Doza and wanted to carry on myself; I wanted that type of influence to be able to deal with everything in a fair and steady way. Young Bloods had been my signing in and The Four Barrels was more my way of signing out, complete with all my knowledge in tow.

Working this door had been a great way to get through some tough times. It was my final band of brothers. The Wild Bunch.

I'm great at looking after my family, I still train and work hard and all of my morals are intact but I became a true man when my ego and the need to fight back against someone had gone and when my only aim was to get home in one piece and to be able to look after my family. It was when I was able to do the job without it being about me. I knew it was coming, I could sense that part of me taking over but I was one step closer to saying goodbye to my Dark Angel and a little step closer to finding my way from the disease of ego and personal pride.

Chapter 16

The happy ending

My first year getting back to Bolton wasn't the best; Me and Andy had very few upbeat moments. We practically survived on skeleton staff. We worked 'til 4am. Our only quiet time was early on in the night; this is when we talked. Andy was similar to me in a lot of ways. He told me about when he lost a boxing match back in the day; how he wouldn't talk for weeks. It was something I related to with my bodybuilding and even sometimes with certain fights I'd lost while working the door. Andy had been a good boxer and had shaken the legs of European and world champions as a sparring partner. He always smiled whilst telling the stories. We laughed at the most stupid of things. He was also a born again Christian but despite his achievements, his prayers and his humorous side he was still very sceptical in his belief of good things to come.

Now both on the back end of our careers as doormen, we were still rolling about with no-marks and not-rights. Any other job where you've had to work this long, you'd be a manager or a sergeant calling the shots from the side lines. I kept mentioning to Andy about working a nice door; somewhere you just open the doors, be polite and have nice customers. A classy venue. Somewhere you get to finish early, not a place you're still having arguments until four in the morning. I was talking about wrapping my door career up with a bow. Andy shunned the comment, "It doesn't work like that. This is it. It's only going to get worse." So despite Andy's venture towards God and thoughts that there was better to come, he seemed to have given up hope as a doorman. This was our main difference.

By 2014 the place I worked was a zoo. Each week it was either fighting in the street or getting spat at. We'd be throwing people out for them to hang around the door threatening to kill us when we'd finished. Then they'd either walk off just when you're about to finish or you'd have wiped them out with little more than a slap then have to go home pent up and unable to sleep.

The change in tide

There was one night while working, a group of idiots were trying to get into the club. All of them were overbearingly noisy, arrogant and clearly off their faces on cocaine. I stood at the front of the crowd, "Not tonight folks." A kid stepped up, cocky lookin' with a short cropped hair cut, suit and attitude. He was right in my face, "You what? You cunt!" He spat in my face as I pushed him out the club. Door staff were soon at the scene and after a brief, yet nasty, argument the crowd got moved on.

It had got to the end of the night; I was standing at the front gate looking on when I saw the same cocky kid with his girlfriend walking by. He didn't seem to want any trouble so I eased off with the stare, looking back towards the inside of the bar. Bang! The guy cracked me from the side. I gave him a quick dig in return and he was on his back. Within seconds the tactical police (who were regularly on the scene in Bolton at that point) were over and had me pinned against the wall. Andy saw and shouted across, "He's just doing his job." But in that minute I was being read my rights and getting told that I wouldn't have my job or badge if the guy I'd slapped chose to press charges.

At 4am I had to go to the police station. Me and the cocky kid were sat across from one another with a police guard watching on. I saw the kid trying to make eye contact. He was getting fidgety, obviously coming down from the drugs. The kid then got the attention of the nearby officer and told him he wasn't pressing charges. He tried to get my attention again. I think he wanted to apologise but I wasn't interested. When the guy had gone I looked towards the officer. "You can go," he said. I was fuming and as I drove home I was thinking that anyone at any time could give me a criminal record when and if they wanted too. And was it all worth it?

Three weeks on and it was the same again, I was on the front gate and it was mayhem. Andy had already had to knock some kid out earlier in the night. Amongst others, I'd had this one guy who kept getting right in my face. He was a big lad with a shaved head and tattoos. He kept putting his head against mine so I kept going on my toes in order to force him back, which forced a clash of heads. "I'll fuck you up, you little dick. You won't stop me."

We were eye to eye as he tried it on.

"Pal, you can call me all you want but you won't get over that line. You won't be getting in." "You're fuckin' dead, fuckin' dead," he kept going on.

This had gone on for around an hour. I really did have the patience of a saint! I'd never kept my shit together so well. Anyway, the guy kept coming back. I was a little edgy at this point and my temperament had started to stray. The guy's head came down again but this time and a little hastily I was back up on my toes. Instead of our heads rubbing together though, my head clashed with his nose. The guy was a big guy but he was obviously more pissed than he was acting. He went flying then cracked his head, full pelt, on the edge of the curb. I saw some blood spitting out from the side. The ambulance was on the way and the place became a crime scene. I was arrested, again. My mates, the tactical police, had me pinned up against the wall and they wanted the footage from the scene.

Fortunately, on this occasion, the lad in question had made enough of a recovery to come over and threaten to shoot me whilst the police were still there. I held my hands up, as if to say, "See" to corroborate what I'd already told them. The police hung about a while whilst they tried to get the footage but eventually called it a day and didn't follow through on the arrest.

After that, I went back inside to use the bathroom. As I was coming out, it had kicked off again. I was in the side street fighting with another guy. The guy had ripped the sleeve from my jacket and even though I'd kind of won the fight, I wasn't feeling like a winner. It wasn't that case of me still having it, it was now a case of, "John, what the fuck are you doing here?"

As I walked back into the venue I'd glimpsed myself in one of the mirrors. My sleeve was ripped and I looked tired. I didn't see a big heroic doorman anymore. I saw a Dad. I saw a nice guy, a guy who deserved better than this. I felt diminished, small. This wasn't me anymore. The problem was, I'd done this job for such a long time and I didn't want it to end looking like this. I felt beaten and sorry for myself. I wanted to wrap all those good memories up in a bow and the only way to do that was with a happy ending.

I headed home that night and at the traffic lights, just as I turned out on to the main street, some idiot jumped on the bonnet of my car. I had to reverse, then drive through the lights and slam on the brakes until he fell off. Was there no end to this turmoil?

Pretty much then and there, I knew it was over; that I'd had enough. I had three weeks until my next holiday then, fuck it, I wasn't coming back. Fuck the happy ending.

It was a week before I was due to go away, when I received a call from a kid called Sam, whom I'd worked with a few years back. He told me about a new place opening in Bury, that it was going to be a classy joint and did I want to run it. I was enthused.

I went down on the opening night to cover the first shift. Sam was on the door but just told me to go in and get to know a few people. Once I was in there, I ran into my old pal Stuart Page. He'd sorted the licensing out for the bar. He told me they had asked him about door staff and he'd mentioned about getting someone who knew a lot of the characters around town, someone who had done the job a while. He'd said that if they could get hold of me they'd be on a winner, like Sam had also said. So, just as I was about to hit retirement on a bad note, the happy ending I wanted had arrived.

End Of Part 2

Part Three
Knowing The Tide

Chapter 1

From fighting to writing

On my post round was where I did most of my thinking; I'd always think back to my past and about how special those times were. The stories of the people I'd come up with seemed too good to just go to waste. I was hoping that someone from my past would want to step up and write a book about the good old days. I knew there were good stories; I just never knew it would be me that was telling them.

It started out like a movie in my mind; that was the original idea. I thought I could turn part of my life into a movie or a series. The only problem was, I couldn't write. You've read the book; you know I didn't study at school. My handwriting is illegible. Grammar? Commas, nouns, I still don't know what they are. Even my Facebook statuses were often mocked for the amount of spelling mistakes they had. Plain and simple, I thought I didn't have the skills to get the stories out.

When God's great plan starts to rise

I'd tried reading a few books, mainly biographies, but they always seemed to start midway through the person's life. I could never get my head around why they didn't just start at the beginning. I'd tried Joe Calzaghe, Bruce Lee, Mike Tyson but I could never get a real feel for the character. I think the books had been written about them rather than being a personal account by them. Either way, nothing had grabbed me so far.

A friend had bought me a book by one of my favourite actors; Rob Lowe. So the same influence that started my wild teenage parties was the one to finally get me into reading then predominantly writing. The start of the book was still a big event, midway through the star's life. I wasn't that interested but what I did notice was that the book actually sounded like Rob Lowe. His persona and personality were all over it. I skipped the initial opening to the book to find out how the star started out.

The book unfolded nicely; from his humble beginning and earliest childhood memories to the set of The Outsiders where he introduced Cruise, Macchio, Howell, Swayze, Estevez, Dillon and the rest of the initial brat pack line up. He took the reader inside of his mind explaining what he was thinking. He showed his strengths and weaknesses, introduced his family and talked about his later success in the series The West Wing. I was hooked.

So a book could be better than a film? This was stage one; a wave on the rise.

While working on the sorting desk, I'd worked next to this same guy for the last ten years; Eamon Kavinar. Like me, Eamon wasn't exactly Einstein. He'd organised his 40th birthday party for his 39th birthday by mistake. He and Julie would discuss TV soaps like real life and he talked about funerals as if he was going to a party. He was a laugh a minute and even though our opinions often differed, we had some decent conversations.

So Eamon, of all people, told me about a book he was writing. I laughed it off at first but as time went by he would talk about it more and he was actually getting through it. I was intrigued. He told me that Kenny's wife was doing the editing and sorting all his spelling and grammar before it went to the publishers where they also did an edit. So out of all the people I knew, perhaps all of Bury, was a guy I worked next to every day telling me every way to succeed at writing a book but without having to be an academic genius.

It had definitely triggered something, but I still wasn't on the wave as yet.

The Four Barrels year: 2012

I'd spent some time hanging with a kid named George Lindsey. He worked with me on the mail, on the door and had started doing a bit with me at the gym also. George was a good character, always a lot of fun to be around. Because George couldn't drive, I took him to and from the gym, and on most weekends, I'd pick him up and drop him home whilst working the doors. Because of the driving here and there, obviously there was lots of conversation and a lot that included old stories about either working the doors, bodybuilding or stories from around the gym. George liked the stories so every now and then he'd say, "You should write a book." When he'd say it, it just kind of hit me like a cold shiver as I knew it was something I wanted to do, but I wasn't willing to accept that I had the ability to do it at the time.

It had got to around Christmas time 2012, after a shift at the pub. I was talking to George before dropping him off, telling him another story of times gone by. George was listening, as usual. I got to the end of the story, when George just looked to me with a serious stern look. "John, you need to write a book. I'm serious pal. You really need to write a book." He said it with such distinction; I automatically knew it was a sign. This was my next venture; this was the tide that was going to take me.

I didn't get much sleep that night, only a clear message that it had to happen and soon. But where do I start? So the very next morning whilst sat drinking coffee, Christina was in the kitchen and Michael still in bed. She had one of her programs on TV, the usual rubbish talk show type of thing. I was about to turn it over when I heard the presenter say, "Next on this morning's show, we have the writer Jackie Collins." Once I'd heard the word writer, I thought I'd give it a minute. She got talking and the presenter asked her: "So what advice do you give to anyone wishing to write their own book?"

Wow, this was the exact question I would have asked. Jackie's reply: "If it's about a person's life, to start at the earliest memory and keep working forward. Don't worry if it's not all quite in sync." She carried on a little more, then finished with: "If you only write one page a day, or just do one hour, by the end of the year you'll have an elaborate book." Boom, right away I'm sold. So the very next day I bought a note book and pen. I was even jotting notes over the Christmas period ready for the start of the coming year's great venture. The new wave was about to arise.

Pen to paper

At the start of 2013 I initially started writing the book. After work and in-between going to the gym was all the real time I was going to get with the schedule that I had. So it was pen and paper sat in Costa Coffee most days; obviously the comfy seats propped next to the window when possible!

After the first couple of weeks of getting started I realised that I couldn't even read my own writing, let alone the fact that I'd not used a single comma, noun, paragraph or full stop. The book read more like a Chinese shopping list. No one was going to be able to rewrite this, not if they couldn't even read it. Ok, first mistake. Instead, I started writing in single letters, slower but a lot neater. I had my A4 pad whilst drinking coffee most days.

I found that whilst writing, there was a vast discrepancy between the bodybuilding story, and the one about working the doors. I also figured that I'd not really travelled far enough back to my childhood in the story. At the time though, apart from initial memories, I wasn't really sure where any of that would fit in anyway, but I still really liked the idea of writing about my childhood.

Around October 2013 I think I must have written around 10 to 12 thousand words but I still wasn't really on the wave, as such. I was thinking that perhaps I should have written two separate books, one more about working the doors and another that's just more in keeping with bodybuilding. But I'd gone so far, the thought of starting all over again just didn't seem like an option. Way too much work done for that to ever happen.

Stepping back to step forward

I'd been doing some boxing with my old pal Daimo Hall and as usual we'd been shooting the fat at the end of our session. Not thinking, I'd thrown my water container in the boot of the car and hadn't realised the top wasn't on.

The following day, after work, I went to get my note pad before going for my coffee. As I went to pick it up, the pad was completely sodden and my efforts were totally destroyed. I kind of wanted to kill someone yet cry at the same time. I started thinking that maybe the book wasn't meant to be. The problem though, as well as the solution, was that the next day, and like most days on my round, the story was still mulling over in my mind. I'd thought about it that often and enjoyed thinking about the stories, that it had become part of everything that I did. This wasn't going anywhere.

Battle plan

I'd decided I was going to go with a format, a plan I wouldn't veer from. So it was going to be the story to do with my bodybuilding first. I could visit part of my childhood in that, then write a book that looked deeper into my childhood and working the club doors; a more personal account. So that was the plan. Then I thought, 'I need a PC, just a cheap one, but really need it if I'm ever going to get through this book'. Christina could always tell when I was proper down about something and also when I really had to do something. She knew my anxious, tunnel vision attitude by now. She knew I was on one.

Christmas day arrived and Christina had bought me a brand new lap top. What a darling! Not only that. She had also bought me one of those badboy, George Clooney, Nespresso coffee makers, so I could have my deluxe coffee at home whilst I wrote.

God being cruel to be kind

January 2014: I'd got my lap top but had done very little in the way of writing. What I had done though was the basics. Turn the PC on, go to file, write then save, then turn off. I'd done this several times, so at least I'd got that for when I did finally get started. This PC was never going to be about going online or downloading music. When I picked it up it was to write and only to write. It was just the case of getting started now.

2014 was going to be a big year for me. I was turning 40. The plan was to get in great shape. I wanted to practice some new break dance, street dance moves ready for my party. Then there was going to be another road trip covering California, then up to Nevada, Las Vegas, Route 66, The Hoover Dam and the Grand Canyon.

Like I've said before, God always acts on the 'what you really want', over 'what you think you want', but all in all he's going to try his best so everything comes right.

It was the third week into January and I'd twisted my back while out on delivery. I couldn't move and the doctor had said that it would be at least eight weeks before I was able to return to work.

So, I couldn't train. Breakin' was completely out of the question. Going out and even driving was a no no. So what did I have? I had my PC, a bad boy coffee machine and a couch to get comfy on. A wife who slept most the day because she worked nights and a little boy who was at nursery from 8 am until 4.30 pm every day. I also had this story. A clear pathway to get the book started.

So for the first four to five days I was literally just sat there. Lap top open, fingers twitching, mind thinking, but not much happening. I wrote a little then deleted everything I'd written. I just needed that beginning. "Come on John boy, think, earliest memory, earliest memory."

"I was sat in class aged around 5/6 years old, when miss asked everybody what they wanted to do for a job when they got older. Everyone was saying the usual things like a police man or a bus driver. When my turn came I stood up and said that I wanted to be a bodybuilder."

Boom, my first memory was on the lap top. I was smiling like the Cheshire cat. I felt like celebrating! It felt like I'd already done it but that was just because I knew, this was it. I remember thinking about Lou Ferrigno as the Incredible Hulk then the files in my mind just sort of went on a roll from there.

So it was one hundred words a day, then a thousand, then three, four thousand, four to five hours a day. I really did make the most of the time I had off.

Even when I was back at work, I was putting time aside to keep up with the book. I got up thirty minutes prior to my normal waking time, trying to add little bits while moving the book steadily along. On my day off from work I caught up the most time, putting in 3-4 hours on those days. I kept to a minimum of never writing for any less than ten hours a week.

My 40th birthday party

I had got in shape as planned. My 40th was an 80s themed fancy dress and I took on being Maverick from Top Gun and even managed to put in a decent break dance performance. I also had the honour of dancing with my original break dance mentor, Graham Gabriel, as well as my cousin Lee Armstrong. Dcza had come and virtually someone from every door I'd ever worked was there. There was everyone, from my first ever friend Sean Joyce, through to my current training partners Alex and Phil. It was a great night. The first draft of the book was also done. Shortly after that I headed to the US on a two-thousand-mile road trip. California, San Francisco, Las Vegas, Grand Canyon then on to Route 66 as planned with great family outings throughout, magic. God had been kind, even if he'd had to be a little cruel to get me there.

From the end of 2014 up until the middle of 2015, I had edited the book several times and although it still wasn't shining as brightly as I wanted it to, at least it now looked like a story and that I had something. At this point I'd got an old pal of mine, John Hartly to go through the book and sort all the grammar out.

Chapter 2

The undercurrent of humanity

In the early days, when at work, it was all about the banter. You'd regularly hear me singing, out of tune and at the top of my voice.

The shouts of "Errrrrrrnnnnnnie" and "Karl Ke Bleeeakly" then Ernie and Karl back to me, "Joooooohhhhnny" along the office floor most days.

You would catch us climbing into mail trucks and slinging each other down the aisle, playing bowls with the York skips; clash bang wallop. Steve Hardman and Jimmy Roberts were the managers at the time, "What the bloody hell are you lot doing?" they'd yell whilst laughing. Me, Ernie, Karl Bleakley and a kid named Dave the Rave were always last out around the Christmas period, wired up on machine coffee. Ernie's favourite saying was 'Get the brews in, or get a bruising'; stupidity at its finest. Me, Julie and Eamon were always laughing when we should be working, with the better end of the sorters, Col Jones (Golden Bollocks, as we used to call him) and Sue Hardman shouting down the line, "We'll do your work for you, you useless bastards. Wouldn't pay you lot in washers", but it was all in good fun. You'd hear Mark Lewis and Kenty having pops at each other, then Kenty would laughingly threaten to bang Lewis. It was like a continuation of school. It was the perfect job for me. The times and the laughs we had back then were priceless. But that was then, this is now.

2014-2015: there was a new wave of management that had just swept up on the shores of where I work. It was mayhem from the get-go. The old school management had moved on and the newer management were usually much more mechanical, more about figures and statistics. A couple of the managers were OK but some were just complete and utter bullies.

The first issue

They'd messed my holidays up. We were supposed to get two weeks off in summer but only one had been written down. We also got six weeks off overall but only five were recorded on the sheet. They seemed almost too happy telling me that I wouldn't be going on holiday: that's what got me the most. So you can see what type of problems this was going to pose when I got home. It was two weeks of stress, then I finally got given the week. Then one of the managers decided to take my August holiday week and move it to the following March for no reason whatsoever. So this was how it started.

In the coming months the place I'd worked became unrecognisable and the people that I'd worked with, even more so. These managers were keen to get on everyone's case. It wasn't just pushing you to do more (this was a business; we know that happens) but this lot were just power hungry. Before long people were going off sick, left, right and centre. Even the bigger characters of the office were affected. Staff had blood pressure worries. Some were even in tears. Folks were on anti-depressants and not wanting to come back.

So my duty was a taboo. I'd been placed on a medical rehab duty for a while because of my bladder and kidneys. It was supposed to be a better option. It had gone from three of us in the office, down to one. I was also taking all the packets from three different walks. The union were arguing until blue in the face but nothing was getting done. Even though everyone was quite badly put-on, they were still big on raising conduct issues every time anyone made a mistake, as well as blaming us for anything to do within our duty, even if we weren't responsible.

If you went to them with a problem they'd basically deny you your rights. If they shouted at you and you shouted back, they'd attempt to sack you. If you threatened to leave because you were being put-on, they'd tell you they would stop your pay. If you asked for help in the front locker they'd question your competence. They jumped from counselling to conduct for one time mistakes. They'd time you on the toilet and degrade you in any way possible obviously hoping you would leave or lose your shit enough for them to sack you. The whole place was on fire with the rage of red hot tempers and burnt-out, battered, demoralised minds.

It gets to Christmas 2015. I was looking washed out, extremely thin and pale. Christmas was busy and I'd been put upon like you wouldn't believe. I was running from start to finish whilst still taking shit off these managers, arguments, and human rights at work were massively undermined. This duty had been put in for me to recover, to go back out on deliveries, but if my body ended up in a diminished state it could end up making me very ill. At this point I felt ok but I looked very withdrawn.

I was out with my family over Christmas and they'd looked at me and said that I didn't look too well, that I'd lost too much weight. This got me a little paranoid so I started to wear my big jacket and extra jumpers to add a little bulk. I was then out with my cousin Phil and was talking to my pal, Stuart Page. He also told me that I didn't look too good. Obviously, it wasn't what I wanted to hear but the fact that I was sat in a hot bar with a big coat and thick jumper on tells you something was wrong. He then told me to get an organ check just to make sure everything was functioning properly. He was genuinely worried and now, so was I.

After Christmas, I'd started to feel even more washed out. I was notably gaunt and tried to appeal to the manager about my wellbeing and that I could do with a couple of Saturdays away from the busy front locker. Again, the manager chastised me. He told me that it wasn't the John Show and that I shouldn't have any special privilege. (I was registered DDA.) Then we had another argument in which he accused me of threatening him this time and surprise, surprise I was down the conduct code again and that I'd have no job by the end of the week.

The only beautiful side to all this was that for the past two years I'd regularly been writing. I had been training my brain to remember as far back as possible, I'd even been eating more fish to help with memory and proteins high in memory engaging amino acids. So over the weekend I wrote out all that had gone on. The witnesses, the times, the dates; I had everything. When I presented my case, the conduct disciplinary was immediately dropped. Ok. So the pen really was mightier than the sword after all.

It was early January 2016. I had made an appointment at the hospital. The news was much worse than I'd expected. My kidneys were functioning at a low percentage and my liver was also damaged through how diminished my body had become. My haemoglobin levels told you that I was near to suffering a stroke. The doctor then told me that I'd have to go into hospital and have a kidney biopsy. I'd avoided any medication and hadn't accepted that there had been any real problem up until now. The start of this condition had first come about some time in 2012.

I was diagnosed with CKD (Chronic Kidney Disease). Protein leaks into the kidneys. The protein becomes toxic which destroys the filters in the kidneys. At this point this was apparent in mine. Obviously the more protein that passes out, the more filters get destroyed then you and your body become badly diminished. If you had a bad dose of flu or infection whilst your body was in this type of state it could eat away at you in the same way cancer could. It was a truth that I really didn't want to accept.

Time to fight back

I was on medication. The doctor had literally said that if I didn't take it, I'd be lucky to make it to 50. But this wasn't the end.

Instantly, I was reading. I got through a stash of new books about self-healing. My initial thoughts on learning about nutrition for muscle growth was now vastly laughable, as the one thing I absorbed the most may just be about to change my life.

I read how spinach neutralises toxins, even metals, cleaning the liver and kidneys. Cucumber leaves the inner organs hydrated, as they are 90% water. Hot water, something I'd done for years over the winter, opens all your organs so hot water became an all year round thing. Broccoli and celery, being very fibrous, cleans the insides. Turmeric, Indian herb' milk thistle would also contribute. So everything I'd done, I just needed to do more of and add a few more options. I read how whole eggs containing choline cleans the internal organs, whilst egg whites take very little breaking down allowing you to digest more protein but without constantly burdening your body. Protein is still needed for growth and repair. Keeping body weight steady or even a touch light means struggling inner organs have less to deal with, making them faster to recover and mend themselves. And of course there had to be plenty of fluids in-between. The body needs plenty of water for everything to operate properly. Eating almonds or adding lemon to water keeps your body in an alkaline state, which is also said to limit viruses(they reckon even diseases like cancer are unable to survive in an alkaline environment) and so the list goes on.

God had prepared me by my understanding nutrition. I now saw the cells in my body like individual lives, all with jobs to do. It was up to me to feed the body's needs. I was now aware that I was a God of my own body and it was my job to answer all the body's prayers of upset. So the problems I could solve, I solved by evolving my new diet ideas. The problem I couldn't solve, the undercurrent of humanity, well that was something I had to work on.

Having an alcoholic drink may deaden the pain of being deflated for a short while, but it won't get rid of the problem. Like prime oil in a fast car or a dock leaf to a nettle, it's like the earth to the body and that's always going to be the best way to fight back. Always full in thought and at your fittest.

I was fighting back physically but the mental strain had taken its toll. I think that all the problems that had emerged from work and through illness had slowly but surely started to eat away at my soul. I found myself only ever half in the room when either with Christina or Michael. I was tending to go out of the way for a while on my own. I caught myself staring out to nowhere on quite a few occasions. My natural brain had always ruled out the negative but there had been so much negative for such a long time that my brain just seemed to be shutting off in order to shut out all the bad stuff. I kept making sure I was putting in time with my family, training, writing, but I clearly wasn't me anymore. At work I barely spoke, I was polite but quiet. I didn't bounce anymore. This went on for a couple of months whilst I was trying to work through everything.

Ghost writer

Around this time, I really didn't think I could put anymore in with the book. I knew I was going through a lot of stuff but I still thought I'd got the book finished to the best of my abilities, so I hired a ghost writer to do the final script.

I got the writer's number and within a week we were discussing the book over coffee. I had told her how it needed chapters and how it needed pumping up at the exciting parts. How it needed a little more feeling at the emotional parts and so on.

She said to me, "Don't worry, when I've finished with your book you won't recognise it".

I asked her to call me if she needed any more info. It cost me £400 which was basically as much as I could afford to spare. But if we were going to do this, I thought, then let's do it right. I sent her the copy of the manuscript and away she went.

Within a week it was back. There wasn't a single change to the manuscript so I gave the girl a call asking what she'd actually done.

"It was very good. There wasn't much that needed changing." She was referring to the grammar which I'd already rectified.

"I'm talking about the chapters and all we spoke about," I explained.

"No, you've only paid for a brief run through so far. Any additional work will cost £25 an hour." Seriously?

She had sent me the manuscript as a PDF, which was a solid file that I couldn't get into. Then she couldn't even open it so I had no book to work from. She then told me she was ill and in hospital and to leave it with her. If she was in hospital, I couldn't really argue. I was sceptical though.

I gave her another week but still hadn't heard anything so I text her to see what was going on. She got back saying she hadn't heard anything from me so presumed I had sorted it.

Now for the best part: after that she blocked my number as well as removing me from Facebook. My pal, who had put me on to her, told me he was also having problems with her, even the company she worked for were having problems with her. A mutual friend had said that whilst on Facebook she was talking about writing her own book. "So Little Polly Poppy Socks is already getting in trouble." She was describing one of her characters like she was getting lost in her writing. Fuckin' ace. Didn't I know how to pick 'em. So hey, ho, it seemed like I was pretty much fucked on all accounts.

My mate, Professor Daggi, managed to get the file back so at least I was able to carry on from where I'd left off. I'd lost two months and £400 in total. So I guess I could easily get bitter but I didn't. Yeah, sure I was pissed off about what had taken place, as well as all the other unneeded shit that was going on in my life at that time but I saw this as a sign, possibly the ultimate sign.

This girl had done me a big favour. I had no more money to spend on the project and wouldn't trust anyone even if I had. God had given me a clear message: "This is your work John; this is your book. You know how you want it now find a way of getting it that way." I didn't actually hear voices; I'd not gone that nuts as yet! But you know what I'm getting at. I knew what I had to do in regards to the book. First though, I had bigger fish to fry.

I remember watching Michael laughing at himself in the mirror as his hair had blown up everywhere. He was so giddy and happy at virtually anything, amused by the littlest detail. As I watched him, my sense of tomorrow's remorse of having to go into work had started to kick in. I'd already had a week of it where even right up to the final second I'd been put on to the point where I'd had to walk out. I looked again at Michael, how happy he was. Now my only real thought was; 'If I can't get through this, then if this kind of thing ever happened to him when he was older, then perhaps he might not be able to get through this type of thing either' (this I couldn't live with) but if I can get through this then so will he. This I could live with. I'd felt psyched and determined the more I thought this way.

I took leave from work the following week. So everything happened for a reason right. For the first time since the start of forever I could write. I'd never been a writer but for the past three and a half years I'd been either stuck to pen and paper or sat at a lap top. So my thing was obviously to write this story but God had seen the bigger picture a long time before things had even started to transpire.

So, I couldn't shout or lose my shit when it came to dealing with stuff at work, I didn't have to. I'd already planned ahead by taking pictures and making videos as back up if anything did. I had a great memory and I could map out a story in occurrence and date order quite easily. Every answer for everything I needed to do.

I felt empowered, from the second I'd wrote out the first series of events. The more I wrote, the quicker the blue returned to my eye and the more I became me. I wasn't the victim anymore. I put in an official grievance. I sent the email to the managers and the Union reps involved, as well as the manager above. Within a week of sending the email the manager I'd had the most problems with had gone. Then the more snakier managers seemed to disappear back down their holes, along with a few of the back stabbers. I felt that the company dealt with the situation very quickly and competently.

The final meeting

With the severity of the case that I'd written, the manager who took it on probably thought that I was wanting to take things further.

The meeting was batting backwards and forward when the manager finally just came out with it.

"John, what do you want from all this?"

I replied, "I just want to be left alone."

He looked a little shocked, as did my wife who, along with quite a few others, thought I should have pursued it to the max. For me though, I had a wave I needed to get on. But whilst swimming with sharks and fighting against the undercurrent that wasn't going to happen and there was only so much time left. The manager I'd had problems with had gone and the other manager couldn't manage me and left shortly after. The grievance was to be handled officially over time. Meanwhile, I could start back at work the following week.

The worse I felt throughout all this, the more I wanted to help others to feel good about themselves. I think this attribute became my greatest strength.

The whole of this period was like when you watch one of those war movies and it's shot in that green, grey colour. Now that I'd fought my battle and won the war, all that was about to change. Soon I'd smell the air, then slowly the blue skies would start to appear from the grim green colour I'd gotten used to. Then the rainbow of thought appeared, putting to rest the dark storms that had taken place in my head. Over the months my life turned back to technicolour and my heart was at full beat. My body's cells were no longer ravaged by the depression. It was time to shine.

Chapter 3

Rhythm and rhyme:

Time to shine

At the latter end of 2016 and into early 2017. I had a book, a good book. The only thing wrong with it was that it still didn't have the edge, the heart. In bodybuilding terms for me it still hadn't peaked. The book had everything but just like the chick from that movie, Weird Science, this thing had to breathe.

Firstly, I started adding Facebook posts about my personal life or about my bodybuilding career mainly. I did this to see what floated people's boats. The more likes I got the more I was able to gauge what people liked as well as what they didn't.

Despite a few good ideas I still hadn't found the edge I needed to get the book to its best. So then I got to thinking about how other writers might phrase things. Seconds later I found myself thinking of William Shakespeare. Right away I started to look up some of Shakespeare's old verse and it didn't take long to get exactly what I needed. I found a piece which was named; All the world's a stage.

The piece described the stages of life, but in a very quick yet thought grasping way. A quick example: "Then a soldier, full of strange oaths and bearded like the pard, jealous in honour, sudden and quick in quarrel, seeking the bubble reputation even in the cannon's mouth." It was quick yet descriptive and it didn't linger at any point whilst still having, a certain urgency about it. It was then able to move on but with you having a full understanding of what's gone on. This was the game changer, the ultimate game changer.

The book had rhyme. It had rhythm, but mostly it had life; my heart and soul were talking out from amongst the pages. I had to set my mood for how I was writing. I thought of something upsetting to reach the lower levels of my thoughts, because things were coming good at this time it was easy to write about the good times and the loved up times. I wasn't trying to get rid of the book anymore. Not now I'd found the magic touch. I was up even earlier, 4-5am most mornings.

I enjoyed the scent of a freshly brewed coffee and the glare of my small reading lamp and my warm blanket. People may think this was a little different from most my other passions where lots of people were involved; perhaps this seems like the lonely man's awakening but it wasn't. This is the time when I was amongst everyone I'd ever cared for, or loved, times that had meant the most, with people as you remember them at their best. You were with everyone, your past, present and future were all coming together in the same place. These dark cold mornings I remember for bringing such beautiful memories. I think this was when I really saw myself as a writer. I'd keep re-writing the book almost right up until the final publishing date.

When it's meant to happen

So it's around October- November 2016. For the first time in forever I realised that I'm physically tapped out, aches, pains, things that really need sorting out before something serious did actually happen. This was the first time in nearly thirty years where I had voluntarily stepped back from training in order to deal with niggling injuries but I'd sensed something great about to happen going into the next year, so both mentally and physically I wanted to appreciate this to the max. I ironically ran into an old school friend of mine named Rachael Caldwell. I was telling her about taking a rest and getting my injuries tended to. As it turned out

Rachael's Dad ran the Northern Institute of Massage which just happened to be exactly what I was looking for.

I met Sean, Rachael's husband and he went straight to work, balancing everything out whilst breaking down all the knots and niggles. He was doing a great job so I sign up for a full eight weeks.

Meanwhile I'd been prep coaching a pal of mine named Alvin Isherwood, helping him get ready for a UK bodybuilding contest. I was at his house at the time telling him and his wife Heidi about where I'd been going for physio and I'd mentioned already knowing Rachael Caldwell.

"I've got Eddie's book, Rachael's Dad, it's really good. Her Dad used to be a professional wrestler," Heidi offered. I stared at the book for a few seconds. The book was totally reminiscent of the 70s-80s wrestling era. I then opened to the pages. The book layout was even better. It had almost a comic book layout capturing that scene so well. Heidi was telling me about Eddie but meanwhile Alvin was just looking up from his seat, a beady eyed, Don Corleone type of look. He had sussed me out. "I know what you are thinking," he said "Can these guys help me with my book?" he smiled smugly.

I nodded and smiled back, "Yeah, that's exactly what I'm thinking." So you see the, everything happens for a reason thing, all coming about at this time.

I bumped into Eddie the very next day and not long after I was working through the book at the publishers.

The final run through at the publishers

We had spent five hours working through everything. It had to be perfect. I'd wanted to get the book looking reminiscent of the 80s as that had been my aspiring decade. The picture on the front also had to be right. And there were various pieces of dialogue I'd wanted changing. It was a long day but as I said my goodbyes I felt confident that I'd got the book to its very best.

When getting back to my car I thought of just driving home but I was way too excited. I figured this was my moment. There were blue skies and a gentle breeze, the first nice day of the year if I remember it rightly. So I took a drive to Heaton Park, nearby. Once I was at the park I quickly grabbed a coffee and took a walk through the picturesque greenery and trees. A gentle wind and mild sunshine brushed against my skin. I sat for a while looking on over the park, I was totally happy. Four years and three months it had taken to get to this point. It wasn't like I'd just written a book; I'd actually learnt how to write. Then I became a writer and wrote a book simultaneously. I had dispelled the myth of old dogs and new tricks. This was an achievement.

Before people even chose to read the book or whether they considered it to be good or not, whether it would fail or succeed and before any opinions came to pass. I was savouring a pure moment, a moment where passion and dreams had met with reality. Where I sat and thanked God, where I smiled and felt totally refreshed. I wasn't worried or having to think about what was coming next.

"You've done it, John, you've done it."

Passionate moments are always the most beautiful.

Chapter 4

I'm a Life Addict:

Time to ride this wave

A couple of weeks went by when I got a call to say that the books had arrived. I'd ordered the biggest shipment there was: 1000 books.

I had no idea what a thousand books was going to look like but around five trips to Prestwich later I'd found out. It was a lot more than I'd expected. I had pilled around thirty boxes in the hall already. I felt the sweat bursting from my brow.

"I love your book Dad, wow, it looks really good," Michael could see me getting stressed and tired as I found new hiding places to store the books.

They were at the back of the dining table and stashed in the downstairs loo. There were still a ton of them in my car and piled up in the hall. Shit, I really hadn't thought this through. Michael came out on the landing as I was launching a few more boxes into the spare room.

He had this bright little smile on his face, "Dad, I have an idea. Come with me, I've found something." Behind his cabin bed there was a large destitute space hidden behind his drawers, a place where these books would be completely out of sight.

"You little beauty," I said to him. I was running the boxes upstairs. Michael helped by sliding them, one by one, across the wooden floor. The little Doosh had brought back the day and the books were now safely out of sight.

The difference between a passionate person and a business person is that the business person is more about selling a product, than about the product itself. Whereas a passionate person puts everything into getting the product to its very best. Then only at the end they start to think "Right. Now I have to sell this." I was a little nervous as all this was starting to unroll in my head.

I was up early Sunday morning. I was excited but was also anxious. I'd been putting together a couple of pictures for my phone. With nothing in the pipeline when it came to advertising, it all came down to this: One picture and a Facebook status.

The pic looked pretty professional and I'd made sure that the status was engaging and honest. Luckily, I hadn't posted anything at all about writing the book so at least that was going to add to the wow factor a little. I went through the status several times. A quick gulp and a nervous laugh, then I hit the send button.

After playing with Michael at the park, then dropping him off at a party, I went back to my phone to see how many people had engaged in my recent status. It was great news. There were over 200 likes and a ton of messages. I headed to the coffee shop so I could rifle through.

"I've seen the book John. It looks great. When do I get my copy?" Adam, the coffee shop manager asked. Then his staff were asking for a copy. I knew quite a few people in there as well and they all wanted a copy too. I quickly went to my car and brought back a ton of books. I did my first book signing at Costa Coffee! It honestly couldn't have happened more magically.

Later in the day I had an absolute mound of messages all from people wanting the book. I knew I could send the books off, but I had nothing at all lined up for taking payment. My pal Simon Jaworski had seen between the lines. I could just imagine him sat at his lap-top,

"John, you thick bastard." He was trying to set me up a simple website and told me to set up a PayPal account for people to be able to make easy payments. Meanwhile, over

Facebook other people were asking whether it was available in Waterstones or in WH Smith. Oh boy!

The web page and the book being in shops were all a long way off. I had an idea. I wasn't sure it would work, but it was my only possible option at the time. I quickly culminated some bullshit about waiting to hear back from Waterstones, kind of like they were dragging their feet. Obviously I didn't want to look a total bozo by telling people I had no sort of delivery method set up; what type of idiot would do that?! So I told people whilst the web was pending, I'd be dropping off books door to door from 5pm onwards over the coming weeks. I told them where I'd be in Bury at a given time or when I was at the gym and even which door I worked and that I'd have my books with me at all times.

"Ok" I thought, "Let's do this."

It went from selling 7 on Monday, rising above twenty a night by the end of the week. I picked Michael up from school, a bite to eat and an hour in the park, then off we went. I was meeting people I'd not seen in a good while. Everyone was welcoming as I arrived at their doors and no one let me leave without signing it.

Everyone also enjoyed meeting Michael. If we were lucky enough to get invited in for a drink, Michael met the family pets, played with their kids or was taken to the kitchen and given some goodies. I met people for coffee endlessly. Everyone was taking a picture of the book or taking a standard book selfie to put over social media. Things happened quickly and it was all a lot of fun.

People were recommending the book whilst reading it. Over social media there was a string of book pics on beaches or at the side of swimming pools and the recommendations were quickly leading to more and more sales.

It also got into the hands of a journalist who worked for a national newspaper. She liked the story so much she did a piece on me for the paper. Even a university lecturer named Pete Deacon, had enjoyed the book. He had me lecturing at Media City. I went and did a lecture on the influence of muscle in 80s movies and am now part of the syllabus. Whether I was at work or down at the gym, it didn't matter. The book was selling fast.

Reviews

I obviously wanted the book to sell but, more importantly, I wanted people to like it. This wasn't a money making project, my heart had gone into this book. After the first couple of weeks I got a message from a lad named John Cooper, an old pal of mine. He wrote an in-depth message on how good the book was and how much it meant to him. He said it was amongst the best books he'd ever read. My aim was to get good reviews, but I'd hoped that at least one person would like the book more than any other. I looked over his message with a massive sense of accomplishment and pride.

Phil Rose then text me at four in the morning. 'I'm really not happy with you. This book has stopped me from finishing a 5000-word dissertation I was supposed to be doing."

Doza rang me to tell me he didn't have his dinner until ten at night. The book had left him starving! He said to give myself a big pat on my back.

Then a less than serious review from my old pal, Sean Joyce: "To say you was thick as shit at school, you've really pulled something out of the bag."

And on it went. A girl I knew named Collette Dabono got through the book in only five hours and Graham, the security guard, read the book twice back to back.

So it ran like that for several months. I felt like a million dollars. The tide of life was back to its best. Again, I wasn't very famous but I was definitely Bury famous. I'm not comparing the book against any proper decent writer. But for a challenged kid who wrote with the wrong hand and got battered off a teacher for not being able to read, I felt I'd done pretty good.

At this point I got thinking. The first movies I loved were the Rocky movies, written by Sylvester Stallone. The first book I ever read to do with training was the 'Encyclopaedia of Modern Bodybuilding' written by Arnold Schwarzenegger. The first autobiography I managed to get through, 'Stories I only tell my friends', was written by Rob Lowe. All the early influences I'd admired for their acting, as well as their physicalities, were imaginative writers. I'd always been a fan of writers.

Chapter 5

Bellagio

Into the early summer and the outside weather was bright and warm and the sun in my heart was always shining. The book was on a roll. I felt like the world (my little world) knew who I was again. Things were great at home and I'd got myself back in good shape.

My only worry at the time was my annual check-up at the hospital for my kidneys. I'd been a little worried as the prescription for my medication kept getting messed up, so I'd not been taking my tablets for the past couple of months. I was feeling good though. But it was now time to see what was going on, on the inside.

At the hospital I'd had my usual series of injections as well as the diagnosed urine sample. The doctor was looking at the screen to tell me the results. He sat up smiling, "John, you look great and I'm glad to tell you that you are also doing great. There's no blood in your urine and your kidneys and liver are working at a high percentage."

I quickly asked, "A high percentage for my condition?"

"No John," he smiled, "a high percentage for anyone."

I started to tell him about my diet, he smiled again when seeing me happy, "Whatever you are doing John, keep doing it. Your recovery has been miraculous." So there was my get out of jail free card you might say. I had a few tears of joy lurking as I walked away from the hospital and as usual I said a prayer of thanks to God for his kindness.

Meanwhile, we had booked to go to my cousin's wedding over in Bellagio, Italy. I'd had an expensive year planned already but because this was my cousin's wedding, and I saw him as a brother, I felt I needed to go even if only for that reason. It wasn't about having a good time; it was about being there for the people that mattered. What I actually got from this trip though would be a world apart from anything I was expecting.

Here we go...

As we arrived at the airport the party had already started. I remember seeing Mark Isherwood, Simon Hayton, John Holt, big Chris, John Dutton, most the Rose family as well as people I didn't know. Everyone was at the bar and on good form. Even the plane ride wasn't a burden. It was photo bombing, jokes and drinks, throughout the whole journey; then from the plane to the coach and from the coach to the side of the beautiful Lake Como. At this point we were greeted with a two tier private river boat, drinks, music and food. It was a full two-hour trip to the hotel with scenery that could only be described as what looked like paradise, a peaceful, dreamy, colourful island.

Everyone was mixing it up, it was a social bonanza. I got talking to my cousin, Kelly Marie. "Isn't it funny, one minute you might be sat at a bus stop in the rain then the next minute you can be feeling on top of the world, surrounded by all this." She was saying it just as I was feeling it. I smiled because I knew exactly what she meant.

Our room at the hotel was reminiscent of old school Italy. The place was unscathed by the modern era, the four poster bed, wooden blinds and floors. There were no mod cons only the most beautiful views coming at you from every angle. An enchanted Italian coffee on the veranda was my first port of call.

The first night was an open top disco with a free bar and food. The whole place was ours. There's no better feeling than going somewhere and knowing everyone and by the end of the first night you really felt like you did know everyone, meeting friends was never easier. As the night drew on, myself and Christina drifted off on our own for a bite to eat deciding on a quaint little restaurant overlooking the lake.

I was on a high even before arriving but now we were there it felt like there was nothing bad in the world; like, nothing at all could hurt you. Christina and I were sat talking, overlooking the lake. It had been twenty years since I'd first fallen in love with Christina. Since then we'd suffered several scars and a much jaded take on what we once were but here in Bellagio none of that seemed to matter. I'd started to look at my wife the way I used to all those years ago.

The world sometimes gets in the way of what's real but on this night it was like starting over; like meeting someone new. The same feelings from when we were young, that holiday romance type of feel. It was in the air. It was everywhere.

The next day you could either opt for a trip to the vineyard or do your own thing. Myself and Christina had spent little time alone in a while so we opted to have the day to ourselves. We hit the road early and decided to tour the island. Throughout the day we visited lake side cafes, museums and scenic gardens. Whilst ascending higher and higher into the hills we came across small fisheries and sculpted cemeteries. An island perfectly clean, peaceful, friendly and without any visible fault whatsoever.

When I saw this place in Star Wars, I thought it was CGI, I didn't think a place could possibly be this dreamy, but here we were. Christina wore her summer dress and looked young and vibrant. Without life's stress she reminded me so much of her younger more carefree self. We were holding each another's hands, kissing one another, looking at one-another like we were glad we had weathered those storms even if only for these moments. I remember this day like a dream: a bewilderment of love, honesty, the feeling of being young and in love. It was a day where I could only remember scenery, kissing and smiling, even laughing. It was almost melodic like a scene from out of a movie. Our eyes shone bright and we were young once more. How magic life is, when all was well.

Later that evening we'd all met at a quiet little tavern set in a narrow back street. It was night time and the lights in the street appeared dim which set a mellow scene. I was stood talking to aunty Cinnie. Cinnie was like a second mum and had helped me and Christina out many times over the years. "So are you two alright then?" she smiled, seeing us close. "I knew you two would get back together," she started, me and Christina were smiling,"I know these things," she said whilst laughing. We ended the night having drinks and sitting overlooking the lake. The moonlight set the scene. It was another end to another perfect evening.

The magic

The big day had arrived. The tuxedo was on, the mirrored shades and I was feeling good about myself. Christina was in a bright summery dress and was also full of splendour. As we set out, people were looking up from their seats as we walked by. It was a Bond-themed wedding so as we got to the party everyone was dressed in tuxedos and ironically all the girls had chosen to wear summer dresses. Spirits were high and you just knew it was going to be a great day.

Soon after, a couple of large speed boats turned up ready to take us across to the island to start the day's festivities. I smiled, as did Christina. I should have been thinking about James Bond but as we crossed on the boats it reminded me more of a Bruce Lee movie. The punters nearby, that were leaving, looked on in awe as we made our way up the island. I threw out a wave and virtually everyone who was looking waved back. It felt like we were superstars; everyone was feeling it. It was one of the couples wedding anniversary and another guest's birthday. One guy had set up a successful business and another guy had just become business man of the year in his chosen field. I, myself, had had my own success so it just seemed like everyone on board was having their own good fortune. Phil's wedding had brought us all together (The angel of optimism).

The harp played and the greetings began. The island was wistful and everyone had witnessed their own success in one way or another in recent times. The positivity of the day revelled amongst the architecture and the blue skies as we all sat to enjoy the wedding.

As the night drew on, we made our way up to the top of the island to a large summer house set in its own gardens. It was night time and the glass panelled windows had been drawn to the side. Outside, there was an open veranda that overlooked the whole island and inside shone a red, warm looking light. There were bongos playing along to the music and the whole room, even the dance floor, was all cream in colour. The room was dressed with various tropical flowers. It was the room were Spielberg and Lucas worked together on one of the Star Wars movies. It was open air with the smell of various perfumes ascending around the room. Everyone looked vibrant and much younger than on an ordinary day, like we'd all stepped back in time. You could feel the energy inside and it started to build as the music played. It felt like God was watching on with a big smile on his face.

Christina and I headed on to the dance floor. We'd not practiced anything but we were dancing with each other as if we had danced together every day. I thought to myself "We've not danced like this in a good while." Then it dawned on me, I don't think we'd ever danced like this. It also occurred to me that I'd not looked at Christina this way in a very long time. She looked at me like I was looking at her and we danced with passion in our step. A blackened love, that had to hide away through life's setbacks, was shining brighter than ever as we locked arms and kissed; almost childlike.

A track named 'Waka Waka' by Shakira started playing. It began with an up-beat tempo then slowed down so you could catch the lyrics. As I listened, the song just seemed to appeal, as if it was covering everything I'd been through over the past few years. I was smiling in the ambience whilst listening to these lyrics.

You're a good soldier, choosing your battles
Pick yourself up and dust yourself off,
and back in the saddle.

You're on the front line,
Everyone's watching,
You know it's serious,
We're getting closer, this isn't over.
The pressure's on, you feel it,
But you've got it all, believe it…

It felt as if everyone was listening, like everyone had their own story, their own torments and their own triumphs but were all happy to be at the place they were in life. Then the track played on, offering a much simpler answer to everything.

When you fall, get up. And if you fall, get up. It's a simple message, but if you want to live, it's what you've got to do. The song then burst into a different language before hitting a sub-tropical beat, to which all the girls were all dancing like Spanish dolls, with all the guys serenading and dancing around them. If you've ever pictured a perfect happy ending to something, this was it.

So over the past couple of years I'd spent a little time with my head down in the dirt, wrestling with the worms and the maggots. Then came the hard graft of working my way back up the stem of life whilst getting poked by various thorns along the way. Now at the very end, I'd made it to where the sun shone and to where the flowers had bloomed. So there was Andy Rose, Charlie, Mattie and Kellie Rose, Danny Rose, Cinnie and of course, the newly married couple, Phil and Mrs Rebecca Rose. So after all that time I was dancing amongst a bed of roses. But on this night, we were all roses, all chic and wonderful in our own different ways; all in full bloom, our most colourful, at our purest and our most beautiful.

Very happy days.

Chapter 6

Some Kind of Wonderful

On our arrival back from Bellagio I had six to seven weeks to organise Christina's 40th birthday party. I'd already done most of the booking, the venue, the food, the DJ and a nice Jag to take us to the event. Christina involved herself by decorating the room and being part of most of the small preparation. The party was initially meant to be a surprise but Christina (the person who says she loves surprises) had organised tons of stuff to do around her birthday already, so I'd had to tell her about the party. The invites were sent.

She knew my surprise and we'd already booked into a spa a few days before the party, so regardless of how the party turned out she would have done something nice for her birthday. She didn't know about the car, but organising a nice car had become pretty standard by now anyway, so it wasn't such a big deal. I really wanted this to be a special event for Christina, though. This was her time just like finishing the book or getting ready for a bodybuilding show. I wanted it to have that edge. I wanted it to shine. It was what the year had all been about. It was about making magic happen.

Flying Sam

A pal of mine named Sammy Gribbon was always putting pictures up of himself flying his helicopter. He'd said to just give him a shout if I'd ever wanted to fly. Sam looked like a film star and was a former British and European Thai boxing champion back in the day. He had helped a lot of kids out with their training and had looked out for them. Like myself, he was always spreading the love and giving back to give forward so I asked him the favour of taking me, Christina and Michael for a ride in his helicopter before her party as a stop off along the way. "Not a problem pal. Just tell us when and I'll sort it." Boom. It was that same message of that one person being able to make all the difference. The event had just peaked. It had the edge. It was time to shine.

I got the idea for Christina's birthday celebrations from an 80s movie I'd always loved named 'Some Kind of Wonderful'. Eric Stoltz was trying to woo Lea Thompson while taking her on a romantic date which had various stop offs along the way. I'd thought more about the Mary Stuart Masterson character though as she reminds me more of Christina. So this is how it went:

It was a three-day bonanza. Thursday and Friday were spa days. Hot stones massages and outdoor Jacuzzi with champagne. A candle lit dinner and a night at the hotel. Saturday I was back at work but Christina had booked herself in for a haircut and was having her makeup and nails done, so her celebrations had carried straight on.

The car place had messed up so I didn't have a car. The weather was breezy so it was touch and go about the helicopter ride and I had to sit with the DJ the night before as he had lost my play list. I was getting stressed. This all had to come right. My cousin, Danny, got in touch saying I could borrow his 75 grand Range Rover and then Sammy was on the phone saying the weather was fine. There were a few glitchy close calls but we'd got there.

The helicopter ride was a blast. Michael battered Sam's head with various questions while looking out from every window. Sam told us that he'd always wanted to fly since being a child; to be like Peter Pan. I realised just how similar we actually were.

Then he says 'This is how they do it in the movies," as he landed half inverted on a hill then sprung straight off again. It was an awesome start to the night.

When we arrived at the venue it had already filled up. Christina held my hand tight as if to say thank you for making such an effort. I finally took a breath.

This had definitely been: Some Kind of Wonderful.

Passing the baton

I'd been dancing for crowds since I was eight years old. Everyone was still goading me to do some break dancing at events but for the first time I was about to be upstaged. I'd been taking Michael to street dance every week. Throughout the week we would roll the carpets back and have our own dance sessions when Mum was at work. I taught Michael how to Break Dance, I also helped him with his street dancing a little. It kind of reminded me of the nights at Alan Hall's house back in the 80s! It was all good.

I started to bust a few moves on the dance floor when little Doosh jumped in at the side of me hitting his crazy legs and swipes. He was then on the stage hitting his little jig with all those on the dance floor stopping and taking videos or pictures. He loved it, and didn't leave the dance floor at all until the end of the night.

At some point in the night I was sitting with my cousin, Tina, whilst watching Michael on the dance floor. I thought back to all those years ago to my first dance at St Bede's and how good it felt. Michael was at that same place. He was beaming, knowing he was the main attraction. I was smiling ear to ear seeing him enjoying his moment. This night, he would remember forever. I looked away from the dance floor to see Tina beaming, a very gallant smile.

"What?" I ask.

She smiled again, "I remember you dancing when you were young and I remember seeing your Dad smiling in awe at you, just like you are with him."

It was a brilliant night for everyone. As the saying goes, this whole year had literally been 'all singing and dancing'. Christina was radiant as she enjoyed dancing with her family as well as seeing Michael enjoy his first major up-beat moment (perhaps the start of his wave). It had been a close call but at the end the effort had paid off. The wave of happiness was pretty much off the scale at this point.

Thirty years of training

Another six weeks to go until the final part of the magic: Florida, USA.

It was fun all the way up until we went. I was enjoying the gym and was back in great shape and feeling fit. Although small in comparison, it had been 30 years since I started training so another little goal was to get in top notch condition as a celebration. I'd enjoyed training at a new gym, Anytime Fitness in Bury. Although clean and smart, the gym and the atmosphere when getting in shape, was reminiscent of a quieter version of Silver's gym from back in the day. I was with my old school training partner, Phil and new partner, Kitty. And like everything else on this year: I'd nailed it.

Florida, USA, here we come. The final part of the wave.

The year was already a bonanza of great memories but it was on to the place where the whole idea started. I had promised to take Michael to Florida when he was 6. I had said this years ago, along with promising to treat Christina to a nice holiday when she hit 40. I'd been saving for over three years and here we were.

On our first day, we were up at the crack of dawn to make sure we were near the front of the early line. When the gates opened we didn't have to rush to get on anything and we saw the whole park before it was busy. We went on the Minion ride, the Mummy, then straight on to the Transformer ride, where they have full size Transformers buzzing around the street. I hit one of the roller coasters then we headed up to Harry Potter Land and on the Hogwarts Express that connected both parks.

We did everything, from a real life safari to Michael's first roller coaster and the big water park, Volcano Bay. Everything from King Kong, to Jurassic Park. The whole holiday was brilliant. The best part of the holiday though was still yet to come.

I taught Michael how to swim at the pool at our hotel. We'd been at the pool most nights, playing about, and doing some practice swimming. I figured he was good to go. It took around thirty minutes then he was going at it like a fish right across the pool. I couldn't believe it.

Michael stood up after his swim with a big smile on his face, "I done it. Are you proud of me, Dad?"

"I'm always proud, Michael."

The holiday turned out to be great, one of the very best, as we were heading to the end of what had been one of the best years I can ever remember. I'd prepared and sensed something good happening on this year but what I got was much better than anything I could have ever imagined.

So on my final big wave to date it had all been based on doing stuff for other people, being there for those that matter. But God had also wanted me to be on this wave; the reason the book was ready and finished at the start of this year. God knew I had tunnel vision, life addict syndrome, that if it's ready then it has to happen.

So why everything in one year? Why not spread things out a little? Why? Because this is God's great tide of life that's why.

Quick re-cap: The positive strength grows as the year goes on

So the writing got busier at the start of year. I was enjoying learning my new skill. I'd surrounded myself with my past, present and future. The excitement was building and the energy was electric.

Over this particular summer Michael and I enjoyed skate boarding and I was back doing a little at the skate parks myself. We went climbing, boxing and martial arts, to ninja assault courses and break dancing. Every passion I'd had as a kid had been drafted and passed on to my own son.

At the same time, the book was out and many people were enjoying it. This was a massive goal for me. I was in great shape, with my ego fully fed (not in a bad way) and the fact a lot of people liked the book I saw it as a way of giving back, which made me happy.

I was at my most positive and in shape as we headed for Bellagio. The upbeat positive energy only got stronger as we were mingling with the happy, the joyful and the successful. More importantly I love my wife. The shades of grey on that subject were well and truly gone.

I was loving gym life again and getting in shape had the same magic as ever but without the overwhelming pressure of competition. This was for the love of the sport and it was healthy. It was also the 30-year anniversary of when I first hit the weights. So all my old loves had come into play: Breakin', skating, training, family time and, now, writing. The book had me remembering everything, everyone and every moment. I was more appreciative of the ones I was closest with. Every stream, every great memory of life was now at its highest.

A drug addict can't get any higher but a life addict that feeds from God, from life and from goodness gets to climb the highest, feel their best, love the most and give a little back because he's just that; A Life Addict. This had been the ultimate wave, God, the ultimate medicine and motivator, the ultimate inner feelings of joy.

I'd walked away from the work incident and the ghost writing incident and anything negative no matter how difficult. For that I received all this, positivity breeding vast positivity. And like I've said earlier in the book 'The devil is powerless against love' and in this year, I was loving everything.

Chapter 7

The last door, the last influence

Like God and the angels, as good doormen we stand on the side lines looking to make sure everyone is doing ok; from talking to people who may be a little lonely and getting people home safely, right through to stopping people getting stamped on and having to roll around in the street. This is what we do.

I'm going to tell you my last story about the last door I may ever work; about the last influence I may ever have.

At the end of 2014 I was working on the new door. The first couple of months were hard to gauge. It was a classy joint so I had to watch who was coming in, plus manners and diplomacy were more essential than ever. The first three months and coming up to Christmas were the most difficult. The place was new so obviously everyone wanted to go to the new place. I had to set the bar early. So there were a few fallouts and a couple of unhappy people who wouldn't be getting in. I was polite and felt I'd got the type of crowd that the management wanted. It wasn't about the clothes they wore (even though the management had said no shorts or football shirts). I based everything on attitude. You can forget about what people are wearing if they are decent people. This way of doing things went down well and we kept more customers because of it.

The only problem I had was the doormen I was working

with. I may have been the head door man but there were two other lads who had already been preselected. They were on their phones or stood away from the door and called me over to every incident; it was like babysitting. I made it known to the management that I wanted my own people but at the time they wanted things to stay as they were.

The Vyas brothers

Back at the end of 2003 I met this kid at the gym named, Phil. Phil Vyas. He was part of the young, upcoming door brigade of the time. Phil just seemed to laugh at everything I said whilst at the gym and so, over the year, we'd built up a good rapport.

In 2011 I was training with Phil and we tended to hang out a little after the gym. We'd been smashing the weights and were around 15 to 16 stone, yet still pretty lean.

I remember one day after a workout, I was telling Phil about how I was having problems with this new TV I'd recently bought. It hadn't worked but the shop kept fobbing my wife off with excuses, saying the TV was fine when they left it with us. So I told Phil I was heading to the shop to see what I could do. Phil said he'd come with me and off we went. When we got near the shop Phil said, "Let's go in, in our vests and scare them!" I was laughing, I was only going to talk but then I thought, fuck it. We went into the shop, fully pumped. I told the guy about my situation. Meanwhile, Phil was wondering around the shop smiling and saying how he liked certain TVs. "I might take this one," he laughingly said. We weren't even doing anything wrong but because we were in this guy's shop and we were of a size (and he knew he'd been a dick with my wife) the guy and his assistant had become massively unnerved. I was trying not to laugh as Phil hammed up the scene. The day later, a brand new, working TV arrived at our door. Happy days!

So Phil was the guy who could be my neighbour, my best pal, my brother. He was already massively influenced by me, so it was all good. Unfortunately, Phil wasn't the one

I'd have to help out. Phil was only the lead, it was his brother, Alex, that was going to be the challenge.

I think Phil was around 21 or 22 at the time and his younger brother Alex was 16. Alex would come swaggering into the gym to speak to Phil. Phil was always abrupt with Alex so Alex started getting arsey with Phil. Every chat they had felt like the start of an argument. You could feel there was a tension between them. I liked Alex, he was overly cocky the majority of the time but there was a spark of niceness that also shone through.

Four months on, Phil's party trick (for many years to come) was to train hard for around four or five months then disappear for a while. I kept running into Alex at the gym while Phil had gone AWOL with his new bird, Eleri. Alex would ask what I was doing when it came to certain exercises. After spending a little time helping him with a few things, we then started training together. Alex, like his brother Phil, were naturally good athletes. A pal of mine at work named Kenny Buckle had told me he used to take the brothers playing football and said they both would have made good pros if they had wanted to. Phil was stocky and Alex was more slender. They both had wide shoulder spans and vast reach with no lagging body parts. Their stamina whilst training was second to none.

I'd trained with Alex for a while. He had this cocky edge to his persona that kind of made me laugh. He was taking the piss out of certain people around the gym (only in a fun sense). I was laughing whilst talking to a couple of the old timers, who had been around when I had first started out, named Phil and Ste.

"Have you heard this dick?" I said to the two.

Phil and Ste looked at each other then grinned. "Ha. I wonder who he reminds us of, 'ey Ste?"

They were referring to me from back in the day. I laughed, and, yes, it was a pretty similar performance. Unfortunately though, our matching egos weren't the only thing we had in common.

As we moved into 2012, The Four Barrels year; it was a

month or so since starting work there. I was working one night when I saw young Alex coming our way. I was stood with Ryan at the time. From the second Alex had got to us and had started speaking, you could already tell there was something wrong. He was loud, aggressive and very dismissive of anyone else trying to speak. "Shut up you dick," he shunned Ryan. The kid was totally wired. His mouth kept going out to one side, whilst his hands kept clasping together and his head was trying to go full circle as he cockily swaggered about and in our faces. There was nothing going on behind his eyes; they darted to the top of his head with a look of menace, pale faced with dominant cheek bones. I thought he was just having a wild night, a blow out as such, but this was Alex most weeks.

The next week, he was back. This time he'd of started a fight inside by belting some guy. Ryan grabbed for Alex on this occasion as I had to take on the guy he was fighting with. The week after that, Alex seemed to be behaving a bit more. Ryan tried wording him up as he was on his way in, but this time a pipe was pulled from the wall. Alex was stood at that very spot but swore blind he had nothing to do with it. A couple more weeks went by and Alex had picked a fight with a group of lads. It was a pretty messy occurrence where me, Ryan and Big Adam had all become involved. The fight went off under the arches and, as usual, we'd taken Alex's side. Some of the other doormen had had enough of Alex by now. Even Ryan said that if Alex hadn't been Phil's brother, he'd be struggling to keep his shit together. Unfortunately, though, it was me that ended up getting into it with him.

As I dragged Alex away from the scene he shunned my arm away and got right in my face. He may have just turned 18 but still he had reach, big knuckles and could handle himself. He grabbed for my top but in that brief second I got him to the ground with my knee on his chest.

"Get off me, you fuckin' dick."

When he was back to his feet he started again. He'd pissed me off this time. I'd kept my shit together until now. I pinned him up against the window of the pub just up from ours. I was trying to help him out but he was making life very hard. My anger was taking over as his insults emerged more direct and in my face.

"He's just a kid John and he's your friend. He's just like you were," my mind was trying to put the situation right. A few more seconds went by when a couple of girls, who had seen what was going on, started getting on my case. I told them the situation and that I was actually trying to help him out.

Alex had started to calm down, "I'm fine, fuckin' ged off me. I'm going."

We glared at one another. "You're barred Alex. I can't keep having this shit with you every week."

"Whatever," he walked off up the street with the two girls.

Come Monday at 5pm, I was making my way into the gym to meet Alex. We'd not spoken since the weekend. As I arrived, Alex was there, waiting at the front counter. As soon as we laid eyes on each other, we both just laughed.

"Alright, dick head" I said.

"Yeah, good."

I was really glad he hadn't taken it personally. "Right, let's do it then." He happily smiled as we headed into the gym to start our session. As we walked in, a kid named Josh Gilmartin, looked at us both, almost having to do a double take.

"I thought you said John had barred you from the club on Saturday?"

"He did. We are still mates though."

Josh just laughed.

A couple of weeks later, me and Ryan stood at the front door of the venue, ready to start the night. Two guys came up to the door, "Have you seen Alex Vyas?"

"No pal, don't think he's out tonight," I say, not thinking too much about it.

Twenty minutes went by when an even bigger group of lads came to the door.

"Where's Alex Vyas? We've heard that he comes here."

"Not anymore, he barred."

Then another crew of lads turned up asking the same question.

"Shit, I think Alex is in trouble," Ryan mumbled. Even though Alex hadn't been over to where we were, he'd obviously been causing mayhem elsewhere still in the Bury town centre area.

Later that night Alex appeared at the pub for the first time in three or four weeks. His head was spinning. He was cocky and aggressive and clearly not in a good way. Ryan had a go at him, wording him up on the trouble he might be in. A few seconds later, Alex turned to me. I gave it about three seconds then quickly got a grip of him and took him around to the car park

"Come on I'm taking you home, pal, otherwise something bad is going to happen to you." I think Alex wanted to have a go but for some reason he didn't. I think he knew I was genuinely concerned about him and the fact that I wasn't shouting or angry might just have been enough to hit home. Alex got in the car and, for tonight at least, we'd managed to keep him out of bother and home safely.

So this was the tussle we had with Alex and over the next year or so, there was a lot of going back and forth.

Around April 2014, Alex was still turning up to train but he wasn't looking great. His face looked pale and gaunt and the underneath of his eyes were often dark in colour. Alex told me that he'd been getting pain in his kidneys and had to go to the doctors to seek advice. I'd had problems with my kidneys, although through different reason. I knew how dangerous a problem it was though. Plus, Alex was only a kid. I knew, at this point, it wasn't just about stepping up to help Alex with his daft behaviour. When the problem became internal, it was about having to make him aware of what was happening within. Alex had to realise that he had to become the god of his own body, otherwise the chapters in his later life may become more blurred, due to the decisions he made if he carried on as he was. It was time to step up.

I started to set Alex more challenges in the gym; various super sets throughout and at the end of workouts. Alex enjoyed the challenges. I told him that even if he had a few weekends without getting wired, that his training would go through the roof. I complimented him on how good he currently looked but I also sold him the vision of how well he could look, along with the performance he'd be capable of. If there's one thing I'd learned about Alex over the years; he wasn't afraid of a challenge and he enjoyed getting psyched. He hadn't gone out for a good few weeks and, like I'd said, he was getting stronger and already looking better. He seemed a lot happier in himself also.

Sometime during all this, he ended up going out having a messy weekend which turned into a lazy week. I didn't like scare mongering but Alex had come so far, I didn't want him drifting back. Come the following Monday, I asked Alex if he was happy with his look and with his training, to which he said he was. I mentioned that if he carried on messing up, that it wouldn't be about him choosing to walk away and that the drugs, sooner rather than later, were going to make that decision for him.

I talked about his testosterone lowering and how his adrenal gland and vascular system were also going to suffer. Then I told him that the last thing he wanted was to be hooked up to a respirator by the time he was thirty. I didn't pass the whole message on in one go, I just kept feeding Alex little bits over the weeks. I saw him getting a little anxious but I wanted him to be aware. I also made it known, that at his age, he was going bounce back with no problems at all. I didn't want him worrying but I needed him to act soon.

If Alex had wanted to walk away I would have understood but I'd grown to like and care for him now, so as long as he kept coming back I was going to help him out. And fortunately, he did keep coming back.

He was filling out his shirts and, like when I'd first met him, he had that upbeat optimism about him. After around four or five months of hitting it hard, he was finally happy with himself. I kept plugging his head about working the doors. I'd lived a clean, upbeat and happy life whilst working the clubs and pubs, so I figured this could be the same for Alex but he wasn't biting. In fact, going up towards Christmas, he was back out doing his usual. I was a little choked to be honest.

So this brings me back to the start of this story. I wasn't happy with the door staff I'd got and wanted my own people. Well, Alex was my own people and getting him off this shite was my aim. So I kept on at him about working the door. He wasn't interested and even Christina told me to stop mithering him but I knew this could be good for him.

After Alex had, had his release, so to speak, he was finally considering what I was saying. I'd even told him that the money would help with his other hobbies (he'd just started getting into motor bikes). Over the Christmas period, Alex had said that he was going out with his pals but in the New Year he was going to get his badge and work the door with me. Boom, magic.

New Year's Eve 2014: Alex had turned up to the Bueller, the three floored pub, restaurant and cocktail lounge, I worked at. He was a touch off his face and kept going onto Brian, the new Manager, about how he was going to be my new partner and how I'd said the other door staff weren't up to much. I was kind of laughing but at the same time hoping he was going to shut the fuck up, even if only for his own sake. Brian was looking at me as if to say, "This is what you have in mind for this door?" Alex's head was half spinning round with him totally wired by then. It was pretty funny though.

When I spoke to Brian about changing the door staff, I wasn't getting what I wanted. He wanted to keep things as they were but for me, I had a promise to keep. I told the other staff that they could take the Friday night and work together; I'd drop the Friday as I had promised a pal of mine I'd get him a spot on the door. The lads were happy with the arrangement.

It was good working with Alex. He was already a far cry

from who he was all those years ago and, apart from the blow out over Christmas, he'd had a pretty steady year leading up to now. Within a month of him being there, he was doing the job well. It was more about airs and graces but when things got a little tense and a situation arose, he was where he was supposed to be; more importantly he was willing to listen and learn. He watched how I dealt with things and seemed astounded with how well I dealt with situations, similar to when I first saw Sean Patrick all those many moons ago. We also went across to help out the other doormen and even the pubs that had no door staff on at all.

Alex said to me, "How come you don't get hold of people? I thought you would have gripped that lad."

"This place wants diplomacy and that's where I'm at with working the doors. If I can get the job done without using any force whatsoever, that's when everyone wins," I told him. We did get hands on, on a few occasions but only when an event had already gone off.

Boot camp

I figured this door wasn't going to be enough to carry Alex's young energy and excitement but I knew this was a good starter door (or retirement home in my case). I thought I could teach Alex everything he needed to know from this venue and at a slower pace. I never left the front door; I believed there should always be a presence. Most the time you can be polite and still turn people away. I made it known to Alex that once you let the shit in, it's a lot harder to get out at the end of the night, so best to spot idiots early. Alex was quick to catch on. The manners thing didn't seem to be a problem. Alex was soon big on spotting the idiots. He was also good at spotting people we'd had trouble with in the past. The door ran clean. I did most the talking but when Alex started stepping up, I was glad to back his play on whatever decision he made (just how Doza had taught me) and together, we worked it well.

The other side to boot camp was self-defence. I'd

recently set up an open martial arts class and I tended to train with various athletes through the week, on my days off or the odd evening. I mainly went boxing with my pal Sharpy (Steve Sharples) who was formerly Ricky Hatton's sparring partner or Glyn Cambell (part of Steve Collins' camp back in the day). I also trained with lads named Pete and Clive doing a mixture of martial arts, usually in the same day. On Sundays I ran my own class. I'd wanted to do this for a while. We had our own class many moons ago, the killer sessions at Silvers. Then we had the cage fighting place, which was a little more relaxed, up in Heywood but all that was four or five years ago now and a lot of the old boys still wanted one more round before having to call it a day. Alex was my number one student and, again, he was all over it. He didn't even seem bothered about not seeing his pals after work and even when he'd arranged a session, he was just having a few drinks or going home early. I was happy at where he was and how active his mind was towards better more natural highs.

I'd managed to get a lot of the old boys down to the gym. We had Mickie Borg, who would basically roll about with you all day. Then there was Mark Holland, another guy who'd done the rounds. Most of the guys were from our original Silvers class from ten years earlier. Omar turned up with a couple of the old school guys but they were all massively out of shape. They fought pretty well for around a minute, then they'd quit. Omar still had everyone laughing. "Fuck this shit!" None of us were anywhere near what we used to be but we still liked to have a go.

A few other kids came and went but not many liked the open sparring at the end of the sessions. Predominantly, it was me, Mike and Alex most weeks. Alex was the favourite; no matter who turned up, everyone wanted to help Alex. He was the clear to see, young and upcoming athlete. He was a sponge when it came to learning and, win or lose, he was never fazed by anything. I taught him most of the take downs, the holds, throws and got him started with his boxing. Mike set up scenarios with the knife attacks, the standing locks and all the other psycho shit that he was into. Mark tended to teach most of the ground work but in general we all offered our own little bit.

Alex was now well trained in verbal confrontation and was handling himself noticeably well. He was eating well and was healthy both in mind and body. The kid was our masterpiece.

The beauty with Alex was that his verbal articulation and his persona were what shone out the most. He didn't become a bully, he just had the confidence to back up his wording. This was the same way I worked.

An example of Alex's confidence: When he initially started working the door, a few door men who'd stopped by were talking to me, then they'd spotted Alex, instantly remembering him from back in the day. "He's a dick head, him." Alex used to step back whilst I explained about him changing his ways and to give him a chance. However, if someone said something to him now, he'd step up on his own and say, "Yeah, well I'm not like that anymore." Even better! Once the other door men got to know him they offered him work at the end of the night. Alex would do a bit and the next thing you knew they were trying to take my best lad. Not a bad word was said about how he performed, no matter what the situation. He earned a lot of respect and in very little time. I was made up that he hadn't left Bury a bad guy. Everyone saw his best side shining through, even working side by side with some of the guys he'd had the problems with.

The thing I liked most about Alex though was his loyalty. Despite all the offers to work elsewhere, even for better money and places just as nice, he chose to carry on working with me until the end. That really was a rarity. Alex was welcomed time spent and unlike most others, he hadn't asked for my help, I'd just wanted to help 'because he was a good kid and I didn't want anything bad happening to him.

God's great tide for Alex

So Alex had matured. It was later into the year 2016 and despite Alex having interest in most sports, as well as taking to most sports quickly, his interest in projecting himself to the next level just wasn't there. Unlike me, who felt the need to compete or to strive for something, Alex just seemed to do things for his own peace of mind and seemed happy just having done stuff.

I'd got Alex set up as a protector but unfortunately over the years the security industry wasn't what it used to be. I kept hoping that Alex would find his own version of Young Bloods and have that band of brothers upbeat feel; he was the perfect candidate. Like the Young Bloods door team, Alex was always smart, polite, lived clean, trained hard and was quick to react and to be a team player. Obviously now he was more mature, he looked the business too. Unfortunately though, there didn't seem like there was anywhere to go with it.

Alex's main interest lay in his work and over the course of time the one thing he'd stuck with was his apprenticeship as an engineer. He was already fully qualified and working on finishing his PhD.

Alex moaned and groaned saying he wasn't happy working where he was. He wanted to be out on site and at the next level. Ironically, whilst working this door, he got talking to a guy who ran an engineering company. The next thing you know, boom, he'd got the job he wanted, or seemingly so. A couple of months down the line; the boss was great, they hung out, had similar interests. Then one day, bang, the guy's a dick and Alex hates his job again and said he wasn't being taken seriously.

Meanwhile, on the job front my old pal Doza (former door mentor now working as a fire fighter) had been in touch. Over the years Doza had always told me when job vacancies came up. In the past I had tried out on a few occasions. The first time I messed up on the hose run but on the second attempt, several years down the line, I'd got through to the later stages then decided that I still liked my job on the post, so I'd left it. But with all the shit that had panned out at work in recent times I fancied another stab at it.

I got the text from Doza and simply applied to the GMC email then they kept me posted when a training day was made available. I got the text while working on a Saturday night with Alex. I started to tell Alex what it was about, then asked him if this was something he'd be interested in. Alex wasn't having a good time at the place he worked so looked it over. He hesitated a few seconds then said, "Yeah, can you send me that link? I'll have a look at it." His wave was on the rise.

Unlike me, who hadn't heard anything, Alex had managed to get onto one of the open days and had got through the first couple of stages. He had been in touch with me as he had to write about a subject he was familiar with. For some reason Alex had chosen to write about an egg. I wasn't sure about his motive but when I suggested we just do the piece on nutrition, Alex just looked up from his seat, "Yeah, that's a better idea" and away we went.

After getting this far with the fire brigade, Alex suddenly changed his mind. He was talking about engineering again. He wanted to work on the designing side of things. So on another Saturday night, whilst working, he got talking to another guy and again in a matter of weeks Alex was where he wanted to be, working in the office side of the job and designing stuff. So again, the boss was great and he was really enjoying it and again, a few months went by and now the boss was being a dick. He wasn't getting listened to and he didn't like some of the guys he was working with.

"You should have stuck with the fire brigade pal," I said to him.

"Yeah, I know, I think I'll go for it again."

So the same as last time. He got his taster day, he then got through the first couple of rounds but unlike last time he saw it through to the end and got selected.

Somewhere into 2017 Alex was telling me about the type of training, the long days and the endless studying that he had to get through. I hadn't even been selected for one training day but as he was talking, it had raised a few thoughts:

1. I wouldn't want to spend all that time away from my family.
2. I'd just released my book and was having a really good time with it, with definite plans to do more.

The penny dropped.

If I had been selected to get on the fire brigade, at the time, my heart would have wanted to be spending more time with my family and my great tide of life lay within my writing (for now at least). God had seen beyond what I think I wanted, compared to what I really wanted, and with all the good that had come from writing the book I was pretty certain that I was in the right place; 2017 being one of the best years of my life.

So Alex was a life addict, always searching for that little more, a place to belong. I spoke to him regularly about God's great tide of life and the 'what's meant to be' factor. Although Alex thought I was full of shit sometimes, for seven years of his life he'd chosen to stick around and, ironically, my full of shit attitude had helped lead him to somewhere a lot better than where he was heading when I first met him. I think I'd spent more time with Alex than Yoda had spent with Luke Skywalker, Rocky with Mickey or even Mr Miyagi with the Karate kid.

The wave of Alex Vyas

I'd trained Alex up to the best of his abilities; mentally, verbally, physically, and (attempted) spiritually but with no place to go with it.

God:
Alex got random opportunities, whilst working the door, to step up to all his engineering goals. Ironically whilst working on this one particular door. Then he decided it wasn't for him. Every answer to every question he'd ever wanted. No regrets.

Doza:
The same guy who taught me the art of thinking, pride and brotherhood had been in touch to help me out again but this time the path wasn't mine. So I passed it onto the young person I had broadened, (same as Doza did for me). The same influence that had helped me had now, indirectly, helped the guy I'd helped the most. God had put all these attributes into place.

Just to go on from this. Alex, who was in an up-down relationship, introduced the fire brigade to his girlfriend, Amanda Kelly. The two then trained together to become fire fighters and are now inseparable.

Lastly:
Alex's first fire was the well-publicised, Winter Hill fires. Both him and Doza would unknowingly work together to put out the fire, whilst God did the job of keeping them both safe as they stopped it from spreading towards the nearby village. Alex became the protector I hoped he'd be with that band of brothers feel I'd hoped he'd get. In the past I'd had the good fortune of working with both of these heroes but on this occasion God had wanted me to write the story and sit this one out.

Ironically:
When the bar first opened was when I got Alex on board. Three years on and literally a week or so after Alex had left to pursue his fire fighting career, the management decided they only wanted one doorman. Almost like the story was meant to be.

The world is magic; you've just got to see it.
Six months down the line and into 2018, actually on my birthday, I received a text from Alex:
"John, happy birthday my mate, I hope you've had a great day. Sorry, been at work all day but just want to say thanks for all the guidance along the way. I did listen to some of it, not all, hahahaha. Only joking mate, cheers for it all."

The Final Chapter

Belief
The Tide
Life Addict

So maybe this whole story is just a load of bull shit, but that's down to you. If you want to believe, you can. And if you don't, no-one's making you. This is my trail of thought that has come about through very humble beginnings and now in my mid forties, my cerebral light seems to be shining brighter than ever. I still can't spell and I'm pretty numb when it comes to certain things but I'm still clever enough never to have wasted thought on things that don't matter or to hold on to hate or negativity any longer than I've had to. My only aim is to smile, to be happy, just like I did as a child.

I know my influences, in the flesh at least, are now limited but on paper that's different. A book or piece of writing is a kind of afterlife, a soul if you will, that could live on beyond your time on earth. Like anything, we all have our secrets and things we've hidden away from in order to keep our peace of mind. However, through writing I've found a much more honest way to rifle through the chapters of my life. Writing has become my sanctuary, my soul. My aim: to help others.

Saying goodbye

At the start of 2019 I moved away from working the doors, over 25 years since I first started. I ran my final door; the cleanest, the most pragmatic and most importantly, nonviolent. The person I am now reflected the place I ran. This great tide of life allowing me to walk away in one piece. The choppy seas of my earlier years were well and truly behind me.

In the whole 25 years I worked, I can't remember ever starting a fight (apart from when I first started seeing Christina) or ever being a bully. And the only thing I ever promised myself when I started work on the doors, was that if I ever buckled when a fight had gone off, that I'd walk that very night and I'm proud to say that I've never had to. Security will always be part of who I am, and has also been a part of everything I ever was.

The wave

Working the doors was a natural progression. Ian Cardoza was putting out the flames in my head years before he even thought about becoming a fire fighter. The bad energy I held on to found somewhere to go. I let it out as a form of violence, but violence to prevent violence, therefore giving back. The most important part of my wave though, was falling in love and having our son. So now as I walk away from the doors I go on to a family that I love and will always protect. It's definitely been a dysfunctional journey but the good part is, we got there in the end. God has been very patient as well as being very kind.

My final message: Gods of our own bodies

In our bodies are millions of cells, just like the world has millions of people. Every cell has a job to do inside our body for it to function at its best. When something goes wrong within our body, it sends a message to our brains telling us about the problem. Then it's up to our brains how we deal with it. But it's our own choice, our own decision.

People look at the world, they say stuff like:

'If God is so great, why are there earthquakes?'

'Why are children dying of rare diseases, suffering with depression?' etc.

Take the earthquake, for example. Scientifically it can be explained as the tectonic plates above the Earth's core sliding back into place, not unlike having physiotherapy on a stubborn back disk to make it slip back into place. You get the picture. We challenge having a God, yet we blow smoke down our lungs, take drugs that demolish sells in our bodies and brains, all killing masses of cells in our bodies. Now imagine these sells as people on the planet. Alcohol, pollutants in the air, shit they put in the food, the processed shit that takes all the nutrients out of the food, stress, unheeded arguments, or insults, and so the list goes on. The human race is the free radical of the planet. It's the creator of all pollutants and breakdowns on this earth.

So what's this got to do with God and belief?

To put this more simply: We all have a choice every day on how we feed our bodies and minds. So first let's take away the factories and the foods, the steel industry and all the other man-made bullshit. What we have is greenery, no guns, bombs, fortified foods. In fact, all we have is what God gave us, the Earth. This Earth supplies every medicine naturally, the prevention rather than the cure, and yes there may be a child who dies prematurely or an old person who could have better been treated with medicines, but all in all, we wouldn't be afraid of guns and wouldn't be questioning how we look. Our minds could secure natural oxygen that comes from the trees and greenery and the iodine from the sea could keep our minds fresh and our metabolic rate higher. Without all of the man-made plagues we face, we could live for love and our beliefs could come from within. In general, all that is green could be gold, a much clearer path to ride the tide of life.

If you can accept that you are a god of your own body and that the cells that cause pain are like prayers for you to answer, then you must also accept that if your body didn't warn you, you would soon die. And if we are the gods of our bodies and we make mistakes then surely God should be allowed to make a few mistakes without being written off. And if you accept that our minds control our inner universe, then you can accept that we, ourselves, can be part of a much bigger Universe (our God). And like the worm holes in the universe can take you out to different dimensions, our minds are the same; from good thought to bad, taking our minds to different dimensions in the split of a second.

Now if we can work on our inner-selves to be at their healthiest and most helpful, then others may start to follow suit. And if we start to believe in something more than just the here and now then the body (the world) we are in may just hear our prayer. If there's enough of us that pray then God above may be able to do something about it, knowing there's a problem. If problems are answered that will lead to belief and if you can believe that's when anything is possible.

In layman's terms

Be good to yourself, be good to others. Don't dispel positive belief of any sort, shine bright and be happy. If you're an addictive person then be addicted to life, so even if there isn't a God or an afterlife, then you still know you've given it your all. Make the bad times interesting and the good times great. No regrets.

But for me, I do believe.

When my time is up on Earth, I don't want to be feeling regret for times gone by and things I should have done better. I want to be thinking, "Yes! I was there for everyone. I was there for myself, and I've done my very best to cherish and nurture my soul for it to now be ready for the next level." I want to be thinking, "I've answered every question, made the best decisions and never pissed on anyone whilst doing it (or made up for it if I have.)"

I want to be saying, "Right God. What's next? Where's the next big wave?"

"I'm a life addict, so let's do this!"

If I was wandering in the forest, lost, hungry and alone. If I'd never read a book, nor knew of any God existing. Then God is the breeze in the wind telling you to change direction. He is the warmth around your shoulders that stops you feeling alone. He is the guide that leads you to water and to food. He is the answer to the questions you never knew. He is the belief on the path that you choose to walk and the guiding light that keeps you safe.

I hope you've enjoyed my tale, thanks for taking time to read it.

Stay Gold.
God bless.

The End

JOHN

Acknowledgments

Gemma Spavin
I'd like to thank Gemma for the constant tutoring and help with the grammar.

Kath Stathem
I'd like to thank Kath for her help with the final proof read.

Gwil and Jane
I'd like to thank Gwil and Jane at Temple for getting the book to its very best.

I'd also like to thank everyone who has contributed their names to being part of this book. The stories are only here because of you.